CW00391472

Mad About The Boys

Mad About The Boys

FAME, FITNESS AND TEACHING LONDON'S TOUGHEST KIDS

LIZZIE WEBB

First published in the UK in 2023 by
Lizzie Webb, in partnership with whitefox publishing
www.wearewhitefox.com

Copyright © Lizzie Webb, 2023

ISBN 9781915036612
Also available as an ebook
ISBN 9781915036629
And an audiobook
ISBN 9781915036636

All photographs and illustrations in this book © Lizzie Webb,
apart from TV-am images courtesy of Ian White, TV presenter and
custodian of the TV-am archives; Gotcha Oscar courtesy of the BBC Photo
archives; England trophy courtesy of Adrian Judd; Take That fax courtesy
of Nicki Chapman; pantomime courtesy of G. Ivan Barnett; prison cartoon
courtesy of the *Henley Standard*; the Royal Osteoporosis Society for the
photograph of the author with Craig Revel Horwood

Designed and typeset by seagulls.net
Cover design by Simon Goggin
Cover portrait by Ilka and Franz
Project management by whitefox
Printed and bound in Suffolk by Clays, Ltd, Elcograf S.p.A.

For Ben

CONTENTS

INTRODUCTION

I'm walking along a graffiti-scrawled corridor on the first floor of a South London boys' comprehensive school. Suddenly, an almighty bang fills the silence, followed by another and then another. It's coming from the end of the corridor to my left, about sixty yards away, near the top entrance of the school theatre.

I stride quickly towards it and I'm aghast at what I'm seeing. A smartly dressed lad is taking running jumps with both his feet high in the air, landing them against the locked theatre doors. He's using all the force he can muster to break them down – *my* theatre doors, where I take the drama classes.

'What the hell do you think you're doing?' I shout in my deep, thundering drama-school voice.

'What the fuck do you think I'm doing?' he replies while taking another flying leap.

For a second I feel myself freeze as I realise who he is. This is the boy we had the staff meeting about, he'd been expelled from Tulse Hill School for violent conduct against the staff. We'd been told that school had the reputation for being the worst in London and, in spite of our own challenging problems, we've now been forced to take him.

'I'm so sorry,' I hear myself say, 'You're new, aren't you and don't know the rules. I've got the key, come with me and I'll show you around.'

He stops and stares at me, his face still etched in anger. I'm unnerved. I unlock the door. The school theatre is in total darkness and I will have to feel my way along the wall to find the switches. We enter in silence; he stands waiting patiently in the dark. Lights on, I shake him by the hand.

'I'm Miss Beveridge, the drama teacher here. What's your name?'

'Samuel Brown,' he says meekly.

I show him around our enormous three-hundred-seater theatre which doubles up for year assemblies, and explain what I do in the drama lessons and in my recently formed drama club.

'Why don't you come and give the club a try Samuel?'

'Yeah, thanks – I will,' he says with a cheeky grin.

Is this the same boy who a few minutes ago was violently kicking down the doors and swearing at me?

Thereafter, Samuel became my 'assistant' and, had I allowed it, my minder – woe betide any lad who dared step out of line, threaten or swear at me while Samuel was in tow.

One day I asked him what had prompted this instantaneous turn around. It transpires this thirteen-year-old lad had been uprooted from Jamaica by his mother, and brought to live with his ageing grandmother in a tiny, cramped Brixton flat. His frustration, his pent-up anger at the isolation caused by adhering to her strict regime was being directed at us, his teachers.

'Nobody had ever said sorry to me before.'

CHAPTER 1

MY FIRST DAY

January, 1970. I'm standing in the doorway of a classroom on the second floor of Henry Thornton Boys Comprehensive School, ready to take my first lesson since qualifying as an English and drama teacher. I'd asked the Inner London Education Authority to give me a teaching job in the toughest school in need of a supply teacher, preferably in the South London area where I'm currently renting a small flat. I'd like to start as a supply teacher, and then look for a permanent post when the new academic year starts in September. The Authority sounded somewhat bemused when we spoke and said it was a highly unusual request.

'No problem,' they said, 'We have several. How do you feel about a boys' comprehensive school that overlooks Clapham Common? It has one thousand five hundred pupils with an eight-form entry; it's a recent amalgamation of a grammar and two very large secondary schools.'

'Perfect,' I reply.

For my final teaching practice at my teacher-training college, I'd asked the principal if he could source a borstal for me, something nobody had requested before, and he'd kindly found one in Sawbridgeworth, Hertfordshire. The invaluable experience of living in the borstal and working with the boys had reinforced my thinking that these were the children I wanted to teach, but it should be *before* they pass the point of no return, where borstal or prison can all too easily become a way of life.

So here I am at Henry Thornton School; it fits my criteria. Arriving earlier this morning as an enthusiastic, fresh-faced, newly qualified teacher, I was warned by a member of staff that the title 'supply teacher' is a euphemism for 'taking the dunce classes that nobody else wants to teach'. Well, I'm about to find out if that's true.

As I pause in the doorway of the classroom, I glance around at these fourteen-year-old boys. I've been ready to expect the unexpected, but not quite as much as I'm seeing right now. Over by the windows at the back of the classroom, one lad is gleefully standing on the windowsill, pulling on the blinds and swinging them up and down. Another is sitting alone, staring into the distance, repeatedly stabbing at his desk with a penknife, while another two boys are seriously fighting. One has picked up a chair and is holding it by the legs high over the other lad's head and it's about to come crashing down; the rest of the room has about twelve boys behaving like a street rabble.

'What on *earth* do you think you are doing?' I boom, as I stride purposefully towards the teacher's desk, my deep voice drowning out the vocal chaos.

The room goes quiet. I glance up as I place my bag on top of the desk. My deep, fearless, authoritative command has stopped them in their tracks. They turn their heads and look at me. What they're seeing is a slight girl, looking more like a hippie than a schoolteacher. She's aged twenty-one with a mop of longish, dark, curly hair. She's wearing an open-neck cream shirt with both sleeves tightly rolled up; a silk scarf is tied loosely around the neck and her body shape is obscured by a purple Laura Ashley smock. Black corduroy trousers and plimsoles complete the outfit.

'Sit down now; we've got work to do,' I command, with a grand gesture of my arms.

The chair is put down, the blinds are let go and the rhythm of the penknife flicking is slowing down. They shove, mutter and juggle with each other to find a desk and lounge back in their chairs, some swinging in their seats, all with a look of defiance. By their body language, they're letting me know they have 'attitude' and I'm about to be their new bait. Clearly this lot aren't used to doing what they're told. Well ... maybe, but it has to be in their own time and of their own choosing.

Am I intimidated by their seemingly aggressive behaviour? Do I feel threatened by their rebellious attitude? Not at all! Why would I? As a child I'd grown up with real fear; my father's heavy hand raining down on me at the slightest childish indiscretion. These boys will have reasons for their behaviour.

'You the latest supply teacher then?' asks a grinning lad with a knowing look. He knows what my answer will be.

I stare at the empty teacher's desk. I've been warned that one of the problems with being a supply teacher is you're asked to take the class of the missing teacher, but they don't leave any information as to what level the class are at, what the class should be learning and what they're currently studying. Studying?

'Right, what did you do in your last English lesson?'

'Don't remember. Do what you want,' comes back a helpful reply from the same lad.

'Well thanks. What's your name?'

'Martin Chivers,' says the confident voice.

The boys instantly burst out laughing, which quells as I scan the whole class with a glowering, stern expression. Why would they be laughing at his name? No time to dwell on it.

'Right, where are your books?'

'We don't have none, the teacher has 'em,' replies Chivers.

More laughter and another problem to get to grips with. I'm going to have find the written books for every class at the start of each morning, presumably they're somewhere in the staffroom, and then lug them around with me. The school's between two different buildings set apart by two hundred yards. What a trek that's going to be. No wonder two boys have just cheekily sauntered in ten minutes late.

'Sorry I'm late Miss, but we was in the old building and it's taken all this time to get here.'

'Ok lads, don't give me that, it might work for some teachers, but I'm not so gullible; you just walked very slowly to be late.' The class jeer.

'What's gullible Miss?' asks Martin Chivers.

He must be the class clown; the rest of the class laugh whenever he speaks.

'Easily tricked,' I say, 'And you're probably not and neither am I. But, I am going to tell you what will happen if you carry on not learning and having a great time mucking around, because that's how you can end up getting into serious trouble.'

I pull the chair away from behind the teacher's desk and place it in the middle of the front of the class. I sit down, I've decided to recount my time teaching in the borstal. Slowly and very quietly they listen; I'm getting their attention. As they start asking probing questions, it soon transpires a couple of these lads have got a friend sent to a borstal, they already have an inkling and a perspective of what it's like and they're interested in mine as a teacher. I answer their questions as honestly as I can. It's slowly dawning on their faces that I'm not the sort of supply teacher they're probably used to – a childminder, a forty-five minute fill-in. I might be somebody who's actually interested in them as individuals if I'm bothering to chastise them for their earlier behaviour, and taking the time to give reasons they can identify with as to why they need to learn. Are they beginning to realise I might be a teacher who wants to teach them on a regular basis? I round off my talk, emphasising I'm not here trying to teach them because I want or need them to learn, I want *them* to want to learn.

''Ere Miss, you don't 'alf talk posh, you sound like the Queen!' I break into a smile; the kids in the borstal said the same thing and my response is going to be exactly the same.

'Well it doesn't mean I'm any different to you just because of the way I speak.' I repeat the same sentence with a cockney twang and then in a French accent. This brings the house down and they clap my performance.

'Why is it that it's people like us that get the supply teachers? We've had three already this year and so we ain't getting the same English teacher.'

I can't tell them the answer that's in my head and anyway it's enough talking. I start writing short sentences on the blackboard to illustrate ways to construct a descriptive passage. I write as fast as I can; I know I can't turn my back on these lads for long. But they're struggling to read the simplest of words either visually or phonically. It's all too apparent that they've either been discarded and left at the bottom of the pile, or they've spent too much time bunking off school. They're full of bravado and loud excuses.

'Can you read ok?' I don't give Martin Chivers time to answer on their behalf. It's clear by their mutterings as they shift uncomfortably in their chairs.

'Right. I'll bring some comics next time and we'll make a start with them. It won't take long before you're able to read.'

How can they go through primary school and not be able to read?

I switch to doing oral work, using the classroom as a descriptive example, showing how we can accurately communicate our thoughts into words. I applaud their suggestions and share their humour, but quickly put them down if they overstep the mark and they accept it. They're beginning to show some interest in learning. It's a start. The school bell goes for the next lesson which means a trek to the other building. They half-heartedly leave the classroom; the noise, the shouting across at each other starts up again. Some of the lads actually thank me as they saunter out cheerfully, saying, 'See ya Miss.'

As I gather my things together, I'm aware that Martin Chivers is hovering near the door, waiting, presumably so he can speak to me on his own.

'Er ...' There's a pause, and then with a cheeky grin he says, 'My name isn't Chivers Miss, it's Martin Jones.'

I look at him with a quizzical expression.

'Martin *Chivers* is my hero, he scores goals for Spurs, loads of 'em and Spurs is *my* team.'

And with that, he saunters triumphantly out of the classroom, punching the air with his fist, singing *'Come on you Spurs, come on you Spurs!'*, his deep, rough voice trailing down the corridor.

I chuckle as I pick up my bag and timetable. Well, at least he's had the decency to clarify it for me, he could have continued with his little joke and they'll all be calling *me* gullible, but they've probably forgotten that word already.

End of lesson notes: Check with the head of English whether I can use comics as a reading resource. Look up goal-scoring stats for Martin Chivers to surprise Martin Jones with

I really have to question why these fourteen-year-old lads I've just been teaching aren't in the 'Remedial Department'. Surely they should be. And what a horrible label for the lads who *are* in the 'Remedial Department'. They might as well call it the 'Backward Department'. I look at the school information booklet.

All boys follow a broad and general course for the first three years in mixed-ability groups, though in the second and third year, setting is introduced for some subjects, e.g. French. Those who show an aptitude for languages also begin German and/or Latin studies in these two years.

Well that's these lads out then. They don't even show an aptitude for learning their own language. Let's read what it says they do in the remedial classes in Hut Y …

A specialist team of teachers is responsible for the remedial teaching of boys with learning problems: these boys are withdrawn from their groups for short periods of intensive training.

I wonder what length of 'intensive training time' these Year 3 lads have had? And the final comment?

The school is structured to give each individual boy the opportunity to develop his talents and aptitudes to the full in an atmosphere of disciplined purposive study.

I have to read that line again. Is that what I've just experienced while taking my first English class?

No time to ponder, it's time for the next lesson, another English class, this time with boys from the lower bands in Year 4. I set off for the old grammar school.

There's a long pathway between the two buildings, with high fencing separating the two huge tarmac playgrounds. I stride past hordes of boys toing and froing in both directions, some loitering and talking animatedly in groups, others charging around letting off steam. A few are walking in an orderly fashion. I enter the old building. It's like stepping back into a different era. Unlike the new building, it has the old style of classroom setup. The bottom half of the walls of each classroom are made up of shiny dark green tiles and the upper half with large, neat square panes of glass; even the door with the old-fashioned latch has glass panes. The pupils and their behaviour are on show. I walk slowly past the first classroom. The teacher must be standing in for an absent one because he's trying to teach his language lesson to an unruly group of lads who clearly have no interest in learning. A few pupils are copying down French words from the blackboard. Two lads are shouting across the classroom at each other, three more are excitedly engaged in a paper-plane-throwing exercise while others cheer them on. It's not this teacher's fault he can't maintain order with this raucous bunch of kids. Here he is in a traditional school building with a set of pupils whose behaviour he has no idea how to control. How on earth do you teach French when some of them can't comprehend nouns and verbs in their own language?

I hasten on to the classroom further along the corridor and get a surprise when looking in at the class I'm about to take. Scattered around the room are twelve or thirteen lads and they're all seated at their desks. I breeze in, apologise for being late to a chorus of 'That's alright Miss, we don't mind how late you are' and smile back at them. They're a cheerful-looking bunch of lads, a mixture of skinheads sitting in the front desks, a group of boys from ethnic minorities in the middle, and three or four dishevelled long-haired individuals at the back.

Sitting bolt upright in the front row is a friendly-looking lad who introduces himself as Jimmy Tag. I resist the temptation to ask if it's his real name. Jimmy epitomises how one expects a skinhead to look. He's got spiky, clipped blond hair, the sleeves of his blazer are rolled up so they look too short for his long arms and his school tie's askew. His grey uniform trousers aren't long enough for his spindly legs and this look is completed by big black bovver boots that protrude from underneath his desk. I compliment him on his unusual take on his school uniform; he grins and tells me I look like a hippie.

I've learnt from the first class that getting these boys in the lower bands to talk and share their thoughts is probably the most valuable experience I can offer as a supply teacher, so I pose a question. 'How much money do we think we all need for a comfortable living?' I start the discussion by emphasising that having a roof over my head and enough money to pay the bills should be enough for me to feel comfortable. After all, there are so many children around the world who barely have enough food to survive, why would I want or expect anything more? Jimmy thinks this is a contentious statement, even though he thinks I'm a hippie. He makes a good case in front of the class as to why he wants a lot more dosh and doesn't believe I don't too.

'Ah, come on Miss, wouldn't ya want a swimming pool?'

The next thing that happens couldn't be more timely. For my 21st birthday, my parents had given me a ring with a beautiful mounted amethyst stone, set either side with a couple of diamonds, but unfortunately the claw setting wasn't very secure.

''ere Miss,' says a grinning Jimmy. 'Your ring's fallen out.' And there, sitting on Jimmy's desk, is my beautiful amethyst stone. It must have landed there while I was waving my hands to illustrate my point.

'See, you *'ave* got more than you need,' he declares triumphantly.

I laugh and try to explain to the rest of the cheering class, who are wildly clicking their fingers and saying 'Licks, Licks,' that I don't *need* this very expensive ring, it's been given to me as a present by my parents so it would be wrong not to wear it, wouldn't it? The class naturally don't agree and they give Jimmy a proverbial pat on the back and declare him the winner of our 'argument'. What a fun, likeable character he is – and, of course, the most important aspect of this story is that Jimmy could so easily have nicked the amethyst, not that I'm suggesting he would have, but if that had been the case, I would never have known.

Don't judge a book by its cover Miss Beveridge!

I make a big show of thanking him for being so honest and when the bell goes at the end of the lesson, this cheerful class filter and dribble out, still triumphantly chanting 'Licks, Licks,' accompanied by a walk that looks almost like a dance it's so rhythmic and relaxed. I feel quite elated as I find my way to the staff room for a well-earned cup of tea.

I join the queue to get water from the big urn and get chatting to another teacher. He's called Andy Webb. He too is on supply and teaches maths, but he's not the typical type I associate with his subject. He's got long, black, flowing hair, round gold-rimmed specs, a fulsome beard and a very engaging smile. Wearing a casual, dark brown, loose leather jacket and a black shirt and tie, he gives the impression of being a smart hippie – another hippie. It seems from our quick conversation he's also interested in teaching pupils who've been labelled 'Remedial', but I don't have enough time to learn more about this attractive, gentle-speaking teacher, I have to seek out Mr Doolan, the head of English, before the bell goes for the next lesson.

Mr Doolan was head of the English Department when Henry Thornton was a grammar school. His thick, black spectacles, his flowing, wavy grey hair and his neat, black bow tie give him a distinguished air and a look reminiscent of Robin Day, the television presenter. I enquire about my previous pupils, but he doesn't seem to be aware of who they actually are. He reminds me about the English stock room where I can find shelves of books by Shakespeare and Charles Dickens as well as poetry anthologies. If these pupils are struggling to recognise the simplest of words, I'm not sure why on earth he expects them to be attempting to read *Hamlet* or Wordsworth.

'I don't think these books will work with some of my classes. I'll buy the latest *Dan Dare* and *Eagle* comics and take them in next week.'

The look of horror on his face and the subsequent gentle but firm ticking off I get for making such a suggestion, certainly puts

16

me in my place as a new supply teacher. But is this suggestion so off-beam? Are these lads realistically going to leave school with any passes in their exams? Maybe I'd best keep my thoughts to myself and not mention any lesson plans in future, not that I've been asked for them for this class, or any others, for that matter. At college we'd learned the importance of preparation, but as I'm only teaching English classes up to GCE O Level, I'm beginning to suspect there's not much interest in these lads. And even if I do get given a register for these bottom-band classes, there are bound to be more kids like Martin Chivers. I won't know their names from Adam. Maybe the staff don't bother with registers for the lowest set. Maybe they're actually grateful when some of these kids bunk off and don't turn up. If Mr Doolan is insisting I have to use books and not comics to teach them how to read, surely something like *Lord of the Flies* by William Golding might be more appropriate: it might even be beneficial to these lads to discuss the feral behaviour of the boys after their plane crash, and what happens to them when there's no adult authority figure.

I don't want to sound arrogant because I'm new to this job, or, indeed, that I'm pandering to the interests of these kids, but if your only experience is with teaching boys who are high achievers with an academic background, who are keen to learn, who sit at their desks and actually work, then let the staff wanting to teach the bottom-streamed lads be given appropriate resources – or at least let them find their own. The important thing is to motivate these kids to learn.

First morning notes: Keep your head down, keep quiet and hopefully the results will speak for themselves.

CHAPTER 2

DRAMA LESSON 1

The theatre is situated on the left side of the quadrangle and accessed on the ground floor by several wooden doors with glass panels. I arrive ahead of the class and unlock the doors. As you enter, you walk straight down the side of a concrete wall that leads into this wonderful, vast, cavernous space. If you stand and take in the whole auditorium, it looks and feels like a real theatre.

In front of me is the stage, which is huge in both width and depth. There are two full-length red velvet curtains that have been swept back and attached either side. The stage floor is made up of twenty wooden cubes, each one can be lifted and moved around to create different heights and working levels. A couple have been left standing on their sides. The seating area of this theatre is well raked and in two sections. The upper level behind me is the largest and steepest, with row after row of full-length, light wooden benches with backs; it's in three sections, one to the right, one to the left, and very long benches in the middle.

The lower level of seats is exactly the same design. Tucked away at the very top of the theatre on the right-hand side is a sophisticated lighting system housed in a big glass room.

I survey the area, feeling extraordinary lucky. How many schools have such a wonderful theatre? I can just imagine this modern, inspirational building lending itself to school productions, but there haven't been any, not yet. I am the first trained drama teacher to be employed at the school. The utilisation of this huge imposing space will certainly need organisation. It will be far too easy for lads to come and hide when they want to skip lessons or cause havoc. It's odd for it to be one of my first thoughts, but it's the reality. There's something about large spaces that boys love when they've been confined to a classroom. And, of course, there are, as I've been warned by the staff, waifs and strays who should be in their classes but wander around the school all day, so if these theatre doors are unlocked, they'll probably make a beeline for it as a place of refuge. I have the keys; I must take care of them.

I look at my timetable. After the mixed-ability classes in the first three years, it looks as if the lower set are the only ones in Year 4 who are going to be doing drama. They're not expected to be taking many O Levels, and drama is probably seen as a soft option. That's fine by me.

I can hear the Year 2 class arrive, so I leave the auditorium and wait outside in the cold. At least there's some concrete overhead to provide shelter if it rains. The class appear, looking engagingly excited. I line them up outside the theatre doors and introduce myself. Mr Allott, the head of PE, wanders over from his block while I'm doing so and stands next to me with arms folded. Maybe he thinks that, as I'm a new young teacher, I'll need a bit of support with these eager and enthusiastic boys. He watches as I tell the class I want them to go and sit quietly in the lower part of the theatre. He has, though, come for a different reason.

'I'm looking for a lad called Terry Timpson; he's gone missing from his classes again, so keep a look out for him in the theatre.'

I don't have a clue who Terry Timpson is, but want to be seen to be helpful and stay for a quick chat to find out more about Terry and then return to the theatre. The class are sitting exactly where they should be and look quite attentive. This isn't the expected behaviour from a Remedial class, so I'm hopeful my lesson will go according to plan. Maybe they're being respectful because Mr Allott was present when they lined up; PE teachers can have that effect on pupils.

I introduce myself once more to the class and start explaining how lucky we are to have such a magnificent theatre and begin outlining what we're about to do in their first drama lesson. As I'm talking, I hear a strange knocking sound coming from under one of the blocks that's been placed haphazardly on top of the stage area. I ask the class if they too can hear a knocking sound. There are some muffled giggles. A lad, impeccably dressed in his school uniform, enunciates in a beautiful, articulate voice: 'Miss Beveridge, they've hidden Omunegbo under the stage.'

To the sounds of 'snitch' and 'sneak', I climb onto the stage and, with the help of two volunteers, lift up the stage block.

Underneath, a cowering, frightened little lad is staring back at me. So that's what they were up to when I was talking to Mr Allott. And this same lad is telling me that this poor little boy they stuffed under the stage block is not only new to the Remedial class, he's also new to the school and can barely speak a word of English. What to do? There's no point in my wasting time trying to find out who the guilty culprits are. I apologise to little Omunegbo, making it as clear as I can with my body language.

I restart the class. The theme I've prepared for their improvisation is classroom behaviour, deliberately chosen on the assumption that for many of these boys it will be poor and disruptive, which will quite probably be down to their lack of ability and learning skills. I hope to find out and right now, given what they've been doing to this poor little lad, it couldn't be more appropriate. Organisation. I need a volunteer to play the role of a teacher. One lad doesn't hold back in his enthusiasm for the chance to be in charge and tells me his name: Tyrone Henry. I tell him his task is to decide what subject he's going to teach (he chooses maths) and think of the type of language he will be using to get his class to listen, and to plan in his head what they will be learning (times tables).

Meanwhile, the rest of the class, who I'm sitting well away from Tyrone, are trying to contain their energy and excitement as they plan what they can do to disrupt his lesson or, put simplistically, make this teacher's life hell. I sit among them, persuading them to keep their voices down so Tyrone can't hear and, in answer to one of the lads' questions, I agree that yes, they can act out the sort of things they already do in their own classes. This agreement seems to ignite a wealth of ideas as they think of all their misdemeanours, each lad clamouring to relate a classroom incident. I'm having to train them not to all shout at once, but to instead raise their hand if they've got something to contribute to the improvisation. Lots of hands go up. One or two of the boys are a little hesitant and not contributing, maybe they're not too happy about behaving badly, including the boy with the beautiful speaking voice who'd kindly informed me about the imprisoned boy. I explain that's the whole point about these drama lessons; it's all about acting. I walk away but keep within earshot to hear them finally establish which band of pupils they will be (they choose to be Remedial pupils, in fact themselves), who's misbehaving and how to misbehave with the teacher. In other words, they will be the ones in charge, not the teacher.

We're ready to make a start. On the stage we arrange the chairs like a classroom. There's no desk we can use for the teacher, so we place a chair opposite the pupils and give the teacher my own bag to carry. I ask Tyrone what his teacher's name is going to be. Quick as a flash he says 'Mrs Fox' at which they all jeer and cheer. My mistake; that's clearly their class teacher. I tell him it's to be Mr Smith, he's to arrive late to teach and to make his entrance when I tell him.

The 'rabble' of the class starts on their cue as they await their teacher. Needless to say, not many of them are seated. Enter Mr Smith and insults are straight away hurled at him. It's an exaggerated version of some of the things I'd just witnessed in some of the classes when walking down the corridors. Well, I hope it's an exaggeration. Mr Smith constantly shouts, repeating the same threats over and over again and tries to teach them their two times table, writing on a pretend blackboard. Sometimes he glares at them to no effect, but in reality, he's had enough. He doesn't know what to do with them. I let it continue. I'll give the class their due, they didn't overstep the mark and get over-silly with their bad behaviour. And who, by the way, was the one 'acting' being the most challenging, disruptive pupil? The one with the beautiful speaking voice. Eventually, Tyrone turns to me and shouts. He mutters a few swear words, and looking totally defeated declares, 'I can't do it, they won't shut up,' and stomps off the stage, back down to the safety of the seating area. It's having the desired effect.

There ensues the most constructive, useful, positive dis-cussion. I feel sure that having the opportunity to act out this situation is enabling them to empathise with the teacher. How does the lad playing the teacher feel? 'Angry! And who'd want to be a teacher anyway?' is Tyrone's sulky reply, said with a great deal of venom directed at his classmates. And what has the class learnt in 'Mr Smith's' lesson? What has the teacher managed to teach them? Their eureka moment – nothing. So, if this was a real class, not of course that they themselves would behave like this, what would the outcome be when they leave school? And is it right to put another human being through such misery, whether it be a teacher, a parent or Omunegbo? I didn't need to hear any response, their body language conveyed their embarrassment.

Before the class go to their next lesson, I ask two of the lads their names, including the one they call a sneak, as they've been outstanding in the improvisation. They've also made some very interesting observations and contributions to the discussion. The one with the beautiful speaking voice is called Patrick. I've just realised who he sounds like: it's the versatile, funny comedian Frankie Howerd. The other more softly spoken lad, but equally smartly dressed, is called Rupert. His school uniform is hidden by a long navy Crombie coat with the collar turned up; he looks quite dapper.

As they leave the theatre, I call these two back and ask them whether, if I were to start a school drama club, they would be interested in becoming members. My idea was that it would probably take place in the lunch hour or after school. They nod their heads in approval and sound really keen and enthusiastic. I ask them to write their names in my book so I can contact them via Mrs Fox, their Remedial class teacher. Patrick very slowly writes his name, passes the pen to the next lad to write his, except he writes Rupert X. Not again, not another football supporter like Martin Jones. Maybe his idol isn't a goal scorer, maybe it's the civil rights activist Malcolm X? I query his name to make sure. The reply from this thirteen-year-old lad takes me completely by surprise.

'I don't know how to write my second name, so I write X for it. Rupert X.'

However did this boy go through primary school unable to write his surname?

• • •

I'd learnt so much about the importance of improvisation and socio-drama when I was in the National Youth Theatre in 1965. At the age of sixteen, I'd successfully got through two rounds of auditions and been accepted for the summer course at Chalk Farm, London in a school opposite the Roundhouse Theatre. The improvisations we did had an enormous impact on me and have influenced my drama teaching ever since. It was the same summer that Helen Mirren played Cleopatra in the National Youth Theatre's production of *Anthony & Cleopatra* at the Old Vic. She was at an English and Drama three-year teacher-training college in Hampstead, the college that I myself was to attend a couple of years later. Helen took time out from her rehearsals to come and talk to us about the play. As she sat on a chair discussing her approach to the role, she slowly and with a very deliberate, almost hypnotic action, brushed her long blonde hair. I'd made good friends on the course with Susannah Clapp, a lively outgoing girl. Together, we sat on the floor at Helen's feet, looking up adoringly, as we, along with the rest of the group, hung on her every word.

Experiences such as the Youth Theatre were invaluable and, for me, a turning point. It was a nurturing environment, a place where you could question and interact without fear of reprisal. A place where you could improvise with other, vastly more experienced hands. Some of the boys at Henry Thornton School are so talented, I wonder if it would be possible for them to audition, even though two of the most gifted lads, Patrick and Rupert, are from the Remedial class and one can't read a word. I need to find a way around it; they shouldn't be penalised just because they hadn't been given the tuition they surely should have had at primary school. I make a mental note and park the thought.

In the following Year 3 class, Jack immediately gets my attention. When lining the boys up outside the theatre, he looks so much smaller than his classmates, and it's obvious why he's close to tears. He's being shoved to the back of the queue in a really rough, jeering manner by the last boys to arrive and they're enjoying ridiculing him. He's hanging back looking pitifully isolated; his vulnerability reminds me of little Omunegbo from the Remedial class. I walk alongside Jack as we enter the theatre to gently probe him and find out more. I sit the class in the lower, more intimate part of the theatre, and decide to switch from my lesson plan to the topic of bullying.

After the boys have defined what they think the word means, with smirks aimed in Jack's direction, I ask one of the worst perpetrators I'd seen pushing Jack outside to stand on the stage. I tell him no matter what abusive comments are aimed at him, he cannot retaliate. He just has to stand there. If he doesn't like it, he can ask me at any time to stop. He cockily and confidently climbs onto the stage and triumphantly looks down at us, his audience. He thinks he's the lucky chosen one. I then (and this might sound cruel) start to jibe and mock him about his appearance. He's taken aback but not showing any adverse reaction, so I single out one or two in the class to pick on him too, and invite Jack, who is initially hesitant, to do the same. The class are enjoying hurling insults at the boy, who is beginning to look visibly hurt and uncomfortable. He is clearly getting the message.

I sit him back down with the class and lead a discussion asking him to describe how he felt standing there. To his credit, he doesn't hold back. He now realises, with a cursory glance in Jack's direction, what he must be feeling. I ask the class if they have anything to say to Jack and they don't need any prompting to apologise. And I myself apologise to the boy for putting him on the stage to humiliate him, but he has the grace to understand why I did it.

An important conversation ensues. The boys say there's too much bullying happening on a regular basis around the school. For example, if there's a group of older lads and you hear 'Gimme money, right', then you know that one of the innocent newbie Year 1 lads is being duffed up and having to hand over his dinner money. The boys ask what they can do about it. We decide the best advice we can give these first years and any others that are being bullied for their money is to hide it in their socks. It'll probably feel very uncomfortable, but at least it will be them that get to eat, and not the mob who share out stolen money at the hot dog van parked outside the school gates.

For all the lads in the class, it's a hugely valuable lesson, one of sensitivity and empathy. No, it wasn't what was planned, but it was about understanding human behaviour and emotions and that is surely what a drama lesson should be about. Drama is so much more than understanding a plot in a play or reading parts from a script.

End of lesson notes: Have faith in yourself and don't underestimate the boys when guiding these improvisations; their response is excellent and shows they're willing to learn from these socio-drama lessons.

Reminder: Next time, check Jack is no longer being bullied.

I'm feeling exhilarated; teaching drama is living up to my expectations. I'm about to try an improvisation I originated after listening to a conversation between two teachers in the staff room; it was about a lad in Year 4 called Fitzroy Williams and I'm about to take his class. He sounds like a very self-assured lad, known for being 'mouthy', but his behaviour and attitude in class isn't causing the concern, it's what's been happening outside of the school that's a major worry.

Fitzroy's been cautioned for molesting a female on Clapham Common, a serious offence that if repeated would see him put away in Stamford House, a Children's Remand Home in Shepherd's Bush, West London. By all accounts, it's a frightening place to be and one that surely should be investigated when so many lads have related despicable accounts of their horrific experiences there. The class seem an affable lot, a small class of fifteen. I introduce myself and ask them to sit in the upper part of the seating area. It's not been difficult to identify Fitzroy when watching them walk into the theatre, his body language oozes confidence, his booming voice drowning out the rest.

Let's see if my planned improvisation will work, but I have a backup if it doesn't.

I ask Fitzroy, without any explanation, to sit at the top of the theatre and out of earshot while I discuss with the rest of the group what we could do to intimidate him and the reason why I want him to experience feelings of vulnerability. We agree a plan. We'll circle round him and one by one verbally insult him and, on my cue, become occasionally physical, but they must assure me it will be in a controlled manner. I'm showing trust with the group and emphatically say that should anything get out of hand, they must stop immediately. I confirm with Fitzroy we have a plan sorted and he agrees that while he stands on the stage, he has to be powerless to do anything, nothing is in his control, he just has to stand in the middle of the circle and take whatever is thrown at him, but, like the lad in the previous class, he can call a halt by asking me to stop, which I reassure him we will do. Fitzroy has no idea why I'm asking him to do this.

We walk slowly and menacingly round him in a big circle, taunting and insulting him, with different boys moving in to push him in the chest or aggressively sneer at him while trying to trip him up. Fitzroy controls himself as the circle closes in and he moves round looking at our faces. He appears physically relaxed, making him even more open to abuse and like a helpless rag doll when he doesn't respond physically. The boys contain their level of role play. I call a halt; it's making the desired impact. This is improvisation at its very best.

In the ensuing discussion, he says he's experienced feelings of vulnerability he's never before experienced and this shared, honest and trusting improvisation is enabling him to understand his victim's reaction. The reason for doing it is unspoken to the class, it doesn't need to be said; Fitzroy's grasped why I've put him through the improvisation. If I hadn't made the right judgement about his character and the trust he's shown in me as a teacher, I wouldn't and couldn't have attempted the improvisation. I like to think it might play a major part in keeping Fitzroy away from both Clapham Common and Stamford Hill Remand Home.

Lesson notes for the lower bands. Drama lessons to be based around improvisation and not from existing written plays. In mixed-ability groups, there are some excellent readers alongside those who really struggle. Improvisations make it more of a level playing field and the confidence and talent among so many of the lads is outstanding.

I'm on a roll. This is where I want to be. I successfully apply for the permanent post for a Scale 2 Head of Drama plus some English teaching. Now I can start recruiting members for the drama club.

CHAPTER 3

THE TENPENNY THEATRE

There are several lads showing an interest in joining the drama club. Lads who are shy and totally lacking in self-esteem, lads who ooze confidence, lads who speak posh like me, lads who muddle up their singulars and plurals, cheeky lads, lads with complex anger issues, lads with aspirations. I can see the potential of mixing them all together. This club might well, albeit in a small way, provide an answer to some of the many complicated and often shocking problems the teachers are experiencing around the school. And not only that, I am also no longer alone in my quest to improve the lives of these boys in need of so much support.

Andy Webb, the maths teacher, and I have become a couple. A few months ago, during a school trip, we had the opportunity to get to know each other beyond the confines of the staff room. The school had hired a whole train for the day to take the first and second years to Hastings. Andy and I volunteered to accompany the boys, as did several members of staff who relished the thought of spending the day relaxing in deckchairs on the beach. But given the fact that all the Clapham shops had window notices saying, 'NO Henry Thornton boys are allowed in this shop.' Or 'Only TWO boys from Henry Thornton School are allowed in this shop at any one time,' we had envisaged a Battle of Hastings, with sea-front shop-shelves being inexorably emptied. The trip certainly had its moments, but it was wonderful to see so many of the boys who'd never been to the seaside before, splashing about in the sea and just feeling free running around in the outdoors. Andy built sandcastles with the lads, who ran backwards and forwards carrying buckets full of sea water to make a moat. I helped Omunegbo bury some of his classmates under a heap of stones. It was an invaluable day out for the boys; and for Andy and me, it was the beginning of a lasting personal and professional relationship.

Decisions about the drama club are made: Andy and I will run it together – we both have the same aims in wanting to make sure it is truly comprehensive and representative of the school. Andy will bring his specific talent for comedy writing with his zany sense of humour and I'll coach and direct the boys. We'll run it twice a week after school. It's not going to be easy to decide who we can pick and mix, or the maximum number we can cope with. There are so many boys needing nurturing, it doesn't seem right or fair, but we know we're going to have to restrict the numbers if we're to have any real influence and make a lasting impact with the most disadvantaged. We'll ask lads such as Patrick and Rupert, who will need help with their scripts, and invite known troublemakers like Samuel, the lad who was trying to break down my theatre doors. Joe, a misfit in Year 4, needs pastoral care, his long curly hair is straggled and filthy, he smokes cannabis and loathes the school. His artwork is superb. He's a lost soul, has no connection with his parents at home and cannot relate to any of the pupils in the school. Unfortunately, he's showing no interest in joining the drama club and will have to be on my list for a home visit. He'll wander into the theatre for a chat, but there's just not enough time to give kids like Joe the day-to-day time they so obviously need. We decide to initially cap the numbers at twenty-two. It might be useful to have some additional assistance with this mix of boys and help is at hand, but it's not in the form of a teacher. It's a lower sixth form pupil called Jeff Thacker.

Jeff is a prefect and is well-respected around the school, even by the most challenging of boys. He was previously a grammar-school boy, speaks with a slight South London accent, and has a confident air of authority. Not long after I'd started teaching drama lessons, he'd wandered into the theatre during one of his study periods and was intrigued by the power of improvisation and the outcomes he was seeing. He asks if he can attend some of the drama lessons during his sixth-form study time as he's thinking of becoming a teacher and I'm only too happy to oblige.

After school, I lead improvisations in the drama club to enhance the boys' relationships, and as they grow in confidence, as their ages and circumstances gel, we become ambitious and start rehearsals, shaping and moulding the emerging scenes for our first production, the pantomime *Sleeping Beauty*. Andy is writing a hilarious, simplistic script. He's keeping the recognisable story line we all know, but writing his own take on it, making it identifiable with the school and using references to the local area. He writes ingeniously funny characters for the club members, building it around their personalities and eccentricities. We have the most enormous good fortune to have Kenny, a fifth-year pupil, who's a hugely talented pianist and composer, the icing on the cake when devising our song-and-dance routines. He was previously in the grammar school and is shy and reserved; the drama club will embrace him as much as he embraces us.

Rehearsals begin in earnest late October. Every available lunchtime and after school time becomes focused on gearing up for our first drama-club play. It's tiring, especially when rehearsing at the end of the school day when the lads are let loose in the theatre. But it's exhilarating. Jeff, with three other sixth formers, starts attending the rehearsals; we're grateful for their support and enthusiasm, especially with the boys who can't read and the ones who are volatile. They're all so different in ages and temperament, but will they continue to get on with each other when under pressure and the reality of performing to an audience hits?

Rupert, from the Remedial class, always arrives quietly, drifting into the auditorium; you suddenly become aware of his presence behind you: smiling, waiting. Wearing a dark, navy Crombie coat with collar turned up, his hair a huge Afro halo, he smiles at Andy and says softly, 'Sorry I'm early, Sir.' It's their joke, their connection. Patrick is the total opposite. A booming voice precedes him as he announces his arrival while confidently striding into the auditorium with his satchel carefully placed diagonally across his torso from the right shoulder. He appears as if it's the start of the school day, his gleaming face shines, his pursed lips breaking into a beaming smile, his school uniform spic and span. Floyd, well, I'm never sure what his mood will be, he can be reserved, or bounce in full of life and enthusiasm. John, a lovable fourteen-year-old is so theatrical, so outlandish, so larger than life, his adoptive ageing parents must find him a total mystery. As for Tom, he doesn't seem to know what planet he's on. A handful of the lads look as if they're ready for a fight, while others look young enough to still be in primary school. And it's guaranteed that Samuel will arrive with a face looking like thunder, which will immediately break into a huge grin as he approaches. Either that or he's already with me in the theatre having bunked off lessons to join in with the drama classes (which is far better than wandering the streets all day, in my opinion). He greets the rest of our mob as my personal assistant. Andy has coaxed along a little lad from his maths class. He's heard from the Games Department that this lad had steadfastly refused to change into his swimming trunks and when the teacher insisted, he could see why: his back is covered in whip marks. This mish-mash group of lads come flying in at lunch times or straight after school, ready to get down to rehearsals which are now happening four evenings a week.

And out of this drama club is born the little production company we're going to call the Tenpenny Theatre. Why the Tenpenny Theatre? Because that's all we're going to charge our audiences. Schoolboys, their families, their friends and locals, we want them to come and fill the theatre for every performance in our three-hundred seater theatre.

We manage to keep our overheads down by hiring scenery from a company called Stage Productions and fancy costumes from the Inner London Education Authority Equipment Centre. We select fantastic outfits at incredibly low prices from their huge theatrical wardrobe collection. Some of the very extrovert lads like Patrick and John love dressing up, and there are squeals and shrieks of hysteria as they try on the lavish dresses and wigs. Others like Rupert show a little more restraint, he needs gentle persuasion to complete his pantomime costume with a pair of ivory silk jodhpurs. When casting Samuel, we make sure he doesn't need to wear an outlandish costume, just in case it triggers an upset. Admittance to the performances will be by programme, bought in advance for ten pence in the school lunch-hour or at the theatre doors on the night. That is, of course, if there's going to be an audience; we have no idea how popular it's going to be. Andy draws an exquisite programme cover depict-ing the pantomime in pen and ink, and my mother types the cast list and the names of the production staff. We can print the programmes in a different colour for each of the two consecutive performances and roll them off in the staff room. Andy does a lighting plot and will operate the sophisticated board in the

Tenpenny Theatre dress rehearsal

Scrooge dress rehearsal, 1974

lighting box, I'm taking charge of the costume rehearsals, and will be the peacemaker should any behavioural problems arise, stalwart Jeff is the stage manager. I make sure I have a good prompt copy at the ready just in case it's needed.

Everything is in place and we nervously await our first night. Ticket sales are going well and the Evening Institute, which is based at the school, have agreed to sell refreshments in the interval. How will this fun, slightly irreverent first school play be received in this comprehensive? Will the staff come? Will the headmaster come? Maybe certain teachers from the English Department won't find it acceptable that a pantomime is the school's first production and won't applaud our attempts to integrate so many pupils with a variety of complex problems into the drama club. Maybe they won't attend the performance. Their loss. We have a huge supporting cast of helpers from the sixth form and invaluable expertise from family and friends. Mick, a lifelong friend of Andy's, has been attending the dress rehearsals with his drum kit, so he's now ready to perform on the night with Kenny, our pianist. My younger sister Rowena is turning her creative hand to doing the make-up and, if required, will help to keep the kids calm and quiet backstage. Everything is in place, we're ready to go.

It's the opening night and ticket sales have been astonishing – it's a sell-out! All three hundred programmes sold! I cautiously peep through the red velvet curtains. Bravo! The theatre is full, with a few latecomers having to stand down the sides. Many of the school lads, their parents and friends haven't been to a live theatre production before. Our performances involve audience participation; we felt that Patrick's booming voice lent itself to asking questions of the audience and the 'he's behind you' act. But can he do it? In the prologue, he bellows a question out several times until he gets the audience response he wants. They finally enter into it with such vocal gusto, we're sure they can be heard as far away as Clapham Common Tube station. What a pro Patrick is: he's completely at home on the stage, definitely a younger version of Frankie Howerd. Even quiet, shy, retiring Rupert, once he's in costume, is finding his voice, and, like Patrick, he has the audience eating out of the palm of his hand. The confidence and self-assurance these lads have on stage is amazing.

We should never have worried about any of them; they all rise to the occasion as one united family and Andy and I are blown away. The prompt copy is never needed. Every minute

Music Hall and Tenpenny Theatre programmes

of the rehearsals in the lunch hour, every minute of rehearsals after school has been worth it. During lunch hour the next day, there is a long queue outside the theatre doors, with boys with tenpenny pieces waiting to snap up the remaining seats for the final performance the following night. We are thrilled. *Sleeping Beauty* is going to set the precedent for our future productions and will enable us to finance hiring more sets and costumes for our next lot of plays.

It seems quite strange that Henry Thornton is a male, macho and violent school and yet inexplicably we're getting away with our lads wearing an array of dresses, miming to pop songs and singing songs from hit musicals that Andy has woven into the plot. Three of the lads, Patrick, Tyrone and Floyd, are dressed as The Supremes singing 'Baby Love' in unison while beautifully performing my well-rehearsed choreography. They looked hilarious in their long, flowing, gold lamé dresses, their big black bovver boots protruding from hem lines, their heads sporting crooked long black curly wigs. It had brought the house down in the middle of the pantomime. We can only assume the warring gangs and the disinterested youths who bunk off lessons and loiter around the school recognise the success and professionalism of this entertaining sell-out production; it's something they and the school can and should be proud of – there's very little else. There's been no sending up of the lads nor duffing them over during school time. It's more like reverence, a 'respect bruv' from the rest of the one thousand five hundred lads. A few staff do come, but not the headmaster.

From then on, each play, whether it's a Christmas pantomime, a summer spectacular, or a revue, showcases the many talents and skills of these lovable lads. The theatre is always full to capacity with what becomes three consecutive evening performances. One of my favourite summer productions is *A Victorian Music Hall*, with the boys dressed in an array of Victorian costumes. The first half of the show is a fun hotch-potch of entertaining acts, linked together by Tony, a popular school prefect, who acts the chairman and host for the evening with great aplomb. Len, a big, congenial West Indian sixth former and talented actor, is the ventriloquist with two first-years seated either side on his lap. He's billed in the programme as 'Len with his amazing dummies'. Jimmy and Timmy are 'death-defying acrobats', followed by a five-piece we call 'The Clapham Crooners' who are all decked out in striped blazers and hats while singing 'popular songs of yesteryear'. Patrick is 'a man of many costumes and guises' and so on. For the latter half of the evening's entertainment, Andy has written a Victorian melodrama titled *The Eye of Wuz-Fur-Denna* (subtitled 'The Stolen Ruby') which has the audiences in uncontrollable fits of laughter.

It soon becomes clear that not only do the lads enjoy taking part in musical numbers, at least a half dozen of them love to dance and do so with great skill and panache. They're quick to learn the steps and really keen to improve their dancing skills. I decide to take separate dance sessions for these lads. Three of them are West Indian and have a wonderful natural way of con-tracting and rippling through their bodies. We all learn from

The boys rehearsing. L to R Patrick, Tyrone, Floyd and Jeff.

them and I incorporate their style into the funky dances I create for them. The boys are becoming our male version of 'Pan's People', the weekly BBC *Top of the Pops* dance group.

Helping the lads who can't read a word of their scripts is a shared task; helping the lads to conform to the school rules and temper their volatile behaviour to avoid expulsion is a shared task; helping the lads to overcome their shyness is a shared task. One night, when we discover all the takings of tenpenny pieces have gone missing a couple of hours before curtain-up, it's shared detective work. Who was the last person to be seen walking past the money? Who is now missing? Andy jumps into his Hillman Imp and drives round to the culprit's house just in time to retrieve all the money. He finds the suspect doling out our tenpenny pieces to his family; their house had caught fire the night before. The play goes on that night as if nothing happened.

Besides his role sitting on the stage with me as my *Blue Peter* partner in the daytime drama classes, Jeff is also the guest greeter and officiator for family and important friends before the performances. He has a natural style, a quality of being in charge in a quiet but authoritative way. When Ma comes to the plays, Jeff lines up the cast and introduces 'Miss Beveridge's Mother' to each of the lads. I'm surprised Jeff doesn't ask them to bow. Ma dutifully and graciously shakes their hands as she works her way down the line and plays her part, her expected 'Royal' position.

The lads' acting, their comic timing and handling of a live audience, their vocal projection is outstanding. Patrick and Rupert from the Remedial class shine in every role they play and calm, dependable Len from the sixth form is also a natural talent. That parked thought from my earlier drama classes with them re-emerges. What an experience it would be for them to widen their horizons beyond the world of Remedial class and our Tenpenny Theatre, to apply for a National Youth Theatre audition. I know what it did for me; it could also do it for them. For the audition they are required to perform two speeches of their choice, one from a Shakespeare play, the other from a modern idiom. There is, of course, that one drawback to overcome. Reading. Patrick isn't so bad; not particularly fluent, but at least he can read most of the words. An obvious Shakespeare part for him, because he's a natural comedian on stage, would be Bottom from *A Midsummer Night's Dream*.

Rupert, like Patrick, is black and often on the receiving end of some very unpleasant racial taunts, I thought he would identify with Shylock from *The Merchant of Venice*, except, and it's a big except, this exceptional, likeable, talented young lad still can't read. With great sincerity, he stands on the stage proudly reciting the lines we'd taught him orally, acting his Shakespeare speech with great dignity.

'I am a Jew. Hath not a Jew got what eyes? Hands. Organs. Direction?'

But when he finally learns his speech correctly, having repeated different lines to us while walking in rowdy school corridors, or leaving Andy's maths classes, or sitting reciting with Jeff before club rehearsals begin, he's finally able to stand on the stage and declare:

'I am a Jew. Hath not a Jew eyes, hath not a Jew hands, organs, dimensions?'

The rest of the soliloquy flows. It is incredibly moving and powerful; it's definitely the right speech for him, he will surely make an impact. His second speech, a modern speech from *Zigger Zagger*, the 1967 Peter Terson play about rioting football fans, the gang mentality and their violent hooligan lifestyle, is equally as powerful and far more straightforward for him to learn. The passion and sensitivity that he conveys in this speech is compelling to watch. Rupert is experiencing violence in the home and violence in the school, he can relate to this speech too.

We take Patrick and Rupert to their audition in Eccleston Square in London. How that brings back memories for me, having auditioned at the same place in the very same room. Against stiff opposition, they pass both rounds. During the summer holidays, they rehearse with the National Youth Theatre for the two-week scheduled performances at the Jeanetta Cochrane Theatre, in the heart of London. Andy and I sit in the audience watching as Patrick and Rupert perform in a revival of the Youth Theatre's *Zigger Zagger*. We're proud parents *in loco parentis*, their own parents having never been to any of our Tenpenny Theatre productions, let alone come to see them in this production in the West End of London. Our two boys are part of the ensemble of very vocal football supporters that chant on stage facing the audience, the set constructed like the terraces of a football stadium. Both of them take it in their stride; we sit enthralled, wondering if they realise just what they've achieved.

The dancers are also beginning to make a name for themselves around the school. Garry, a very reserved fifth former, saw a couple of our previous plays and has become our latest addition. The lads in the drama club nickname him Illya Kuryakin because he's the spitting image of the actor David McCallum, who played a spy in the hugely popular TV series *The Man from U.N.C.L.E.* Garry has never danced before and wants to give it a go. He lacks confidence and hides in the back row when learning new dance routines and needs gentle persuasion and encouragement to come to the front. Garry told me the other day the teacher in his maths lesson tried to break up a fight by hurling the wooden board duster at them; it hit them so hard they exploded with anger and the boys fought all the more. No wonder Garry hid cowering under his desk.

I feel really fortunate. Garry's enthusiasm and willingness to learn dances matches Jeff's so I have five promising dancers, all talented and all different in temperament. I happily spend lunchtimes and any spare time after school training them, choreographing dances, perfecting their presentation. And as they are so popular with our audiences, we can happily incorporate a dance routine into the future storyline of every play. And via the drama club, Andy and I have found our own happiness and get married during the summer holidays.

CHAPTER 4

DR HOOHAA

After the success of our highly acclaimed pantomimes and revue, we start mulling over ideas for our next play. Andy and I feel the time is right to do something completely different, something that will utilise the many talents of this wonderful, incongruous bunch of lads, something more adventurous and original than our previous productions.

'Got it!' exclaims Andy. 'Our play is going to be a parody of *Dr Who* and we'll base it around a comprehensive school, a *fictitious* one of course.' There's a twinkle in his eye and a very knowing look.

What a great idea, what a superb opportunity to show what's really going on in our school. The impact of the day-to-day violence, the constant, aggressive disruption in the lessons, the unacceptably low academic standards. Our boys in the drama club will relish the chance to replicate some of this behaviour on the stage, and for some, they'll be able to play themselves. I have every faith Andy will write it with the zany humour that our audiences have grown to love, and I'm confident that with a bit of artistic licence, we can attempt to get a very serious underlying message across. The staff are struggling to cope and so are most of the pupils.

I've already hinted at some of the day-to-day chaos, the *laissez faire* attitude around the school, the dominance of some of the many roaming gangs, the menacing undertones of violence that permeate the seething corridors. One thousand five hundred pupils spill out of classrooms at the end of lessons. The sheer volume of boys sauntering, milling around, pushing and shoving, is like the London rush hour. How can these lads fulfil their potential in such an environment?

I love the freedom we have with our grass-roots productions; there's no interference or, indeed, the slightest bit of interest shown by the powers that be, so I don't think we're about to sail too close to the wind with this one. The headmaster has never attended any of our highly successful sell-out plays and this will be our fourth. It's full steam ahead.

Our spoof version of *Dr Who* starts to emerge; Andy has an endless wealth of material. Often he bases his dialogue around the many theme-related improvisations we do in the club and the ensuing conversations we have with the lads about the extraordinary incidents they witness during their lessons. We're also eavesdropping on enlightening, amusing, and very telling conversations in the staff room. *Dr HooHaa*, Andy's title for our play, is genius.

The scenario and script are finally in place. The Doctor will be a force for good, the Master a power for evil. Somewhere in the stratosphere is an anarchic school totally out of control. The boys are in a feral state because the school is run by a totally ineffectual headmaster who hides and hibernates in his office every day. The local school inspector will be summoned, the headmaster sacked and the education authorities forced to install a new headmaster. He will instantaneously transform the behaviour of these rebellious boys; their conduct will become impeccable and each and every one of them will achieve straight As in their GCE O Levels. But there will be a twist. The new headmaster is not a proper headmaster, he is the Master, aka the baddie in the real *Dr Who*. The Master will rule these pupils with a quirky robot that completely controls their minds. They will become his subordinates and help the Master with his evil intent to take over Clapham, England, the United Kingdom, the whole world. But help is at hand. Just in the nick of time, Dr HooHaa will turn up in his Tardis, defeat the Master and return the school and the pupils to ... their normal, anarchic, chaotic state.

Next: the main casting. It's not a problem, there's never any disagreement among the lads, the character and personalities of the twenty-five members are so strong, it's obvious who is suited to any given role. Because of the drama club's previous successes, there are lots of new lads wanting to take part in the shows. They want to be seen on stage by their mates, but haven't grasped the time, effort and dedication that will be required. Much as we would happily welcome lots of new members, we need to resist expanding our numbers in order to retain the original reasons for starting it, though Andy and I do readily agree we must accept a couple of extra Year 3 lads called Max and Terry because they're on the cusp of permanent expulsion. Terry with his mischievous smile and endearing character is a 'bovver boy', Max, more straight-laced, is prone to outbursts. Both are wildly spirited and rebellious lads with their own agendas and are very keen to join; they will certainly give extra gravitas and realism to the bedlam of the classroom scenes. Plus Andy and I, not too unrealistically, hope it will give them a good reason for staying out of any further trouble with the law.

Patrick, our beautifully dressed and well-spoken lad, is the obvious choice for the role of the teacher. Like Rupert, he's permanently in the Remedial block, not for any challenging or disruptive behaviour, but because his English and maths are woefully below the expected standard. Rupert, you may remember, is the lad who is still writing X for his surname.

How on earth did so many of these boys go through primary school barely able to read and write?

During rehearsals, in spite of his powerful persona on the stage, Patrick experiences genuine feelings of helplessness while trying to control this melee of boys shouting out to each other as they amble around the classroom. Some are throwing coins on the floor, others jeering and swearing as they pull the chairs away from the couple of lads trying to work. A few of our lads look very sheepish when they see a reflection of their own behaviour on the stage. Samuel, in particular, finds it difficult and is clearly embarrassed when reluctantly trying to act out challenging the authority of Patrick the teacher. It probably reminds him of my initial chance meeting with him when he was breaking down the theatre doors.

We cast Gary as the teacher's pet; he's a tiny first-year boy, petite in stature with long straight blond hair and choirboy looks. Like Patrick, he is beautifully well-spoken, his uniform always immaculate. This tiny, intelligent first-year boy is very amusing acting being dim and sycophantic and looking aghast at the classroom bedlam. He looks so out of place, as he does in real life in this aggressive school. He's well protected from the numerous school bullies during the day by his fellow drama club members. The all-important role of Dr HooHaa will be played by a delightful Year 3 pupil called Jermaine. He has the most pliable facial expressions, his huge eyes conveying the most wonderful air of incredulity and astonishment. The Doctor, if you're familiar with the television series, needs a female assistant. I ask Aaron, one of our excellent dancers, if he will bravely volunteer for the role, brave because he will be the only one wearing a skirt, but that doesn't faze him – he's used to it from the pantomimes. Rupert I'm casting as the Master. Unlike Aaron, it takes a bit of persuasion to get him to wear something a little out of the norm like thigh boots, but he's happy with the wrap-around black cloak. We record his scripts onto a cassette so he can learn his words. Max is now minus his friend Terry, unfortunately we've lost him to Stamford House Remand Home and will have to share his lines with the rest of the cast playing our classroom boys. It's sad to see such a congenial lad being banged up in a Remand Home. We're giving

Max a new role as a robot; he'll enjoy wearing his outfit because he'll be hidden by a helmet and a big silver-painted cardboard box and be unrecognisable should any of his raucous mates be sitting in the audience. Finally, we cast Sammy as the headmaster; I mean, of course, the fictitious headmaster.

While I direct the play, Andy is busy writing and adapting the lyrics to some well-known popular songs. Kenny, our talented pianist, is doing his usual stellar job of arranging them. Here are some typical examples. Try humming the tune of 'I'd Do Anything' from the musical *Oliver!* while picturing Gary, the teacher's pet, fawning all over him at the teacher's desk.

I'd do anything, for you Sir, anything, for you mean everything to me

Would you clean my boots?

Anything

Would you press my suits?

Anything

Would you bring me fruits?

Anything (while producing an apple from his school blazer)

I'd be top of the class (looking smug)

Like hell you would (as an aside)

The first verse of another example is most appropriate. It was a number 1 in 1972 called 'Black and White' by Three Dog Night. The song is about racism and was inspired by a US Supreme Court ruling that segregation in public schools is illegal. Andy changed the lyrics and the classroom of lads belted this song out while tying up the teacher with a rope.

The ink is black
The paper's white
We don't care
Cos we can't write
Read or write

The lads are really excited at the chance to perform in something so innovative and experimental and I'm enjoying improvising around the script, finding different ways of being creative with them. For example, when the Master arrives from outer space with his robot, to contrast their riotous classroom behaviour I'm doing the theatrical trick of slow motion. The class go from the thundering noise and organised chaos of fighting, throwing chairs and missiles around the room to instant silence. They walk as one, in hypnotic slow motion to sit bolt upright, arms folded behind their desks. Later on, towards the end of the play, I'll reverse this device when Dr HooHaa arrives to free the pupils from the clutches and spell of the Master. While they're reciting in unison with their controlled learning, they start making a slow, menacing, growling sound. It grows louder and louder until it escalates into a huge crescendo of an erupting cacophony of roaring noise as they burst into action, leaping over their desks, shouting and swearing as they revert back into their uncontrolled classroom chaos. Everyday normality will be restored.

Andy and I are delighted with the way rehearsals are shaping up; it's all looking extremely professional. We've now got financial support from the Clapham and Balham Evening Institute who are based in the school, so we're able to hire costumes and scenery, although this particular production needs very little. We're hiring costumes for the main characters from the Inner London Education Authority Wardrobe Department and apart from Gary, who can wear his own immaculate school uniform, the rest of the class can look scruffy and unkempt in their own clothes to match their defiant behaviour. We'll borrow desks and chairs from the school, and from LEA's School Scenery Department we can hire tall, dull-looking painted flats. We'll hinge them together on the stage to resemble classroom walls, a couple have wide bookshelves with books painted on them, so it'll give the set more of a classroom feel. We decide to pin big posters on the remaining flats, one saying 'No Smoking'.

The technical run-through and dress rehearsal go well at the end of the school day and carry on into our early evening classes with the evening institute. We've acquired a lovely, cuddly border collie dog called Watson from Battersea Dogs Home. When we know we'll be rehearsing late, we bring Watson to the school in our Hillman Imp and let him join us in the school theatre. Suddenly, during this all-important, concentrated dress rehearsal, six huge lads appear at the very top of the theatre stairs, jeering loudly and threatening us in a very intimidating manner. Andy shouts at Watson, the meekest and mildest of dogs, to 'go get 'em'. Quick as a flash, he bounds up the steep theatre stairs, probably expecting to be greeted and stroked at the top, but instead, is greeted by nobody. The abusive, hulky lads have fled terrified, screaming and swearing, never to be seen again. Perhaps we should employ the services of Watson during the school day.

At the end of the dress rehearsal we're really pleased and excited with *Dr HooHaa*. It's innovative, powerful, very dramatic and will clearly have a very effective message: at the same time, it can be enjoyed as a stand-alone comedy with recognisable characters from the television series. The whole production gels and I'm proud to say that not once do the lads, who are considered by so many of the staff to be unteachable, get out of control as they enact the scripted scenes of riotous behaviour. A good dress rehearsal, a poor performance? I hope not.

It's a nervous time by day as we await opening night. There's a buzz and a growing interest at the school; questions are being asked about *Dr HooHaa* as Andy and I are jostled along the corridors to teach our respective subjects. Some of the most notorious miscreants are intrigued and perhaps hoping to achieve some claim to fame upon seeing and hearing their words and behaviour replicated on the stage. It's good they're interested in coming; it might make them think about their own conduct around the school.

It's the first night and it's a full house, but we're nervous. My younger sister Rowena is standing watching with me in the wings, struggling to suppress her laughter as we watch many of the chaotic classroom scenes, including the 'Black and White' song they sing to Andy's lyrics. She listens to the words and whispers to me:

'Do you think you'll get away with this Lizzie?'

I turn to her grinning and nod as the audience laugh and let out a resounding cheer when Dr HooHaa overthrows the Master. They applaud wildly at the end, cheering and whistling, stamping their feet and demanding more and more curtain calls. Are they associating what they're seeing on stage with what is happening in the school, their school, or are they just seeing a fantasy stage version of *Dr Who*? The few teachers attending certainly seem to be getting the message.

The next day, queues are quickly forming during the lunch hour and after school for the remaining two performances: it's a sell-out with standing room only. At the end of the last performance, the father of one of the drama club boys stays behind to speak to us. He's a theatre director, praises what he's just seen and wants to arrange for us to put on our play at the Oval House Theatre in Kennington, not far from Clapham. They're renowned and respected in theatreland and have a great reputation for experimental theatre productions. Our play absolutely fits their criteria.

Life is full of coincidences. Oval House is a very well-known venue to me and I am both thrilled and grateful to have this opportunity. At my teacher training college, the boyfriend I was with at the time was part of a small theatre company called the Pip Simmons Theatre Group, mostly made up of past college students. They'd performed at Oval House in my last year at college. As a pioneering fringe theatre group, they'd managed to make *Hair*, the sixties American rock musical where everyone gets naked on stage, look tame by comparison. I'd been to see one of their productions at Oval House a few years ago and now, what an honour, we have an invitation and the privilege of taking our lads to perform Andy's very original school play there.

The date of this special performance is set and the parents of the pupils invited. We're so proud of these lads' achievements and saddened only a couple of the parents attended their sons' productions. Our talented club dancers' parents, for example, never came to a single performance. It's right for this Oval House performance to issue them with a personal invitation; besides, we need their permission to perform on a Saturday night at a different location.

Andy and I decide the audience at Oval House would welcome and benefit from some background information about the play, the origins of our drama club, how we want to make it all-inclusive, embracing disparate walks of life and including boys with complex needs, boys on the cusp of permanent exclusion and some that couldn't even read.

The theatre at Oval House is a very big, dark open space with a flat black floor, no proscenium arch or front curtains, just side black drapes. The audience is seated in rows on chairs very close to our lads, but we feel confident the lads won't be put off by that in spite of them being used to being on a raised stage performing to audiences that are seated well back. In fact, the close proximity of this audience could well be to our advantage, given the aggressive nature of the play. We hire a van and take a load of desks, chairs, a blackboard and an easel from the school; no other set is required, just the few costumes and props. Before the performance commences, we place an information sheet about our club on each seat. It doesn't include a named cast list; this is an ensemble, nobody is singled out and anyway, given the audience is being made aware of the ethos of the drama club, it would be wrong to name any of the cast individually.

What a spectacular performance on this special Saturday night! With no dress rehearsal, the lads go straight into the play and perform to a full house of a totally different audience. They are hugely impressed and enthralled at the effectiveness of the message that we're trying to convey, the theatricality, the professionalism and the talent of the cast. They unanimously agree it is totally original and unlike any other school play they have ever seen. They invite us to do some extra performances. It's all so overwhelming and incredibly exciting for Andy and me to suddenly have some support from somewhere other than the Evening Institute, and such professional acknowledgement. Could this be the start of us collaborating with Oval House on more creative works? But that is not how it turns out at all.

We return to the school the following Monday with the applause still ringing in our ears. I go to teach my English classes that morning, Andy to his usual maths lessons. It isn't long before both of us have a visit from Mr Edgerly, the deputy headmaster. He's been dispatched to escort us to the headmaster's office because he is demanding to see us. We naively assume it is to congratulate us.

Wow! Any pupils walking in the corridor past the headmaster's door that morning would instantly know that Dracula really does exist behind his office door. His shouting is totally out of control. A parent (probably the only one who attended) has complained, saying that our play reflected very badly on the school, not especially because of the content, but because of what we had written about the pupils in the drama club in the leaflet we'd left on each chair for the audience to read. This parent was absolutely furious, fearing we'd implied that his son was 'one of the pupils who couldn't read or was on the cusp of permanent expulsion'.

We stand before the headmaster listening to him ranting on while he stays firmly seated behind his desk. He yells at us for ages, suggesting our play was subversive (well, not in our eyes, but in truth we did want it to make waves) and repeatedly saying we didn't have his permission to write a leaflet, the leaflet we had both signed. This is true, we can't deny it; we hadn't asked his permission, but then he had never shown the slightest bit of interest in what was going on in his school theatre, or in any of the productions we had so successfully put on in his school, helping to bring in the local community. And, I must add, immeasurably helping control some of the most challenging lads' aggressive behaviour. Never once, even though he is the headmaster, had he appeared at or attended any of the sell-out performances of our highly original school drama club productions. And this one was our fourth. Why then, would we seek his permission to write a leaflet about our drama club?

We agree, of course, with the headmaster's emphatic statement that the play is entire fantasy and we had never said, nor indeed implied on the leaflet, that the play was based in any way on his school, although I did then say to the headmaster that, unfortunately, we do have some lads in our drama club who can't actually read. Once he finished shouting, he rounded off by asking us:

'What have you got to say for yourselves?'

Wisely, I leave the answer to Andy.

'Nothing,' he quietly replies.

'Will you have something to say for yourselves?' he barks.

'Yes,' replies Andy, his calm demeanour contrasting with the headmaster's overwrought tones.

'When?'

'When we've had a chance to think about the accusations.'

This might sound arrogant on Andy's part, but it isn't. We can both see the sack looming and we need to think very clearly about our next move. If we do stay, would we be shackled and not allowed to do any more productions, or, if we are allowed to continue with our drama club, will we be dictated to by the headmaster and have to do, for example, a Shakespeare production? It might keep Mr Doolan, the head of English, happy, but there will be no pupils left in the drama club; they wouldn't want to do one and neither would we. We'd just created our very own hoohaa.

Andy and I decide to let things cool and just quietly carry on with our daytime teaching. During the next three days, Mr Edgerly keeps asking us to go and see the headmaster, but each time Andy replies we need more time. I was given the full-time Drama and

English post two years ago, but Andy is still a supply teacher and therefore in a very different, very difficult position. Throughout the time of rehearsals and performances of *Dr HooHaa*, he'd been considering applying for the advertised full-time Maths post at the school with an upgrade to a Scale 2. Has he jeopardised his application and future at the school or, for that matter, at any other school? But now is not the time to look weak or to throw in the towel. He decides that in spite of what has happened he will go ahead and apply, expecting not to be given an interview.

Mr Edgerly by now is getting extremely anxious and almost commanding us to see the headmaster. Before we agree to do so, we decide that should we get the sack, we will go straight to our Local Education Authority and invite them to come and see the production for themselves so they can make their own judgement. We will also suggest they might like to pay a surprise, unannounced visit to the school, to see what actually goes on in this comprehensive.

It is with both reluctance and an air of defiance that we finally agree to go to the headmaster's office. We have our sleeves rolled up, metaphorically, with our much-rehearsed script in our heads. We stand before his desk with our heads held high, no longer looking and feeling like naughty schoolchildren, and await his verdict. But much to our utter, utter astonishment, he apologises. He stays seated and very quietly says that Andy's application implies he really is a dedicated teacher and that the whole issue is best forgotten. And that was that! Just like that, the matter is closed as far as he's concerned. It's the end of our very own hoohaa. We were utterly incredulous.

When we'd recovered from the meeting, we debated the outcome. What could have prompted this complete turnaround? We knew we'd sailed too close to the wind, more perhaps than we had originally intended, but we had never, ever in our wildest dreams expected him to climb down. From his initial, verbally aggressive reaction, we had assumed he was going to demand an apology from us, maybe our resignations? Chairman Mao's *Little Red Book* had recently been controversially published in a blaze of glory; did he think we young teachers had been influenced by its anarchic preaching? No. We are influenced by our pupils and fellow teachers, who are confronted on a daily basis by a relentless barrage of ill-discipline and violence from so many of the pupils, while being given zero support from the top. The pupils deserve better and so do the staff. It seems totally unacceptable and unthinkable to us that this can be allowed to carry on. That aside, what might have been the reason for this extraordinary turnaround of his decision? Does he think if he sacks us we will take this whole unsavoury episode a stage further and expose the fact that both the Local Education Authority and he, the headmaster, don't have a realistic idea of what goes on in his school? Well, how could he possibly know when he never comes out of the safety of his office? Maybe, just maybe, he knows that.

We decide to carry on with our drama club and make sure to base the next production on something light-hearted. I happily announce we are having a baby and Andy is promoted to a Scale 2 Maths teacher.

CHAPTER 5

OPPORTUNITY KNOCKS

Our four dancers are following Floyd's meteoric rise with great interest. He's instantly gone from being a school drama-club member – one of us – to being one of the most famous dancers on television. Floyd, the very lad who Andy had tried to persuade me to ban for his rude behaviour, has arrived – and how! Every Thursday evening, he's there dancing on *Top of the Pops*, one of the BBC's highest-rated television programmes. He's with 'Ruby Flipper', the newly formed dance group who've replaced 'Pan's People', the phenomenally successful, all-time iconic dance group. They're still choreographed by Flick Colby, the founder, but she's moved with the times, keeping her original female dancers and including new boy dancers. Sixth-former Jeff had seen an advert about auditioning for them as the credits had rolled at the end of a show. Three of the lads were adamant they wanted to go. Garry, because he was the last to join the dance classes and felt he had more to learn, was still lacking in confidence and elected not to audition. Tyrone wasn't interested. None of the lads are aware of the existence of dance academies or stage schools; I hadn't the heart to tell them and warned that the audition wouldn't be at all easy. I have no desire to dampen their enthusiasm, but I'm very wary of raising their hopes. I've heard how crammed the changing rooms and winding staircases can get at these mass auditions with dancers milling around waiting to get into the studio.

The audition was held at the Dance Centre in Covent Garden. I thought it best to leave them to it; a whole new world was about to open up to them. Jeff, being the oldest, said he would phone me after the audition. I hoped it would be a positive experience for the three boys and fire their enthusiasm for the future. Privately, I wasn't at all optimistic about their chances.

Later that afternoon I got the call. It absolutely took my breath away. The audition had been overflowing with hundreds and hundreds of lithe male dancers, all clad in an array of coloured T-shirts and dance tights, and Floyd, our very own Floyd, had been offered one of the two places, with Jeff himself being offered one of the two reserve places.

Wow! My heart skipped a beat. It was utterly unbelievable. Our boys, from the battleground of this unruly, violent comprehensive school in run-down Clapham, had triumphed with our very own unique style of dancing, a style I had developed with our wonderful West Indian lads: now it's making waves in the dance world! Their dedication, their love of dance, their rawness and purity of style had just been recognised by one of television's most successful choreographers. All those endless hours of training squeezed in during lunch hours and after school, me heavily pregnant in long flowing dresses: little could I have foreseen it would result in something as extraordinary as this. They had achieved something beyond my wildest dreams. The wonderful opportunities my mother ensured I had as a girl have been passed on to this next generation. Thank you, Ma. I wonder if these lads understood the enormity of what they'd just achieved?

All four of them, Garry and Tyrone included, become hugely ambitious; after all, if Floyd could make it to the top and walk into, or rather dance into, the biggest pop/dance show on television, why not something similar for themselves if they continue to work hard?

They so deserve to make it too, but could they? I begin training them with an even greater fervour and enthusiasm, perfecting the dances every available lunch hour and after school. Andy even finds a place to weave a dance into his script for *Scrooge*, our seventh Tenpenny Theatre production. I'm having the easiest of pregnancies in spite of the intense summer heat, and it doesn't affect my dance teaching.

Time passes. I take time out to give birth to our wonderful son Ben, the most affable, easy-going baby imaginable. He slips into my life and I continue on my journey; I don't stop teaching for long. When I do return, it's not to the day school; we decide

I'll just teach the dancers and be employed by the Evening Institute. We hold a meeting and collectively make an all-important decision to form our own professional dance group. The boys readily agree that if I am to take them to another level, it needs total commitment. Jeff is about to leave the sixth form and start a teacher-training course, it's fairly local and he can return in the evenings and at weekends to continue his training with us. Tyrone is a natural dancer and performer, but doesn't have the necessary staying power or the discipline to attend all the required rehearsals. I know it won't work out for him and need, for everyone's sake, to tell him, and he readily agrees. Garry and Patrick have complete focus and dedication, I have no qualms about their resolve. I realise that to enhance the group, to make it a more appealing commercial product, we will have to do the opposite to Flick Colby: we need girl dancers, probably three. We place an advert in *The Stage*, the fortnightly show-business newspaper, and hold auditions. We select three lively, outgoing girls, all with a history of dance training, either with dance academies or stage schools. We hire a hall in Clapham and start rehearsals. The boys live at home, are local and don't have to travel, but the girls are renting flats and two travel from the other side of London. After a while, it becomes very difficult to sustain the group financially. Viv, one of the girls, leaves, while Mandy and Jo stoically carry on with the hope that one day we will get a lucky break. And once again it's Jeff who makes the suggestion as to how we might get it.

'Why don't we audition for *Opportunity Knocks?*'

Opportunity Knocks is a great title for a television show because it describes exactly what it does. *Opp Knocks*, as it's affectionately known, knocks on the doors of performers from every sphere of entertainment, giving artistes a fantastic opportunity to showcase their acts. Singers, comedians, dancers, poets, impersonators, puppeteers, fire-eaters, an eclectic mix of speciality acts, all clamour to take part. After they perform, a panel of three showbiz faces make comments about these diverse acts, the studio audience vote with the notorious 'clapometer' for their favourite act, and the public vote by post. The combined votes result in the winner returning to compete the following week.

But, and it's a big but, I'm unenthusiastic about Jeff's suggestion. I'm not at all keen and really don't think it's a good idea. I don't view the programme with the same affection as its millions of viewers. In truth – I must confess the real reason – I am being very snobbish. I think the show is far too downmarket and cringe at the idea of looking so desperate that we need to audition for what is in my eyes a lowly, albeit popular, ITV entertainment show. My background and associated viewing for dance is far more upmarket programmes: the popular BBC Saturday night variety shows such as *Seaside Special*, or Mike Yarwood with the 'Young Generation' dancers, or a Tom Jones special. I'm no fan of Hughie Green, with his annoying catchphrases, weird mannerisms and odd facial expressions.

I'm embarrassed to reveal such an appalling attitude; how wrong and stupidly short-sighted I'm being. We need Hughie

Green's *Opportunity Knocks* so that unknown acts such as ourselves can have that one golden chance, a platform with huge viewer ratings on which to showcase our talent. I get my head round my appalling snobbish attitude and, for the sake of the dance group, agree to give it a go. We apply and wait for news of an audition date.

A letter arrives with the date and suddenly it all becomes very real. We have just one chance at the audition to captivate the panel with our style of dancing. What music will I choose to use to choreograph? Should it be to 'Don't Go Breaking My Heart' by Elton John and Kiki Dee, the dance for our last school production? The boys' strength, rawness and energy as they dance suits this pop song, but now we have the girls, it's probably a good idea to choose music with them in mind too. We settle on 'Get Back' by The Beatles. Rehearsals go well, with the girls adapting to a style of dancing they have now become very familiar with and it's gelling as a group, looking promising. We need to find a name for our newly formed group. Andy suggests that in spite of their ten legs we could call it 'Spider', a play on our married name. Will it bring us luck?

Before the audition, we go shopping to buy their outfits. We have very little money and need to get some appropriate, inexpensive but fashionable ones for them to wear. In *Scrooge*, our Christmas production, we had a dance number where the lads wore dungarees; we'd laboriously sewn sequins all around the bib of each pair to add some sparkle. Understandably, they want something different, something new. In the end, for the

Spider

three boys, Jeff, Garry and Patrick, we choose bright, tight-fitting T-shirts, a denim waistcoat and tight jeans. The girls opt for a white shirt which will be tied in a knot underneath their chests, jean hotpants and colourful, long, hoop-striped leg warmers that finish above the knees. It all looks very seventies. Somebody has to be prepared to speak on camera about the group should they get through the audition. Unfortunately, only one person can really talk knowledgeably about 'Spider' and that one person is me. I dread the thought of it; the group are the performers, not me.

The audition is held in a hall near Twickenham. On the panel is Doris Barry, the producer of the show. Good heavens! On hearing her name, I know my mother – who's at home looking after Ben – will be over the moon. Doris is the sister of Dame Alicia Markova, a ballerina my mother revered and had seen performing many times at the Sadler's Wells Theatre in London. And what a charming, encouraging woman Doris Barry is. She absolutely loves the grit of our lads; she recognises their lack of formal dance-school training and contemporary dance technique and sees it as a help and not a hindrance. They dance from the soul with uninhibited abandonment, with energy and a passion that can so easily be lost with gruelling technique-training. They have natural talent; I've just provided the tools. She applauds their dancing and is totally taken aback and marvels when hearing these lads have only learnt how to dance in lunch hours and after school in a tough South London boys' comprehensive school.

They get through the audition.

On the day of the filming at Thames Television Studios in Teddington, we arrive early for the technical rehearsal, then we're told we'll break for costume and make-up, before filming our routine in front of the live studio audience. Jeff, as ever, is taking everything in his stride, the rest of us are nervously watching the clock. We walk onto the studio floor to do the technical camera rehearsal and are introduced to the director. It's Keith Beckett. Oh my goodness. Here's a ballet dancer who I revered as a little girl, he's now directing us on *Opp Knocks*. I am transported back in time. I can feel myself sitting excitedly in the audience watching him dance with the Festival Ballet Company, dancing the role of the drummer boy in *Graduation Ball*. How amazing! Here I am now, standing next to him as he's directing the cameras for these dancing boys from Henry Thornton Comprehensive School. How mad is that?

Our moment comes. The group are looking fresh and youthful in their outfits. I'm no longer looking like the hippie teacher, dressing for the occasion in a black and light blue crushed-velvet top and matching patchwork skirt; knee-length dark pink suede boots complete my outfit. I am ready with a rehearsed script to introduce the group and sit opposite Hughie before they perform. I am far more nervous than the dancers.

The floor manager takes the dancers onto the studio floor and places them in their marked camera positions. We're third on the performance list, after the first commercial break. I speak with what appears to be confident ease as Hughie asks me questions, the group perform with great energy. They look and dance like true professionals, they could not have performed it better. It's all over in a flash. All that build up, gone in just over six minutes. At the end of all the acts, the studio audience vote and we wait with bated breath. We've come third on the leader board. Katie Budd, the singer, has come first and a comedian second. We are elated.

The wait for the postal vote seems to take an eternity. With all the votes added together we come second. What a fantastic result! Jeff had been right all along about auditioning for *Opportunity Knocks* because straightaway we're booked for two gigs. Our first one is at the Town Hall in Stratford, East London. Again the group want to wear something different. We buy rugby tops with hoops in three different colours so we can pair each colour with their partner. Worn with their jeans, it gives them a young, fresh, sporty look. The compere for the evening is Sally James, well known for fronting ITV's *Saturday Scene* and *Tiswas* with Chris

Tarrant. We're asked to perform before the main act, supporting a singing group called Guys 'N' Dolls. What an honour: the
group are very well known. 'There's a Whole Lot of Loving', their
first single, is currently number two in the charts. We perform
two lively numbers, including 'Get Back' from our success on
Opportunity Knocks, and our very own guys and dolls are thrilled.
It's their first professional engagement and for the first time they
experience fame, signing autographs for hordes of excited teenagers who've been patiently waiting outside the stage door.

The boys have arrived.

Our next gig is for a boxing promoter. It's their annual
black-tie dinner at the Savoy Hotel in London. This causes great
excitement. The hotel in London is considered to be *the* hotel, a
true icon, a monument where the wealthy dine or stay overnight
enjoying the grandeur of luxury suites with butlers in attendance.
Here we are from Clapham, our lads from the second toughest
comprehensive school in the whole of London, performing in
this glamorous hotel just off the Strand in the heart of the city.
Who would have guessed it?

We take two lads with us from the drama club to help backstage. We don't need them, but we want them to share in the
experience, to savour being in one of the most beautiful hotels in
the world. The stunning River Room restaurant has a stage erected
especially for the cabaret singers and our dance group. The front
of the stage has been beautifully decked out with an enormous
row of tightly packed hydrangeas, the huge blooms alternating
in stunning colours of pink and blue. We perform 'Get Back'

and a contrasting number I've choreographed to Diana Ross's 'Love Hangover'. It starts very slowly and builds into a lively disco number.

At the end of the evening after this, our second success-ful professional engagement, we pack up our things with the applause still ringing in our ears. But there's a problem. We can't find the two lads we've brought with us from the drama club. We seek them out backstage, the foyer, the cloakrooms and finally return to the River Room and, horror of horrors, there they both are helping themselves to armfuls of these wonderful, potted hydrangeas plants that have adorned the front of the stage.

'What on earth do you think you're doing?' I whisper looking absolutely shocked. This is theft.

'It's Mothers' Day tomorrow,' comes back the response, 'our mums would love these.'

• • •

It's time for the boys to leave the fold. New encounters to expe-rience, wonderful opportunities, new pathways to be pirouetted down. It's become impossible for us to sustain 'Spider' financially. I feel a huge tinge of sadness at the thought of saying goodbye to them, but the lads have a great future in dance, they've already proved they can hold their own among the very best trained dancers from stage and dance schools. We've grown together like a family and they've acted like godparents to Ben. Floyd left a long time ago, but it will be farewell to the omnipresent Jeff, the affable Garry and Patrick the fearless extrovert. At the same time, though, I'm excited for them. We're also having to part company with the girls; I'm grateful to Mandy and Jo for their input and their brief stay, and hopefully they too will find work.

An advert in *The Stage* catches my eye, it's for an audition for boy dancers with Dougie Squires. He's one of the best choreographers in the business, if not *the* best, and he's seeking dancers for his ever-expanding domination of the commercial dance scene. He's looking for dancers for several TV entertainment series, summer seasons, pantomimes and venues around the world. This audition is for his new dance troupe that'll be called 'Second Generation', the follow up to his hugely successful 'Young Generation'. Those dancers included Nigel Lythgoe and Kenny Warwick. I adored watching them dancing in their shows; they performed with the very best popular singing artistes of the sixties and seventies including Shirley Bassey, Vera Lynn, Engelbert Humperdinck and Lulu. Will my boys be good enough for Dougie's new dance group?

At the end of the audition in Covent Garden, after whittling down the dancers to his final selection, he takes Jeff and Garry aside. He asks them where they've trained, not having encountered them before in any of his previous auditions, and can they sing as well as dance? Well, having sung in our revues and pantomimes they're entitled to give a resounding 'Yes!' Have they done any partnering work, pas de deux work as in ballet? Er no, not really. Have they really done any tap? (Jeff had initially implied they had at the start when Dougie was asking all the auditionees). Er no. So who has taught them all the funky dancing to enable them to be chosen ahead of hundreds of other trained male dancers who didn't pass the audition?

Dougie takes Jeff and Garry under his wing. He not only puts them in the dance group for a summer season in the theatre on the end of the pier at Southport, but also arranges for them to take some classes at the Italia Conti Academy of Theatre Arts, to learn the things I wasn't able to teach them at the boys' school. But it isn't just Jeff and Garry who benefit from this incredibly caring, famous choreographer and teacher; their success at this audition isn't just to irrevocably change their lives forever, it will change mine too.

'The way you've taught these boys to dance is remarkable, you should be teaching in stage and dance schools, I'll introduce you to Italia Conti, so they can benefit from your style of teaching.'

What an absolute honour! I have to pinch myself – how has this all come about? But a cat has just been thrown among the pigeons. I'm about to be torn between my passion for teaching dance and my passion for teaching disadvantaged, discarded, vulnerable pupils consigned to remedial classes or homes for disturbed adolescents. But what an opportunity is being presented to me. With my love of ballet, of contemporary dance, choreography and the joyous experience of teaching in the boys' school, I can't turn it down. I have Ben to think about, too, will Andy and I manage between us or should we get an au pair? Instead, we decide to engage a very good daytime local sitter; Ben really is the most extraordinarily contented baby, happy with whoever he's with.

Sometimes talent is rewarded, sometimes it's sheer, grinding hard work, and if you're lucky enough, people like Dougie Squires can use their position to transform lives. Often, it's being in the right place at the right time and sometimes it can simply be connections, or who it is that recommends you, that snowballs your career. It can also be where you are living.

CHAPTER 6

REACH FOR THE STARS

East Twickenham in Middlesex was a great place to live in the seventies and eighties. Andy and I have bought a small terraced house in a street just over Richmond Bridge, not far from Richmond Ice Rink. From two flimsy flats we're converting it back into one spacious two-floored Edwardian home. At weekends and during the school holidays, Jeff and Rupert travel on the 37 bus from their homes in Vauxhall and Clapham to muck in, helping us to knock through rooms by smashing down the dusty lathe-and-plaster walls. They stand precariously on top of ladders patiently chiselling out the layers and layers of paint that smother the decorative moulded plaster on the ceiling, and shovel bags of cement for a kitchen base and a garage extension. In Ben's bedroom, Andy has painted a wonderful mural of Snoopy the dog; his bedroom is the calmest and brightest room in the house.

Across the road from us lives Douglas Camfield, a well-known BBC television director who's married to the actress

Sheila Dunn. Living next door to them is Arline Usden. Arline's the current Beauty Editor for *Woman* magazine. Aware of my teaching history and my current classes at Italia Conti and the Dance Centre in Covent Garden, she commissions me to write a book for Marks & Spencer titled *Fit Together*. It's based around couples exercising together, a fun, pictorial book combining photographs and painted backgrounds that give it a bright cartoon image. I'm able to use Jeff and Garry for some of the illustrations, alongside professional models. When Arline and her family move out, the actor John Challis from *Only Fools and Horses* and his actress wife Debbie Arnold move in.

Further along this little road and on the same side as us lives David Benedictus, theatre director and BBC Radio readings editor. He's there with his actress wife, Yvonne Antrobus, they have a daughter called Chloe and a son called Leo who's the same age as our son Ben. Andy's dog Watson has become very attached to their dog Magpie. Not only had Magpie been responsible for introducing Dame Judi Dench to the actor Michael Williams, her future husband, Magpie also found a mate of her own in Watson, and beautiful puppies are born several months later. Opposite David and Yvonne, and tucked down a narrow track, is a small car repair garage, very handy for when Andy's Hillman Imp needs fixing and for keeping Rupert on the straight and narrow. When our house is near completion and Rupert nears the end of his school days, Andy asks Wilbur the owner to give Rupert a job. It's the start of Rupert learning his trade as a motor mechanic and a step closer to his dream of owning his own E Type Jaguar – the legitimate way.

At the top of the road and round the corner lives the voice coach Joan Washington and her new partner, the actor Richard E. Grant. Joan's son goes to the Montessori school with Ben and Leo. Sam Walters, the artistic director of the Orange Tree Theatre lives close by. The Orange Tree Theatre's a tiny, trendy theatre, housed above the pub of that name, opposite Richmond railway station. Pub theatre is a new concept in theatreland in the seventies and the Orange Tree features regularly in the arts pages of the *Guardian* and *The Stage*.

Andy has made good use of the smallest room in our house by turning it into a dark room, where he develops and prints all his photographs. I love watching the photographic paper swishing around in a tray of chemicals, being held aloft by a pair of forceps before being pegged on a line to dry. Slowly a beautiful, blurred, black-and-white image transforms into an artistic masterpiece of gorgeous clarity. Often they're photos of actors from the plays. Andy attends the dress rehearsals at the Orange Tree and Sam pays him to photograph the latest productions. David Benedictus doesn't pay Andy for his images, but swops his hobby of acquiring antiques in return for Andy's technical expertise. We gain some interesting possessions, not least an original Charing Cross Underground sign.

Our road holds the occasional moveable feast, inspired by the Ernest Hemingway book of that title. It's David's suggestion that each of our houses (there are five in our group) prepare a course. We go from house to house, feasting and imbibing, with nobody needing to drive home or produce a full-blown meal, just one course. When it's our turn to make a dessert, Andy makes a Baked Alaska and I put together a Pavlova, the pinnacle of my seventies culinary expertise.

A little further away, across the main road and round the corner, lives Nikki who has two sons at the same Montessori school. We mothers don't bump into each other at the school gate, but instead in our local park, fitting exercising our respective dogs into our hectic working lives. It's later, when events take a dramatic turn, that I'm more than grateful for this quiet and attractive environment I live in. Nikki's a television producer at Saatchi & Saatchi which is how, just when I need a diversion from my personal life, I come to choreograph television commercials including K.P. Discos, Quality Street and Anglian Windows.

In 1982, other work opportunities away from home come rolling in. I'm teaching Frances Ruffelle at Italia Conti, and she deservedly becomes a Tony Award winner for her musical performance in *Les Misérables*, when her mother, Sylvia Young, asks if I would also teach my funky dance classes once a week at her new stage school. Bridget Espinosa, a renowned and revered ballet teacher and guest teacher at Conti's, offers a day's teaching at the London Studio Centre, a new dance school she's in the process of founding and would I also be interested in making the journey from Waterloo to Guildford to teach a half day at the Guildford School of Acting? Besides all these classes, I'm running my own evening class for Dancercise at the Sundance Club in the Tottenham Court Road in London, incorporating John Travolta's moves from *Saturday Night Fever*; teaching on the

Teaching at Pineapple Dance Studios, 1980

flashing disco floor is heaven sent. Saturday mornings are spent teaching at the Dance Centre in Covent Garden and the newly opened Pineapple Dance Centre. Before Pineapple, the Dance Centre was *the* place to teach dancing. Molly Molloy and Arlene Phillips have their own classes and every Saturday, in the middle of my teaching, I'll look out of the studio window and wave at the teacher heading to his class in the studio next door. It's Bruno Tonioli, who'll later become a judge on *Strictly Come Dancing*.

In all these centres, aerobics class posters are everywhere. It's the populist umbrella term for group exercise to music. 'Going for the burn' is the phrase that's being made notorious by Jane Fonda. It's become the exercise fashion of the decade which means that classes are called aerobics even if they're a form of toning and stretch. Some of us, though, keep to our love of dance, so there's still an eclectic mix of jazz dance, dancercise, disco dance and funky dance on offer.

In 1983, I'm asked by the Dance Centre if I will go to a trade fair in Japan with Prime Minister Margaret Thatcher as part of a twelve-man delegation representing the best of British manufacturing. I'm invited with another teacher because Covent Garden is considered to be the mecca of the dance world. What an absolute thrill, of course I will go. The economy in Japan is booming. We have the remarkable experience of travelling on the Bullet train, gliding effortlessly and silently past tea plantations and rice paddies at the most extraordinary high speed. We whiz from Tokyo to Kyoto past Mount Fuji, we gaze out of the windows and luxuriate in the design of this incredible train. Once arrived, we sit on cushions and drink green tea out of delicate tiny cups and cleanse our hands with fresh hot towels. Then it's on to Osaka. Everywhere we look there are never-ending skyscrapers that seem suspended from the clouds, all just inches apart, with cultivated green gardens planted on their roofs. There's no space for greenery down below in the narrow streets, teeming with people.

Wherever we went we were bowled over by the hospitality and courtesy, the tradition of bowing; we experienced a whole new culture. I feel hugely grateful to have been offered the opportunity to take part in such a successful trade mission.

If ever proof is needed that dance and exercise is a universal language, it's here in Japan. The courteous interpreters are redundant while I'm teaching in all these cities. The classes are always held on the top floor of a store called Takashimaya, a chain of stores that are all rather like Harrods. This keeps the whole delegation together, including two women from Wedgwood China who display their wares and Lord Lichfield who showcases his photographs. I'm not sure if the PM is ever in the stores; we never see her during the entire trip. I come home laden with presents, with the smallest, sophisticated toy cars, buses and lorries for Ben. And for dear Ma, some beautiful pearl earrings.

They are heady days. In two ex-Conti pupils, Nica and Dawn, I have two invaluable assistants who will step in at short notice to take the classes in my absence. And Garry too, if he can fit them in while performing in West End musicals. Somehow, as the mum of a young toddler, I manage to keep all the balls

I'm juggling up in the air. Except I haven't. My personal life is in disarray. Andy is about to leave home.

We'd both left teaching at the boys' comprehensive school during the day, with me, for a short while, becoming the tutor in charge at the Home for Disturbed Adolescents in Isleworth and then Spider, our dance group. Andy no longer enjoyed teaching mathematics in a constant atmosphere of negativity and aggression; the drama club had been his mainstay, it had given him a sense of purpose and now it was gone. He'd successfully applied to teach in a London polytechnic, and later found his niche by going into partnership with a medical computing company. It was owned by the father of the family that lived at the end of the terraced houses in our East Twickenham street, next door to Wilbur's garage.

I hadn't seen any of it coming. All my energies had been diverted into Ben and travelling to teach in all the different dancing institutions. I have little energy or time left to share with Andy. I also have to contend with a working mother's guilt. We parted knowing that we must do everything possible to ensure that Ben, who would live with me, could see Andy as often as possible.

At times it's bleak, very bleak. The Clapham boys are totally mystified as to why Andy and I have parted when we'd seemed so happy. Friends, Ma and the boys rally round and I manage to get on with my life; there isn't another option. I carry on travelling to all the different dance schools and centres, often taking Ben with me. He's been the easiest of contented babies and is now, at four years old, just as contented. I can take him anywhere with me when he isn't at school. We travel on buses and trains (I still haven't learnt to drive) and he sits quietly drawing at the back of the studio in the Pineapple Dance Centre, at Italia Conti or staying at Ma's flat in London while I teach at the London Studio Centre. My father had died a few years ago and Ma's now living the life she had always yearned for. The student dancers and adults adore Ben and he benefits from everyone's affection. While I get on with teaching, he contentedly plays with his collection of toys, the ones I've brought back from my trip to Japan.

I engage Pum, an exceptional, young Norwegian au pair. When Ben stays at home with her, I don't ever recall him asking me, 'Where are you going and when are you coming back?' It's me, at times, who finds it difficult. Sometimes coming home at the end of a long day, I'll be briefly acknowledged while he carries on drawing exquisite pictures or playing fun games with Pum. I'm so lucky; he enjoys everybody's company and they enjoy his. It's just wonderful to have him in my life.

It feels for a while as if time has stood still, has overtaken me or left me stranded. Gradually I start to walk, to run and catch up. Exercise and dance have great healing powers. The shared physicality and freedom with class groups during this time is an escape from my imprisoned recurring thoughts, which dissipate with the music, the focus, the freedom of expression. But I never lose, throughout this short space of time, the desire to teach, to see the pupils progress, the fun, the sharing, the happiness and the enduring friendships.

And yet again, connections are about to catapult me into another unexpected, extraordinary life-changing experience, a completely new phase in my life.

At the end of one of my Saturday funky dance classes in Covent Garden, I'm approached by a girl whose face I'm familiar with, but not her name. When you take open classes in a fitness club that doesn't require membership, people pay at the end of the session. You have a nod of recognition with your regulars, they become part of your faithful following, the mainstay of your classes. This smiling, friendly girl has stayed behind to speak to me and introduces herself.

I'm Jane Tatnall and my boss is Greg Dyke who works in television, I'm his PA. He's taking over the new breakfast television station called TV-am, it needs a complete overhaul and he's been brought in to change the entire format. He wants to counteract the popularity of the Green Goddess on BBC *Breakfast Time* with an exercise session. He's asked me who I recommend because I used to be a dancer. I love your classes and said you're mad, a totally different teacher and he wants to meet you.

Hold the front page. I've seen Jackie Genova on Saturday mornings doing a short aerobic routine on TV-am, haven't they already got someone who could do it in the week too? And the Green Goddess on the other channel, the rival channel, she looks stunning, with the most perfect body and a radiant smile.

No wonder she's called a Goddess. Do they really imagine I can compete with her? And your reason, Jane, for telling Greg I'm mad is because I make dancing fun. That's a great compliment. It might sound a slight exaggeration, but people following the trend in the dance centre take their classes very seriously. Dressing for the part, they arrive colour co-ordinated with matching wrist and headbands, calf-length leg warmers all complimenting their brightly coloured leotard and tights – and they leave after an hour's class looking exactly the same as when they'd arrived. The people who come to my classes leave dripping with sweat and looking bedraggled having laughed and mastered their way through strenuous dance routines.

'No thanks,' I say, and tell Jane to pass my answer on to Greg. I'm a very strange mix of being confident in my ability with my work and with some of my achievements, but totally unsure of myself as a person, and that causes a conflict. I can look self- assured and sometimes do a good job of covering up when I'm most definitely feeling insecure. At other times, I say the daftest of things and ruminate on them for months. Would I really cope working in television? My Clapham boys will think I'm mad to turn it down, but then they've always been the per-formers, not me. Jane returns to the class the next Saturday with her next request.

'Greg says "Mad Lizzie, at least you can give me the courtesy of coming to see me."'

So I do. I arrive at the studios at Camden Lock to the most impressively designed modern building with an array of huge egg cups sitting on its top, and meet this dynamic, fast-speaking, enthusiastic, persistent, persuasive director of programmes at TV-am. He happily tells me he knows absolutely nothing about exercise and that he will leave everything to Jane and myself, it would be up to us to work out what we will do with our daily slot at 6.50 every weekday morning, which is the same time the Green Goddess is on the BBC. Such faith, but can he turn around this ailing new station that's only been on air for just six weeks? Plus there's no money, the 'Famous Five' heavyweights in broadcasting – Robert Kee, Angela Rippon, David Frost, Anna Ford and Michael Parkinson – with their very newsworthy three-hour programme format, have not only haemorrhaged viewers, but also haemorrhaged money. There are no viewers to speak of, therefore no advertisers and no money left in the kitty to pay their staff. As a single working mother, I can't afford to take up Greg's offer, so I turn it down again. His response?

'How much are you making each year with your teaching Lizzie?'

'Twenty-three thousand pounds,' I quickly reply.

'Done. We will match that.'

And that's what happens. I'm called 'Mad' before he's even met me; a clever, concise, identifiable nickname that will capture the attention of the media. Suddenly, out of nowhere it seems, I'm about to be thrust into the world of television. Panic stations, organization required. I'll keep my evening class and my Saturday classes in Covent Garden, plus the one at Richmond Ice Rink because that's close to home. London Studio Centre

TV-am exercisers: Dr Hilary Jones, (R) Ben and Steve (B), Overleaf: the Chelsea footballers, Frank Bruno and the Chippendales

Exercising *The X Factor* finalists in their house, 2007

Accompanying a Children's Peace Mission in 1986.
Pictured in Yoko Ono's New York apartment

In George Harrison's
garden, 1988

TV Times, second
anniversary of TV-am, 1985

TV Times cover, 1987

Top of the video
sales chart, 1987

Pantomime at the White Rock Theatre, Hastings, 1985

With Craig Revel
Horwood: patrons
of the Royal
Osteoporosis Society

With Ben, 1992

Training the GB
Women's Rowing
Squad, 2002

Artwork by Ben

Spreads from the
Go! London 2012 brochure

Welcome to the competition!

This is your chance to tell us at the London Bid why you think London is the best venue to host the Olympic Games in 2012. But it's not just London that's involved – if the bid is successful, events will be staged in the cities of Manchester, Glasgow and Belfast as well as areas such as Broxbourne in Hertfordshire and Dorney in Berkshire.

And you don't have to be the next Kelly Holmes or Amir Khan to take part. Lizzie Webb, the television fitness presenter, has devised "Go! London 2012" which includes all sorts of activities such as singing and painting, as well as fun, sporting games.

And this is what you do. First of all, visit the website www.london2012.org and take a look at the amazing new stadiums and facilities we can provide. Then research the historic buildings and traditions of London (plus other UK cities) and list all the advantages to be gained by bringing the Olympics to our country.

And don't forget to include our current Olympic Champions and our many past medal winners.

There are five different categories in the competition and when your teachers have selected the best entries from each year in your school, all you have to do, is send them on video to us.

So get started – you have until June

There are some "oarsome" prizes to be won!

Best wishes,

Sir Steve Redgrave

Ryan & Billie

Making their dreams
come true...

Express your support for London

'It's no secret we're backing the "Go! London 2012" competition – we'll be keeping watch on all your entries!'

Matthew MacFadyen, Keeley Hawes & David Oyelowo
Cast of the BBC series, *Spooks*

Wessex Junior School – Cox Green
Lowbrook Junior School – Cox Green
Royal Grammar School – High Wycombe
Redroofs Theatre School – Maidenhead

and the others might be difficult, thank heavens for Nica, Dawn and Garry. Now, TV-am.

I'm too nervous to tell anyone but Ma. I want to practise a few days on air first, make any mistakes and then announce it to friends, sisters and the boys. They're probably not going to find out, the viewing figures are so bad they don't even register on the official ratings. Before the first live transmission, Jane comfortingly advises me to just be myself, be how I am in class. She'll watch from home and be on hand at her desk at 9 a. m. upstairs outside the presenter's office in the huge open-plan work area.

At 6.40 I'm taken into the hushed studio and wait with trepidation for the floor manager to tell me where to go. During the commercial break, I'm seated on the sofa next to Nick Owen, one of the new anchor presenters who's busy talking to the director via his earpiece. Then we're on air. A quick chat and it's Nick introducing 'Lizzie's first shake out', but, horror of horrors, nobody has thought where I'm actually going to do it. Where am I going to stand? And here we are live and I haven't a clue what to do, no experience. Realising the situation, quick-thinking Nick pushes back the coffee table to make a small space in front of the sofas, shifts discreetly to the farthest point, hoping to keep out of the line of the camera, and tells me to start.

I don't remember much about those three minutes, just the floor manager inexplicably waving his arms as if helping to land an aircraft. I haven't a clue what any of these signals mean, not until he appears to be slitting his throat which must mean stop. I've no previous television experience as a presenter, only sitting as a guest with Hughie Green on *Opportunity Knocks* and, to cap it all, this is live television. No wonder I shake with nerves. I'd originally called my slot 'Shake Out' because it's what I do at the start of every class I teach, shake out all the tension before exercising. 'Mad Lizzie's Shake Out' has just taken on a different meaning. I carry on shaking live on air throughout the next two weeks.

But can this whole new format really work? Will I be able to make a living? Instead of three hours of heavyweight rolling news, the station is now extolling their new look with an upbeat advertising campaign:

> Start your day bright with TV-am and switch on your colour TVs for competition time with Timmy, TV news with Jimmy Greaves, cartoon fun with Roland Rat, the latest pop videos and pop news with Timmy Mallett, Lizzie shakes you up and shakes you out and Wincey makes the weather look brighter. Join Anne and Nick and get the latest news.

In spite of the programme content being the complete antithesis of the one that had won the TV-am contract from the Independent Broadcasting Authority, the station is allowed to try out this new snap, crackle and pop format. If it doesn't work, ITV's first breakfast station will be shut down; the banks are already on the verge of pulling the plug.

It's not surprising there's a constant state of insecurity, of fragility and impermanence at TV-am. Anne Diamond and Nick

TV-am publicity

Owen, the two sofa presenters, have given up their successful presenting jobs elsewhere and all of us are having to go in person to the finance department and beg, literally beg, to be paid. The advertising money isn't accumulating, that's evident from the few adverts that are being aired, they're paying next to nothing to advertise their wares and the ads are repeated over and over again throughout the entire three-and-half-hour programme. The advertising agencies don't want to know. The seemingly fun camaraderie that's portrayed on air doesn't exist in reality, well not with me at least, probably in part due to all the uncertainties and the very early morning alarm calls, but perhaps it's because of the status and the positioning. I feel like an outsider. I only do a few minutes on air and because it's a light-hearted 'cabaret' contribution to the programme, it probably looks to some of the presenters and the editors of the day as if I walk onto the set, cue in the music and make up any old exercise that comes into my head. Nick is one of the exceptions and happily agrees when I ask him to join in exercising with me, as does another anchor man, Richard Keys. I feel like the new girl, a teacher with imposter syndrome, all the other daily presenters seem so self-assured. I get a great confidence booster when Nina Myskow, renowned for being the acerbic television critic for the *News of the World*, praises me in her column. Little does she know how it helps boost my morale.

And so does Barbara Hulanicki, the founder of Biba, a unique, amazing store in Kensington that started in the sixties. She contacts me at the studio and offers to design and make several outfits using soft material in different colours and textures that will allow freedom of movement. It's in keeping with my concept for the viewers of not needing to be in exercise gear, but to keep on the move throughout the day. Yes please! What an honour for me. When I was a student, Min, my college flatmate, and I would go to Biba, Barbara's shop in High Street Kensington, and look lovingly and longingly at her clothes. They were so original, so sixties, but we couldn't afford them. And here she is, knowing that TV-am is struggling financially and charging me a pittance for these wonderful designer outfits, making them just for me. I often wonder if I showed enough appreciation for her designer outfits that helped create an individual style and boosted my confidence. A very belated thank you, Barbara.

I don't want to sound ungracious, or indeed critical of this new world I've joined. What a gift of a job to have, especially when

The TV-am presenters. L to R Wincey Willis, Jayne Irving, Gordon Honeycombe, Anne Diamond, Nick Owen and me in one of Barbara Hulanicki's outfits.

Greg's letting Jane and I get on with producing the 'Shake Outs'. Here is my own opportunity to reach for the stars, an opportunity hundreds of exercise and dance teachers would give their right arm for. It's just very different to any of my previous work experience. In teaching, you work with people, you pull together; this feels like the total opposite. Off camera and out of the studio, I hide away in my dressing room. I'm fortunate to have my own large one, space in the building being at a premium. It's appreciated by the powers that be that I need to use my beat box to warm up and go through the routine before going into the studio and sometimes rehearse guests. Jane feels out of place too and finds it very different to her happy experiences of working with Greg at previous television stations. She inveigles me to stay with her every morning after we come off air, to sit with her outside the presenters' office until lunchtime. We have dance and the 'Shake Outs' to happily chat about and letters from viewers to answer – it's the least I can do.

I begin to seek out guests for my 'Shake Outs' to add more interest, guests of all ages who will inspire the viewers. But there's still no money for them, let alone for ourselves, so I have to rely on my contacts. Plus, this little exercise slot is going from strength to strength and Greg has asked me if I would also close the show every morning with another 'Shake Out' slot at 9.18 a.m. This gives me something else to aspire to because Greg has been absolutely right with his new format, TV-am's beginning to build a loyal following of viewers.

With this later slot, I need some variety and a different approach because it's a different viewership to the 6.50 'Shake

Out'. With no money, I have to rely on past pupils. Jeff and Garry both come and exercise with me. They've been dancing in many television shows and Garry is now roller-skating in the West End musical *Starlight Express* and Jeff is a choreographer with the BBC. It's taken them a while to forgive me for not telling them I'd got the job at TV-am right away, but I'm forgiven so they happily come into the studios and I proudly present my past pupils to the viewers. My nieces Anya and Beth join my son Ben to encourage younger viewers to join in at home, not that this age group need much encouragement, my postbag is full of photos of children copying me on the screen. I contact pupils from my previous classes. I'd taught a young schoolgirl who'd enthusiastically attended my weekly Saturday classes at the Dance Centre. She's the daughter of the writer Hunter Davies and novelist Margaret Forster. Flora is delighted to appear and it's a lovely item. I've promised her a very modest appearance fee for joining in with both workouts. For weeks going into months, I badger the finance office to pay her this meagre amount. Hunter Davies is not amused, he's used to giving interviews with broadcasting companies that honour his fees, and quite rightly wonders why Flora isn't getting paid. I eventually secure a cheque from the department and for a while don't invite any more guests.

Audience ratings continue to increase, and Greg has the novel idea of taking TV-am to the viewers for the summer holidays. For four weeks, Chris Tarrant is going to tour popular seaside locations and after my Thursday 'Shake Outs' in the studio, I'm to take a train to the seaside so I can be ready for the first slot on

The *Good Morning* team

Friday morning. Although I'm no longer feeling like the new girl, I'm really nervous. I've just got used to going live in the studio and now I'm about to do live outside broadcasts. Will holiday-makers join in with the early 'Shake Out' at 6.50 a.m.? I have visions of an empty beach and me exercising with just the sea. The location producer thinks it's a good idea to contact fitness organisations in each of the locations to swell the numbers. It's a good idea, but if I can't rehearse them, it could look very messy. A brainwave, I'll turn it into a 'Shake Out' seaside theme. In the studio Monday to Thursday, I'll teach the same routine. Blackpool is going to be the first location, so, for example, I'll call it 'The Blackpool Shake Out', and tell viewers each morning that if they're in Blackpool on Friday they should come and join me live doing it from the beach. What I'm not taking into account is that the guests, who are appearing in theatres and on the piers at these seaside resorts, will also be joining me. In Blackpool, I discover it will be Freddie Starr. Now Freddie is notorious for wrecking shows. Whatever will he, could he do, while I'm exercising live in Blackpool?

I arrive in Blackpool and nervously await the first 'Shake Out'. Before we go on air, I check the sound levels while the floor manager positions me on top of the high seafront wall. Joy, oh joy, there are at least a hundred holidaymakers and lots of exercisers from local health clubs. They can all look up from the beach and follow my instructions. And, a bonus, Freddie Starr is nowhere to be seen. Anne and Nick hand over from the studio to Chris who introduces the 'Shake Out' and, after a brief intro, I begin. It isn't long before there are huge smiles and howls of laughter from the exercisers down below. I look over my shoulder and see Freddie marching up and down, saluting with one arm in the air and the fingers of his other hand across his mouth for a moustache. He's doing his Hitler act while I'm giving instructions. Before I can think how to react, Freddie pushes me with one almighty shove off the wall and I fall way down into a heap on the sand. Fortunately no expletives escape from my mouth. I get up as fast as I can and carry on. And if that isn't unsettling enough for my nerves, to close the Blackpool outside broadcast, I've been told to climb on top of an elephant to join Chris Tarrant so we can wave goodbye as we lumber into the distance. It's a doddle compared with the Freddie fiasco.

The ratings shoot up, aided by the very popular Roland Rat travelling the beaches in his ratmobile, and in no time at all,

Greg has completely transformed this ailing breakfast station into a success story. American film stars, singers and soap stars become the norm, along with Greg's added list of populist features: Diana Dors with her weight loss programme, Michael Barry the crafty cook, nosey parker Loyd Grossman taking a peek *Through the Keyhole* and Nellie the clairvoyant. Just like my boys, I have unintentionally reached for the stars, but things, once again, are about to take a different turn.

CHAPTER 7

MONDAY TO FRIDAY, FIVE DAYS A WEEK

Jane has decided to leave TV-am. I'm not surprised, just saddened and hugely grateful for the support she's given me. She leaves knowing this newbie presenter is feeling less green about the gills thanks to her. I'm confident I can take on the challenge of producing and presenting 'Mad Lizzie's Shake Outs'. The viewing figures scrutinised by our ratings department are proving the 'Shake Outs' are an important feature of the morning show. I'm not aware of just how detailed the audience research and monitoring is until I'm stopped one morning and congratulated by David Frost. I have to enquire what for and I'm amazed to be told the latest poll figures have shown I'm the most popular presenter on TV-am. I'm taken aback, delighted but at the same time slightly embarrassed given I'm on air for such an infinitesimal amount of time within the whole programme. His relating of this accolade has come just at the right time. It gives me an added fillip to see if I can maintain this popularity, to start thinking more creatively about my airtime. After all, there are only so many fitness warmups and exercises I can devise for two arms, two legs with a core in between.

I know from the multitude of viewers' letters and feedback that lots of them of all ages and abilities are joining in. In addition, the demographics for the viewership is different for each of the slots. Of course there's a huge viewership who aren't the slightest bit interested in kicking their legs or strengthening their abs at that hour of the morning: 6.50 a.m. is very early. I've met countless people who recognise my voice and it's not because they're doing the exercises, they're too busy hastily getting dressed or grabbing a piece of toast while I'm on their television in the background. But there are thousands of viewers who cue their morning routine to the timing of my daily appearances, as well as those who join in. So, for this eclectic mix of viewership, the aim is to inspire people to 'have a go' and to make it fun and entertaining for those who aren't. Greg called me 'Mad Lizzie', which gives me licence to live up to my name.

I decide to dispense with any further hint of exercise gear like leg warmers and instead wear a variety of outfits to help brighten up the mornings with a splash of colour. Using my generous wardrobe allowance, I go shopping for jumpers, interesting tops, sweatshirts and T-shirts adorned with sparkle or ones with an appropriate message, jumpsuits, casual trousers. Nothing with block white, it can cause a problem for the lighting guys, and definitely not fine stripes as they will strobe. Eye-catching patterned jumpers seem to exist in abundance and I get offers from the public to knit them for me. Gyles Brandreth, our very own woolly man and the doyen of breakfast television, notes my variety of jumpers and invites me to feature with my son in *Knitability*, his charity book for the London Playing Fields. We wear intricately designed jumpers, the photos featuring alongside the meticulous pattern instructions. Mine has an elegant black cat and Ben's a colourful fly-away kite, but as the extent of my knitting ability has been the obligatory primary school scarf, I make no attempt to give them a go.

My effort to seek out colourful clothes is appreciated and goes down well with Bruce Gyngell, our imposing, statuesque Australian managing director, recently appointed following Greg Dyke's departure to pastures new. Bruce watches the first hour at home before travelling to the studios. He commends me on my choice of coloured outfits and says it's exactly what he wants to see first thing in the morning, and declares mine is to be the look. Presenters are no longer allowed to wear black; he bans the colour, saying they all have to brighten up to look like Lizzie. This doesn't go down too well with all of the sofa presenters, but I think he's right, viewers want to be awakened by cheerful faces and bright outfits, it creates a positive start to the day, especially if the news stories are pretty grim. Outfits sorted.

Other components are needed to make an impression, to hold the attention of the viewing public. There has to be music. It's always been such an important part of my life and so often it's been my saviour at the lowest points, as it must for countless others, too. But at this stage, TV-am still can't afford (or won't pay for) the licence to broadcast commercial music. Thankfully, I have great connections with KPM, the music library for EMI music.

Prior to my TV-am days, I'd learnt about the invaluable existence of library music and used it when choreographing television commercials. Musicians, assigned to KPM and other libraries, compose and record a wealth of music for TV film producers, record companies and television stations to access. The composers get a royalty when their music is used, all very lucrative if it's a nightly programme or a long-running series. So many unforgettable TV themes and popular songs come from these companies. Can you recall the BBC's *Saturday Grandstand* theme, the *Wimbledon Fortnight* tune, the catchy pipes for *Blue Peter*, the staccato, bouncy opening for the long-running TV drama *The Bill*, the dramatic intro to *Mastermind*? And what about the striking chords and catchy bongs that for decades has preceded the nightly ITV *News at Ten*? All these memorable tunes come from composers and musicians commissioned by KPM.

The year before I'd started at TV-am, I'd worked with John, one of the producers at KPM, when needing music for commercials. He'd subsequently arranged for me to choreograph two routines for eight dancers performing at a corporate dinner in the Grand Casino in Monte Carlo. What a magical experience, an unforgettable four days in such a spectacular city, and now, it's a great connection for finding music for the 'Shake Outs' at TV-am. I go back to their offices in Denmark Street, just off

Tottenham Court Road. This little street used to be known as 'Tin Pan Alley', because of the recording studios used by such famous groups as the Rolling Stones and the Sex Pistols. I sit for hours with John in their offices, listening and selecting endless uplifting, orchestral tracks for my TV-am work. Music sorted.

'Mad Lizzie's Shake Outs' still need something more than just the exercises and dances, the outfits and music: it needs to be bound and linked together. Of course, a weekly theme! The weekly summer seaside themes were so successful, I need to think of other weekly ideas. Choosing a music theme, like a James Bond week, would be a really good one to start with, there have been so many exceptional songs written. Sports stars, especially Olympians, if I can get them, are an obvious tie-in and would make great guests for a week. I'll approach Steve Redgrave and, if he agrees, I'll ask Ben to join in too, as a junior aspiring rower and a very promising one, Ben will be thrilled to have the opportunity to meet Steve, let alone do a 'Shake Out' with him. It might in some small part make up for me not being at home in the mornings. I make a list of suggested names for as many different themes as I can think of, and the celebrities I can approach to go with them.

Five days of sports stars

Steve Redgrave – Olympic rowing medallist

Sharron Davies – Olympic swimming medallist

Nigel Benn – World Boxing Champ

Suzanne Dando – Gymnast Champion of Champions

Eddie the Eagle Edwards – Ski jumper in training

Thames Television had invited Ben and me to take part in a show called *Whose Baby?* and that's given me another idea. I think viewers might enjoy trying to work out the famous parents of the children joining in with me and I can give hints as to who they are with the type of exercises. Here's the list of famous personalities who agree to bring their children to the studio to take part:

Five days of 'Whose baby?'

Ruth Madoc (arms in the air for the TV series *Hi-de-Hi!*)

Lesley Joseph (exercises executed with a haughty expression for *Birds of a Feather*)

Dave Willetts (the lead in *Phantom of the Opera*, so mysterious moves)

Judy Loe and Richard Beckinsale (a 'Shake Out' with their daughter Kate Beckinsale; I can't think of any moves to go with his series *Porridge*)

Frank Bruno the boxer (lots of punching exercises)

Invariably guests will be promoting something when they join the presenters on the sofa, so they'll surely be more than happy to be invited to promote their panto, and if they come in costume, it'll give an added, colourful dimension to the 'Shake Outs'. They can kick their legs in colourful breeches and silver buckled shoes, wave their glittering fairy wands and cast spells in their tutus. I make a list of very approachable stars and their forthcoming panto season.

Five days of panto guests

Bonnie Langford

Christopher Biggins

The Roly Polys

Barbara Windsor

John Altman

A lot of television commercials are set to classical music, so the products come to be identified with the associated music. While we exercise, viewers will have enough time to try and recognise the commercial and it might encourage those not joining in to listen and participate. And now TV-am can afford to pay the music licence fee, I can go ahead and it'll have a different feel to the other ideas.

'Guess the Commercial' week: five days of advertisements

British Airways – 'Flower Duet' from the French opera *Lakme*

Coca-Cola – 'I'd Like to Teach the World to Sing' by The New Seekers

Hamlet Cigars – 'Air on a G String' by Bach

Italia 90 – 'Nessun Dorma' from the opera *Turandot*

Hovis Bread – Dvorak's *New World Symphony*

Five days of musicals will, from past experience, be easy to arrange. Whenever a new musical is about to open in the West End, I invite their publicity people to send some of the cast to the studio. They always oblige and I love having the luxury of working with professional dancers. For this themed week, I'm going to arrange to work with a team of eight dancers from *42nd Street* in their rehearsal room at Drury Lane Theatre. I'm devising an appropriate routine for our TV-am viewers to the show's title song and, because there will be so many dancers, we can perform it live on the forecourt at TV-am. And for another morning I can work with Garry again; he's now the dance captain and assistant theatre director for Arlene Phillips in the West End production of *Starlight Express*. I'll ask him if he can bring four of the cast to work out to 'Rolling Stock', one of the show's hit songs. This is the boy from Clapham who used to try and hide in the back row of my dance class and he's now looking after the welfare of his own team of dancers. What a wonderful morning that will be.

There's another great musical in town called *Miss Saigon*. I've approached the PR company and they're sending four dancers including their dance captain. I chat briefly with him and ask him what he does in his role.

'What's the role of a dance captain in a musical, Craig?'

'I crack the whip!' was his laughing response.

(Well, that's good practice before becoming Mr Nasty on *Strictly Come Dancing*.)

Five days of workers

Police

Firemen

Postmen

Nurses and doctors

The forces

I've just tried the police workout; it really captured the public's attention. The five police arrived nice and early so I could teach them a dance routine to 'Let's Hear It For the Boy', the hit song from the film *Footloose*. We rehearsed it several times before performing it live in both 'Shake Outs' on the steps of the atrium. What fantastic sports they were, cheerfully swinging their hips, and doing the famous John Travolta moves in unison all dressed in their immaculate police uniforms. It lit up the morning programme.

There are lots of other themes with accompanying guests I continue to devise, some perhaps a little off beat, including the five mornings of 'Page 3' girls, with a different one joining me each morning. The only way I can exercise with one of them is to do the exercises kneeling on the floor, because she is somewhat top heavy. And a memorable week is with both the Chippendales and the Dream Boys (to redress the balance of the Page 3 week). Even when I have guests that are very fit, be they sports personalities, pop stars or the public, I always rehearse them in my dressing room or on the studio floor before going live on air. I've already learnt the hard way what happens if you don't.

During one of the earlier half terms, the last forty-five minutes of TV-am was taken over by children's television shows hosted by Timmy Mallet. I was asked to do a week of 'Shake Outs' in my usual 9.18 slot with Timmy and his guests. I was happy to oblige, it meant I didn't have to seek out any agents, book guests, arrange their transport or look after them. Except it was television for children, so I should have expected the unexpected.

First up was Rod Hull and Emu. Now, a decade ago, I'd seen Michael Parkinson, television's iconic interviewer, being set upon by them, with poor Parky ending up wrestling with Emu on the floor in the most undignified manner. Could I cope with this potentially unruly, attacking bird? And it's live television! I'd no option as I'd agreed to Timmy's guests doing the 'Shake Out'. No sooner had I started the swivelling foot work, thinking it was something Rod and Emu could at least join in with, when I too was attacked, tipped flat on my back, pecked and unable to move. I managed to flippantly dismiss him as I staggered up. Rod got the message and left the set as I, bird like, flapped my arms and quickly wrapped up the attempted 'Shake Out'.

The next morning the guest on Timmy's show was Gary Davies, the popular, smooth-talking DJ. No problem! He quietly obliged by following the exercises. But the calm of the week was about to be disrupted once again the following morning. Lenny Henry was Timmy's guest as well as Sue Pollard, the lovable and popular *Hi-de-Hi!* actress. Timmy can behave in his slightly bonkers way and so can his guests, and although I'm called Mad Lizzie, I'm not quite that bonkers. Comedian Lenny had decided he wasn't going to make it easy for me. Oh no. Unfortunately, I was wearing a top that was very similar in colour to his, and as I repeatedly reached out with my arm to the side for a waist exercise, Lenny, standing next to me, chose instead to repeatedly pluck at my red jumper to get my attention. Timmy and Sue meanwhile were trying to copy the exercises in the row behind while I quietly died. I decided at the end of that week it was much easier for me to choose my own guests, in spite of all the organisation.

Over time, several politicians join in to inspire the nation to get fit: Jeffrey Archer, David Mellor, Ken Livingstone, plus an array of politicians taking part in the annual House of Commons v House of Lords tug of war for charity. There are hundreds and hundreds of charities in need of support and there are several opportunities for me to include them in my daily workouts. Bob Geldof's and Midge Ure's Band Aid single 'Do They Know It's Christmas?' is an easy record to devise exercises to: I could do arm exercises, as if pulling down church bell ropes to the sound of the ringing bells each time in the chorus. For Sport Aid's 'Everybody Wants to Run the World', I was asked to join Arlene Phillips in leading the warmup on stage in Hyde Park to prepare the thousands of runners, so she joined me in the studio on the previous Friday with some of the dancers from *Starlight Express* in support of the event. And who's joining his schoolteacher this time from his Clapham school days? Floyd, no longer dancing with Hot Gossip, but still dancing for Arlene, this time in her latest West End hit musical *Starlight Express*.

The very first idea for a theme I ended up calling 'Guess the title of the James Bond film from the music'. I started on the Monday with 'Goldfinger' sung by Shirley Bassey. I'd bought a toy water pistol so I could have a joke with the unsuspecting Richard Keys, who presents the first hour of the programme. When he introduced me from the sofa for my first 'Shake Out' of the morning, I fired back at him with the water pistol from the study area where I was doing all the 'Shake Outs' that week. I knew he wouldn't actually get wet and that it would appeal to his sense of humour. He enjoyed the joke, but I should have known better that Richard wouldn't leave it at that. In the study area the set has been built so it looks as if there are real windows in the wooden frame with a garden beyond. In my 9.18 'Shake Out', I'm introduced by the After Nine presenter, start the exercises for the Bond theme week to Shirley Bassey singing 'Goldfinger' when I notice the cameraman and the floor manager in front of me suppressing their laughter. I quickly glimpse behind me while

The TV-am study area

exercising. It's Richard. He's standing in the window doing the iconic James Bond pose from the film's opening title, and then intermittingly firing it at me throughout my routine, with the water hitting me. Would any other TV station allow such antics?

One morning I wander into our little green room and sitting in a chair is John Travolta. To this day I don't know what possessed me. Out of my mouth come the words, 'Oh, I didn't know you were on the show today, I would have asked you to join me doing the exercises, that would have been wonderful.' Very calmly and politely and with a lovely warm smile to this person who had so noisily accosted him, someone he couldn't possibly know from Adam, he replies, 'Sure, the next time I'm in.' What a star, what a gentleman. And one person who does take up my offer when I suggest doing something together is a very attractive, youthful-looking blond guy who's about to run the transport system for presenters and the show's guests. He and I immediately gel and for our first date we go to my sister Rowena's for dinner, where the family dog my father used to terrify is living happily with her and her partner. So happily, in fact, that during our main course he manages to eat the entire cheesecake she'd left for us in the kitchen. A fun introduction, and as I get to know Dougie and his background better, I fall for him all the more. I marvel at how he manages to appear so serene despite his complex, emotionally difficult childhood, although I learn far more about that from his sisters. We quickly become an item and happily fall into a relationship that combines work and family life, and, together with Ben, we share the amazing life experiences, opportunities and luxuries that being a face on television offers. I understand all too well that what I'm doing at the moment is a luxury eloquently summed up by Lenny Henry when I was chatting with him one morning at TV-am.

'Let's face it, Liz,' he says, with a twinkle in his eye, 'what you do is money for old rope.'

I totally agree. When I'm driven to work, I pass office cleaners, milkmen, kids doing paper rounds, all on foot. I've been given the role of producer and am able to decide the content, the music, the clothes, the guests: it's an absolute privilege. But there are many times I question whether I should be continuing. Should I be back in schools teaching disadvantaged kids, doing a real job, not just looking into a camera? My mother reassures me that instead of teaching just a few, I'm reaching so many more, inspiring them to get fit and therefore affecting many more lives. I'm also getting lovely letters from viewers writing to thank me for encouraging them to become fitness and dance teachers and they're now in a position to help create a fitter, healthier nation. Ma's answers suffice for a time.

The only tiring aspect of the job is getting up at 3 a.m. every weekday, five days a week. Viewers might think work finishes when I come off air at 9.25 a.m., but the day can be long. There are letters to answer, constant preparation to be done, music to

With Gyles Brandreth introducing award winners
at Buckingham Palace

TV-am's healthy eating campaign

Gym Bunny

Charity baseball match at the Oval with the organiser
Paul Gambaccini, including Timmy Mallett, members
of the pop group Madness and Jonathan Ross

find, agents to be contacted, guests to be booked. Also taking
part in chat shows such as *Blankety Blank, Family Fortunes, The
Krypton Factor, Give Us A Clue, You Bet!, That's My Dog* and
guesting on news and radio regional shows. Then there are the
numerous exercise videos to devise, nine in total, three exercise
books, weekly national newspaper columns and magazine articles
to write, countless interviews and hundreds of photoshoots to go
with all the text. There are several charities to support, along
with personal appearances that can be as far away as Scotland or
Northern Ireland, and I'm hugely honoured when I'm asked to

be photographed for Gemma Levine's *Faces of the Eighties* charity book in aid of The Sharon Allen Leukaemia Trust that also includes Margaret Thatcher, Bob Geldof and Robert Runcie, Archbishop of Canterbury. It's an extraordinary whirlwind time in my life, all originating from teaching my Clapham school boys. And, once again, I have another marvellous opportunity to work with Jeff.

One day while I'm at TV-am, Dougie receives a phone call with a request for me to take part in a new children's series, and it's Jeff doing all the arrangements on behalf of the BBC because it involves exercise. He says he'll forego his role as a choreographer when making the arrangements and get rostered as the floor manager (it's not live) so he can look after me on the studio floor. How very kind of him. I am delighted to be asked; it seems surreal this young lad I taught for many years at the Clapham school is now going to be in charge of me. I've been busy creating my own children's character called Joggy Bear to encourage children to enjoy participating in dance and exercise, and the first video was so successful, I'm about to do some more. It's probably why they're asking me to be in this new series at the BBC. Or so I thought.

I go to the BBC at Shepherd's Bush to record the item, having previously chosen the music and carefully devised the exercises I would be teaching. They've worked well with Joggy Bear, and it's flattering to be asked by the BBC. I don't imagine Jeff had any say in the matter of casting me for this role. But during rehearsals on set, it all keeps going so horribly wrong. The character inside the costume keeps making mistakes and we have to keep retaking every scene. Jeff is very apologetic, probably remembering how well-rehearsed and experienced we must have looked with our own dancing in the school plays. The actor inside the costume isn't very professional, and you'd really think they would have found one that has better balance and can actually move. Poor old Jeff has chosen to be the one on the studio floor to help me feel at home, and is probably now having to listen to some abuse through his earpiece from the director. I feel quite embarrassed for him, especially when this character swipes me across the face a few times while trying to master the exercises. It isn't really this actor's fault; they haven't given us enough space, even though the studio is big enough, and this character's costume is so ridiculously huge. But I don't want to make any negative comments to Jeff so do my best to soldier on and try not to catch Jeff's eye; he keeps turning away, he's definitely trying not to catch mine.

Putting my own feelings – and the fear of this all looking very naff – aside, I do also sympathise with the actor inside the costume. It's no wonder he keeps going wrong, he's probably dripping with sweat like the actor who plays Joggy Bear. When he takes the head off his costume for a break, and comes up for air panting, I tell him not to worry, to stop apologising; he's very much got my sympathy. I tell him about Joggy Bear to make him feel better and say that he shouldn't feel in any way hassled, to just take his time. We restart. I want it to look good, I don't mind being patient, there's no need to apologise. I'll keep smiling, I really do understand. Except I understand too well.

I don't know at what point this character disappears – for a loo break or for some fresh air to get away from the claustrophobia of the costume, perhaps – but when Jeff cues us in to do yet another take, I'm still happily trying to get it right, but if anything the character is getting it even worse. The director in the gallery tells Jeff to tell us to stop. The actor takes off his big, ungainly costume head. I turn to speak to him.

But it isn't the same actor, it's Noel Edmonds from *House Party*, the massively popular Saturday night show on BBC1. For a second I can't think, I am utterly confused, baffled, bewildered. What is happening? I don't understand. I'm concentrating so hard on what we're doing and trying to help the character get it right. Then it very slowly dawns on me. In his hand, Noel is clutching my Gotcha Oscar. Oh my goodness, I've been had. It's the first recording of a series using a big floppy character called Mr Blobby, a new children's character for the BBC. All the faux pas we've been doing, all the smashing me in the face and falling over is going to be shown on *Noel's House Party*. Aaaaagh! What a fabulous way to get your old teacher, but I can't be mad at Jeff, he's Gotcha'd me in the best possible way.

CHAPTER 8

THE POWER OF MUSIC

Every weekday morning a car arrives at 4.45 to take me to the studios. Capital Radio is quietly on in the background, and then I hear it. The most captivating, soulful romantic song. The DJ at the end says it's a new release called 'Can't Be With You Tonight' by Judy Boucher. I arrive at the TV-am studios, and straight away phone Capital Radio to find out the name of the record company to get a copy sent to me. It's been made by a small indie company I've never heard of, and it transpires they're really struggling to get radio stations to play it. I think it deserves a huge audience.

It's going to be a challenge to choreograph a set of exercises to the slowest music I will probably ever use on TV-am, it's long too – over five minutes – but I love it. I feel sure that if I can emulate that continuous round shape of the music and repeat the same moves each time with the chorus, it's going to strike a chord with the audience. And even if they're not joining in with me and instead they hear it in the kitchen, bedroom or bathroom, they will still be captivated. If I use it three times in one week on both slots, I'm pretty sure it will make the charts.

It gets a great viewer response, with calls inundating the switchboard. I use it again twice more the following week and, sure enough, it leaps into the charts. Jason Pollock, the showbiz editor, shows me a copy of the *New Musical Express*, the music industry's biggest-selling magazine.

'Look Mad Lizzie, you've singlehandedly got this record into the charts!' he beams.

'How come? How do you know that?' I reply, thinking it sounds a bit far-fetched.

'Because records that make the top one hundred have their airplay – the number of times they're played on air – listed. The information's from mainstream radio like Radio 1 and the commercial stations. Everybody's asking how did this record get in the charts because it's not playlisted. Well, it's you.'

'Wow, I'm amazed! That just shows people love moving to music, or seeing music interpreted and, anyway, with such a beautiful song, you can't help but listen to it.'

'Every record company is going to inundate you with their latest releases, and no doubt offer you their artistes, too,' Jason replies while walking in the direction of the TV-am press office to give them the story.

Very quickly, 'Can't Be With You Tonight' climbs higher up the charts and reaches number 2; Judy Boucher is booked to appear on *Top of the Pops*. And Jason's right, I arrive at my desk every morning to be greeted by another heap of singles.

All that experience from choreographing and studying the violin has really helped with producing my fitness slots. I know within a few minutes of listening to the opening bars of a record if it's going to grab the viewer's attention, and whether I can put together the right exercise sequence or dance. It's not always to my own personal music taste, I have to wear a commercial hat too. One record is massively successful and it's right to use; the viewers' response is enormous, although others disagree and choose it as their 'wally song of the year'. It's not a single I would perhaps have in my record collection, but it's bubbly and catchy and would surely wake up the doziest of morning risers. I don't have to work out any moves for Colin and Alan, the two singers from this group called Black Lace, they're all sketched on the back of the record sleeve. I teach them throughout the week in both slots and viewers, especially children, love copying the simplistic moves. The following week the two singers join me. Because it climbs into the charts, radio stations start to play it, except Radio 1, the most important radio station for reaching a wide audience and therefore influencing record sales; they ban it, saying 'it's not credible'. I guess it isn't to their musical taste either, but the record does go on to become the eighth best-selling single of 1984 in the UK. It doesn't register at the time with me that if I hadn't used 'Agadoo', it might possibly not have seen the light of day for this small independent record company. And I've been awarded a framed gold disc by Flair Records to thank me for using it. And that's without singing a note.

Presented to Mad Lizzie to recognise sales in the United Kingdom of more than 500,000 copies of the Flair single 'Agadoo'

One morning, instead of a record plugger just sending me a record, he contacts me by phone. He says he's a co-director of a record company called Fanfare Records. Like Flair Records, it's not one of the big boys like EMI, CBS or Polydor. I'm interested, it's not easy for these small independent companies to compete and I like the idea of being able to kickstart someone's career, just like my boys back at Henry Thornton School. Perhaps this small-time plugger has an artiste with a single that he thinks would be great for 'Shake Out'. I arrange to meet him at their offices just off Oxford Street.

There are only two of them in the company. Ian Burton, founder and director, introduces himself. He's a quiet, unassuming young man, and was previously a dancer with the TV dance group the 'Young Generation', the acclaimed forerunner to the dance group Jeff and Garry had successfully auditioned for. Although Ian's used to performing, he happily leaves the 'pitching and selling' role to his co-director.

He's young, slim and attractive, with dark bouffant hair, a hirsute body and a rich warm tone to his voice. His dress code is a tight-fitting white T-shirt worn with unusually high-waisted jeans and a black bomber jacket. His outward appearance is soft, and I'm quickly learning his charm hides the guile and astuteness of his salesman's patter. With a packet of Marlboro Lights always to hand, this amenable and very confident guy is called

Simon Cowell. He's recently joined Ian and has one hit single with his artist called Sinitta.

Simon is very aware of the popularity of 'Shake Out' and how the connection between the song and the physicality of the dance interpretation has an impact on the viewers – and the immediacy of television exposure. Sinitta's single 'So Macho' has been established in gay clubs and discos and, although it didn't take off straightaway, it had been a good learning curve about the importance of timing. Collaborating on future songs for Sinitta with Stock, Aitken and Waterman, a team of writers and producers, hands Simon a winning tempo and disco format. He gives me a copy of 'Toy Boy', her new single, another clever catchy title. As soon as I hear it, I know it'll sell, it has that same easy-on-the-ear continuous up-tempo beat that builds and rises, and the all-important singalong chorus. It typifies what we call 'bubble-gum' music. And he's right, it will work for both of us. Sinitta is the perfect guest for me, I'm gifted with a trained dancer and a lithe mover with an appealing perfect teen image for several of my 'Shake Outs', and it's brilliant for Simon, it showcases his star, giving Sinitta the TV exposure he craves and hasn't managed to get elsewhere. Once it enters the charts, mainstream radio stations can no longer ignore it and then Sinitta's booked for the ultimate Thursday evening music show, *Top of the Pops*. It reaches number 4 in the charts.

Simon knows how to get the best out of people. He asks if I would like to make three albums myself, but not singing. Oh no, I'd already shown performing in the pantomime at the White Rock Theatre in Hastings that I don't have any natural abilities in that area. After hearing me sing in rehearsals, the director had suggested I speak the words of the fairy rather than sing them. (You probably can't recall a fairy in *Mother Goose* and that's because there isn't one – they had to create one for this non-singing fairy.) Fun though it was, it's not an experience I want to repeat. Simon asks if instead I would like to record three exercise albums. It both surprises and flatters me. Jane Fonda has burst onto the scene with her highly acclaimed worldwide bestselling aerobics videos, and although the sales of exercise vinyl albums had been significant when fronted by well-known television personalities such as Felicity Kendall and Angela Rippon, it seems a bit passé. I'm surprised Simon still wants me to do them. The sales of video recorders are huge and video cassettes in all categories including film, pop and exercise videos are taking off in a big way. But, of course, I'll happily go along with his proposal.

The albums cover three different age groups and involve finding a huge amount of appropriate instrumental music and recording carefully placed instructional voiceovers, plus long photoshoots for the accompanying eight-page booklets. It's a lot of work to do while organising my TV-am workouts, but I enjoy it. He always has an aura of cheerfulness and optimism about him whether we're recording the albums at Fountain Studios or on one of the many photographic shoots he attends. Failure and negativity aren't in Simon's vocabulary.

In 1987, at the same time as all this preparation, I'm in the process of devising and about to film *The Body Programme*, my own exercise and lifestyle video, with Kathy Rowan, the editor of the After Nine half hour that closes the programme every morning. We hire Barbara Daly – Princess Diana's wedding make-up artist – to make me up on camera, providing a step-by-step guide. We also include a section on healthy eating with nutritious meals by Arline Usden, my neighbour in East Twickenham, who's become editor of *Successful Slimming*. The contract for the video is drawn up by Tony Vickers, the head of sales at TV-am, with Video Gems, the company distributing it. Tony announces, 'If we made a video with Page 3 girls it will sell, but this video with Lizzie won't,' and signs a contract that gives me probably one of the worst royalties deals ever in the history of sell-through videos.

My wall of gold and platinum discs is expanding. I've been awarded another gold disc for the tracks I've used from Jonathan Butler's album, but my framed disc award from the little independent company for Judy Boucher's 'Can't Be With You Tonight' holds pride of place. But these awards aren't only for helping to create hit records, I'm also having a number 1 of my very own. 'Body Programme' has gone straight to the top of the sell-through video charts. As an apology, Tony Vickers presents me with a bouquet of flowers. The video stays there throughout March, is the biggest selling video title, topping the charts in June as well. I'd like to think it was the content, the instruction and the trust in my abilities that helped the immediate and ongoing sales, but I also know it's the power of television and my repeat daily appearances. It's something Simon has always known, too.

• • •

The UK Video Awards

(based on the annual survey of the Video Business charts for the period December 1986-November 1987)

TOP COMPANY – **Warner Home Video**
Runner-up – CBS/Fox Video

★ ★ ★

TOP RENTAL TITLE – **Back To The Future (CIC)**
Runner-up – Aliens (CBS/Fox Video)

★ ★ ★

TOP INDEPENDENT COMPANY – **EV**
Runner-up – Guild Home Video

★ ★ ★

TOP RENTAL TITLE (INDEPENDENT COMPANIES) – **Wanted Dead Or Alive (New World Video)**
Runner-up – Soul Man (New World Video)

★ ★ ★

TOP DISTRIBUTION COMPANY – **CBS Records**
Runner-up – CBS/Fox Video

★ ★ ★

TOP COMPANY (SELL-THROUGH) – **Video Collection**
Runner-up – BBC Video

★ ★ ★

TOP SELL-THROUGH TITLE – **Lizzie Webb's Body Programme (Video Gems)**
Runner-up – Jane Fonda's New Workout (Video Collection)

★ ★ ★

TOP DISTRIBUTION COMPANY (SELL-THROUGH) – **Screen Legends**
Runner-up – Video Collection

★ ★ ★

TOP COMPANY (MUSICVIDEOS) – **Picture Music International**
Runner-up – Virgin Video

★ ★ ★

TOP MUSIC TITLE – **Queen Live In Budapest (PMI)**
Runner-up – U2 Under A Blood Red Sky (Virgin Video)

The Number One Awards

(given to titles which topped the Rental Chart or the Sell-Through Chart)

RENTAL TITLES

CBS/FOX	CIC	WARNER HOME VIDEO
Aliens	*Ferris Bueller's Day Off*	*A Nightmare On Elm Street 2*
Big Trouble In Little China	*Golden Child*	*Heartbreak Ridge*
Commando		
Crocodile Dundee	RCA/COLUMBIA	
Jewel Of The Nile	*Critters*	
The Mosquito Coast	*The Karate Kid 2*	

SALES TITLES

BBC VIDEO	CHANNEL 5	VIDEO GEMS
Scotch & Wry	*Status Quo: Rockin' Through The Years*	*Lizzie Webb's Body Programme*
Double Scotch & Wry	**MISSING IN ACTION**	*Transformers: The Movie*
Watch With Mother	*Hero: World Cup 1986*	**WEA MUSIC**
CBS/FOX		*Madonna Live: The Virgin Tour*
Hits 6	**VIDEO COLLECTION**	**VIRGIN**
CIC	*Jane Fonda's New Workout*	*Comic Relief 'Utterly Rude' Video*
Beverly Hills Cop	*Jane Fonda's Prime Time Workout*	*Genesis: Visible Touch*

Video Awards, 1987

It's 1987, and Stock Aitken Waterman (SAW) are dominating the charts. They release a single – 'Never Gonna Give You Up' – by an unknown artist called Rick Astley. The single's a smash hit. Simon also wants another hit with them – a third for Sinitta. He chooses another song from her self-titled album called 'GTO' and invites me and Dougie, my partner and now my manager, to the launch. It's held at a trendy, swanky restaurant on the Thames Embankment. Naturally, Simon's placed a brand-new red Ferrari 250 GTO on the forecourt to mark the occasion. It's a fun record, but doesn't quite have the same winning formula that Stock Aitken Waterman are now turning out prolifically. It's still a good beat for me to use, but it lacks that X factor; it gets to number 15, no mean feat as it's Christmas, the most lucrative and competitive time for sales.

Both Simon and I end this pivotal year on a high. My video carried on topping the charts in October and won the coveted prize of 'Top sell-through title' in the 1987 UK Video Awards (not to blow my own trumpet, but it outsold Jane Fonda's latest workout video and Michael Jackson's 'Bad' music video) and Simon has completed his year on a high with two more big hits with Sinitta.

The many record companies whose records and artists I'd promoted on breakfast television are generous in their thanks, supplying the very best tickets for concerts. We're enthralled by Whitney Houston, Chris de Burgh, although backstage he's clearly not a TV-am viewer so is a bit baffled when introduced. George Benson surely must have been primed to comment 'if you want your record to chart it must have Lizzie do it'. Ben, now a music-loving teenager, is particularly chuffed that he could get to see Dire Straits, as well as being given a prized Pink Floyd CD boxset. Simon is the most attentive and generous of them all. He and Ian invite Dougie and me to the 1988 Brit Awards at the Royal Albert Hall. We sit in a prominent box with them and celebrate our combined successes, cheering on the live stage acts and the artists collecting their awards and splashing the champagne at the following Grosvenor House dinner.

The Simon empire is starting to build and we carry on creating hits for another few years. There's one act I feel sure will spark an idea for the future. He gives me a copy of an album by a group called Rondò Veneziano. They're an Italian chamber orchestra who merge classical compositions with a rock-style rhythm section. They play all their instruments, whether it be violins, cellos, the synthesizer or drums, in huge powdered white wigs, the women in long crinoline dresses, the men in brocade jackets and knee-length silk bloomers; all look as if they've been transported from the Baroque era. This unique interpretation of pop classical music is a bonus for me. I use several tracks over and over again, whether it be by myself or with guests, it's such a bright, uplifting unique inspiring sound and for viewers not acquainted with my own passion for classical music, a perfect introduction. It affords me another gold disc the following year and another delicious lunch with Ian and Simon at L'Escargot in Soho. Album gold discs are so much bigger, but hey, my wall's expanding with my own exercise and dance video awards.

It doesn't always go according to plan. Simon's discovered what he considers to be another Sinitta, and gives me her single 'Rhythm of the Night'. She's called Princess Sheeba. Her up-tempo song's perfect for waking up the viewers. Except, she does more than wake them up. When she walks into the studio to do the workout, she's wearing very skimpy fitness gear which doesn't leave much to the imagination. I, with my concept of not being in exercise clothes and encouraging viewers to keep on the move to build fitness into a part of their daily lives, look like a thoroughly over-dressed parent next to Sheeba. I'm in white trousers and a white jumper, a pure, clean-looking outfit. I'd also talked to the editor of the day, suggesting Princess Sheeba would make an interesting guest with Lorraine on the sofa before we dance in my second slot. They'd thoroughly agreed and Lorraine does a lovely chatty interview with her. She proudly announces to Lorraine that her 'grandad was a Zulu king and I am a princess.'

I think everything's gone really well until I open the *News of the World*, the biggest-selling Sunday newspaper. There, emblazoned at the top of the page, is a headline:

Vice Secret. Sexy Singer Sheeba didn't tell telly viewers she also worked as a high-class call girl. Pop beauty offers sex for £1,000.

And next to a big photo of her looking cheeky in a very provocative Page 3 pose is me. A screen shot has been taken with us dancing side by side captioned 'Dancing to "Fame"'. I gulp. I was certainly 'unaware of sultry Sheeba's secret life of vice'. And presumably Simon was too. Somehow we rode the storm.

With several guests, I'm able to use them in photoshoots, and then interview them for my weekly page with the *Sunday People* newspaper. I was initially approached to write a fitness page for the paper by Mary Riddell, a journalist and newspaper editor. I'd had the good fortune to sit next to her at a celebration lunch for a magazine for *Woman's Own* magazine when she offered me the page. It's good fortune because I'd lost touch with Min, my best friend from my college days, while she's been travelling the world with her husband, a senior executive in the oil business. It transpires that Mary's husband is working with the same company and they're all very good friends. How small the world is and how grateful I am to Mary for reconnecting me so Min and I can continue our own great friendship.

So it's another new challenge, it's onwards with newspaper writing and double-booking the guests I'm exercising or dancing with on TV-am, and then doing a photoshoot and an interview with them; it's a system that saves me coming up with new ideas for the column each week. It's also a lovely opportunity for me to have a get-together with some of my past pupils. The five boys, Patrick, Jeff, Floyd, Garry and Rupert, top my list so we can catch up and celebrate all their ongoing successes, and I do the same with several of the girls I taught at Italia Conti; they too have become big names in the entertainment world.

Simon doesn't sign any more singers or pop groups himself, but carries on introducing me to other groups and singers that Pete Waterman and other producers are recording. One of them is a wonderful singing and dancing duo called the London Boys. Dennis and Edem are charming lads and possibly the first boy band to, with their honed, gyrating, athletic bodies, disco dance their way through their songs. Their energy is infectious as they backflip and spin on their heads. They are unique and rightfully considered to be one of the best acts of the eighties. I arrange for them to come into the studio many times, I love working out their dances and then watching their acrobatics in the instrumental break. Will they be an inspiration for future television ideas and acts for Simon?

In the early nineties, Simon and Ian part company. Simon has successfully paved his way, joins BMG and is able to use not just one high-profile TV star, but two. With his instinct and experience, he must know he'll be on to a winner with two very popular lead actors from a highly rated ITV television drama series called *Soldier, Soldier*. In one of the episodes, Robson and Jerome sing a version of 'Unchained Melody', last seen and heard in the film *Ghost* with the iconic pottery scene performed by Patrick Swayze and Demi Moore. Simon, with his well-worn commercial hat, relentlessly pursues Robson and Jerome and persuades them to record a cover version, only this time produced by the successful partnership of Stock and Aitken. His uncanny nose for a hit proves right yet again. It reaches number 1 and stays there for seven weeks, becoming the biggest selling single of 1995 at the same time as their album becomes the biggest-selling album. Simon had learnt the power of popular television exposure at TV-am, the rest is history.

• • •

Would you believe it if I said someone from the most famous pop group ever in the world phoned me to say 'thank you' for making his record a hit? No, me neither.

One day, I arrive home from the TV-am studios to a message on my answermachine.

'Hi Lizzie, this is George Harrison.'

I don't hear the rest of the message. Have I heard right? No it can't be, play it again Lizzie. It sounds like George, with that unmistakable Liverpool accent. I rewind the tape and start it again. Not only is it George speaking, if it really is him, and I think it is, he's thanking me for using his music, helping it to climb up the charts. George Harrison, a former Beatle, is thanking me and wants to take me out to lunch?! Well it has to be a send-up, a big wind-up. Is it the comic Rory Bremner secretly recording me and pretending to be George, or is it someone in security at TV-am passing on my phone number to a television show like *Game For a Laugh*? A few years ago, I'd been in the extraordinary position of finding myself sipping cinnamon tea with Yoko Ono in her apartment in the Dakota building in New York, and all to do with the power of music, but George? It's too good to be true – definitely a send-up.

It isn't. George has tracked down my phone number to ring me personally and thank me for devising exercises to 'Got My Mind Set On You', his solo release. Nobody else is playing it on its release in the UK, and I've exercised to it three times in both exercise slots so that it's reached two different audiences, a total of six plays, and this has subsequently helped it to become a hit. George has just taken my breath away. How can someone of his magnitude bother to go to such trouble or even consider thanking me in the first place? And if he wants to convey his thanks, wouldn't you designate one of your team to do it? And more than that, who was the Beatle I had a crush on when I was a schoolgirl? Yes! And little did I know when I choreographed the routine to 'Get Back' by The Beatles for the Clapham school-boys' appearance on *Opportunity Knocks* that George Harrison would actually one day be phoning *me*.

I return his call. It's on answermachine. My turn to leave a message saying of course I would be delighted to have lunch with him. I put the receiver down, never expecting to hear anything further. Anyway, by now radio stations are playing his record because it has a chart position. But I do hear back from him.

Several weeks later, a Christmas card arrives in my post bag at TV-am, the words 'Merry Christmas and A Happy New Year' printed on it. The rest is in George's handwriting.

Dear Lizzie. All the best to you and your family. I'm afraid the lunch will have to be next year now — sorry I have been so busy — thanks for the promotion on my record — the next one is in January called 'When we was FAB' – could be 'When we had FLAB'! See you when I return to England in February – lots of love – George Harrison

And does he keep his word? No. We don't have lunch. It's better than that.

When we do get to speak, it transpires that George lives in Henley-on-Thames, just twenty miles away from where I'm currently living with Dougie. So instead, he invites us to his house. We go, both a little nervous and hugely excited, not knowing what to expect. I press the button on his intercom. I can still hear his voice saying, 'Keep coming up the drive and then you'll come to my bungalow.'

A bungalow indeed. He must know how overwhelming it is for people like me when they eventually get sight of his 'bungalow', because after driving for an eternity up his driveway through this massive country estate, it is, of course, anything but.

It's the most magical, unforgettable day. I think what best sums up our time with him is something he says while we're sitting drinking tea with him in his kitchen. He points to a tiny black and white photo balanced on a ledge. It's of a little boy sitting on the front doorstep of this tiny terraced house.

'That's me. I keep that there. I don't forget.'

George had agreed we could take a photographer with us to record this memorable occasion. We take several photos in his stunning grounds, some with me posing in an exercise position while he plays his guitar, others in big bear hugs. My face in these pictures says it all. People from my generation from Russia to Timbuktu will know just how out of this world it must feel to be in the company of one of the Fab Four. Imagine who you would like to be sitting with having a cup of tea in their kitchen and that dream comes true.

For some of you, it could be a member of a more recent boy band.

In 1992, I'm watching the *Junior Royal Variety Show* on a Bank Holiday afternoon when a group of five lads catch my attention. The song they're singing is their new release, it's catchy, up-tempo and they're exuding a boyish energy as they dance; two of them look like professional dancers. I've not seen them before and take a note of the group's name. It's Take That and their single is called 'It Only Takes a Minute'. It's their latest release, and none of their previous singles had made it into the charts. They would be ideal for waking up our TV-am viewers.

The next morning, I track down their manager and ask if the group would like to join me in the studio, but could they do so in the next couple of days? They won't have to come in early because I can do a pre-record with them. I'm about to go on holiday and always leave recorded material for the programme. I can film three mornings' worth, so that will give them six slots and with that amount of television exposure, this boy band with such a catchy single should have a sure-fire hit on their hands. Nigel Martin-Smith, their manager, is more than happy with my request.

I ask Nicki Chapman, their plugger with RCA Records, for a copy so I can work out a dance/exercise routine in advance.

I have to keep the routine quite simple; many of the viewers are joining in, so it still has to be achievable. I choreograph a series of lively repeat moves for the chorus, and keep the rest more exercise based. The instrumental break in the middle of the song is theirs to do with whatever they like, and for the two athletic lads, it'll be an opportunity to demonstrate their impressive acrobatic skills.

I meet the lads at 9.30 a.m. as arranged so we can rehearse before filming. I find them slumped in their chairs in the green room looking somewhat bleary eyed. I introduce myself and find out their names. I'm really surprised, my enthusiastic greeting is met with a muted response; there's an air of reluctance about them. I expected them to be keen and full of energy and raring to go with this opportunity. It surely isn't that early in the morning, well, not to me it isn't, and I've been up since 3 a.m. Ah, maybe these lads have been gigging the night before and aren't yet awake. One of them called Mark breaks the awkward silence.

'My mum's really pleased we're dancing with you,' he says, clearly the friendliest of the group.

Well that's lovely, but is that a problem for these boys? Perhaps the lads are seeing this gig as something they have to suffer because their manager insists on them appearing with me for some TV exposure. A shame he hasn't arrived yet, because he'll know of Simon Cowell's success with singers like Sinitta and others, including Sonia and Black Lace, who shot up the charts after their 'Shake Out' appearances. Sonia says dancing to 'You'll Never Stop Me From Loving You' so many times on TV-am in 1989 resulted in her very first number 1 hit single.

Sonia dancing to her single 'You'll Never
Stop Me From Loving You'in 1989

Maybe these five lads are never up in time to see TV-am and what we do. Hopefully they'll get their energy up when we go into the studio to record. I must say my hackles are up a bit when I think of my five Clapham boys.

I take them into the empty studio so we can rehearse while the technicians are having their breakfast. We run through the routine a few times. I can see the one called Gary with the blond hair isn't a natural mover. He's quite gauche and spending the time grinning, looking a little awkward; he'll be more comfortable if I put him in the back row. Mark's a slick dancer and is coming across as a really sweet lad, he looks as if he's enjoying learning the routine, and if he's not, he's got the sense to keep smiling and sell it, that's after all why they're here. Robbie's clearly the clown of the group, he's quite clumsy with big feet and apologises every so often as he treads on my toes. He larks around making funny whoopee noises during the chorus as we neatly and quickly jump backwards. Hmmm, he's coming across as a lovable cheeky chappie, but I'm not sure if he's sending it up. The taller boys, Jason and Howard, the two that had previously caught my eye, are much quieter, and both fabulous dancers with great-looking bodies. Both of them really add to the energy of what we're doing and I would think are essential to the success of the group's promotional video.

Their manager arrives and stands watching on the studio floor. When we start recording, I chat at the beginning with two of the lads, so they can fill the viewers in about themselves. All is going well. The instrumental break is great to watch, it's giving

Jason and Howard a chance to showcase their slick mirrored backflips, Mark his spins and when Robbie's turn comes, he chooses to attempt the splits, which of course he sends up, clutching his crotch area each time we do it. It's really very funny. I've made sure there's no time left for Gary to do anything; he's still looking uncomfortable. I hopefully make the lads feel more at ease at having to dance with me by saying, 'Come on, keep up with Grandma!' while leaping back into view to join them with the chorus. For each of the recordings, I change my outfits to make it look less like a recording and for the final one, I position Robbie next to me and ask him if any of them have had any dance training?

'We're from the streets, man,' is his hip reply.

They maintain their energy and perform well, maybe they were just tired after all. Before we leave the studio, I take Nigel aside. Robbie's brought out the schoolteacher in me.

'Watch out for that one, he enjoys being naughty.' Nigel says nothing and nods his head, he probably knows that already.

The lads go back into the green room and Nigel and I go to our open-plan offices upstairs so I can find Jason, our showbiz editor. I introduce him and suggest the lads will make great guests on the sofa with the show's main presenters. It'll really help them to have a much longer chat than I can do, plus the programme planners can also link their sofa chat to one of our three recordings. Jason readily agrees and books them to come in the following week. Before going away, I schedule my running order and spread the recordings out, timing the

6.30.1992 13:22

RCA Records Bedford House, 69-79 Fulham High Street, London, SW6 3JW
Tel: 071 973 0011 · Fax: 071 371 9296 · Telex: 920896 BMGRCA G

Via Fax
(071) 284-2044

Lizzie Webb
TV AM
Hawley Crescent
London NW1

Dear Lizzie,

Just a quick note to say a BIG thank you for all your help with **Take That** on TV AM - it certainly made a huge impact.

I've actually been on holiday for the last few weeks - imagine my delight on their chart position when I returned! I know for a fact that their single rose dramatically after their appearance on "**Lizzie's Workout**".

The boys have a new single scheduled for release at the end of July, and if you would ever like them in again, they would be delighted to join you.

Thank you once again.

Kind regards,

Nicki Chapman
RCA Television Promotions

BMG
RECORDS (UK) LIMITED

RCA Records is a Division of BMG Records (UK) Limited,
a Company Registered in England, number 1471066,
at the above address. VAT Reg. No. 440 6258 65
A BERTELSMANN MUSIC GROUP COMPANY

Take That success, 1992

third morning for when the boys are in the studio chatting on the sofa.

When I return from holiday, not only do I hear the switchboard has been flooded with viewers wanting to know more about Take That, but there's a fax on my desk from Nicki Chapman, sent after the first week's transmission. How kind of her to take the trouble to write such a lovely fax. I do question, though, whether they really 'would be delighted to join me again', and anyway they won't need to, 'It Only Takes a Minute' has reached number 7 in the UK singles chart. They're on their way.

CHAPTER 9

MY EARLY YEARS

When I was six years old, my mother said my headmistress at Underhill Infants School in Barnet had told her, 'With Lizzie's warm voice she should be a teacher.' I remember feeling really chuffed; it was such a positive, kind thing to say. I wasn't a high achiever when I moved up into my primary school, so her comment comforted and influenced me, especially with my lack of self-worth.

When I took my eleven-plus, I failed. It was no surprise to me. I had two older sisters who had sailed through this exam and, several years later, my younger sister did too. I never felt I was as clever as them. Forty-five pupils had sat the exam in my school and only four failed to get into a grammar school. I was one of the four; it meant I would be going to a secondary school. The shutters quickly came down on my future learning as far as I was concerned.

The local secondary schools were mixed and didn't have a good reputation. My parents decided I would be better off travelling to an all girls' school in Friern Barnet called Southaw Girls' School. It was a long bus ride, but they felt it would be worth it. It wasn't. The time I spent at Southaw Girls' School was not particularly happy. The little confidence I had after my failure of the eleven-plus, let alone what was happening at home, quickly dissipated when attending classes. I felt like a fish out of water. In lessons, I sat next to a very assured girl called Elaine Bickerstaff. We always had to sit at the same desk in the same place; she was my desk partner. We had music and dance in common, but neither of us was interested in learning maths or science and, eventually, I think she got fed up with my meek and mild ways,

In the middle with my two older sisters in 1959

she was too much of a ringleader for me. But at least throughout that first year, I felt I had a friend and ally. Much of what happened around that time I've locked away in order to move forward. I didn't want to dwell and have never discussed with either my sisters or close friends, because the things I'd experienced as a child were so deeply unpleasant. I'd been in too many dark situations that I couldn't control. I think I subconsciously built a protective mechanism around myself, which gave me the ability to park the memories. Now, as I relive those times, I do so in the safety of my adulthood.

After a year at Southaw, my mother made a decision that was to completely change my life. She was determined to send me to a very special private school called Potters Bar High School, later renamed Anthorne. It was like a stage school, but was more of a ballet school; a few pupils had successfully auditioned for the Royal Ballet Senior School and one had even joined the Royal Ballet Company. Each day was spent doing academic lessons, but they were interspersed with ballet classes and other forms of dance. It was another long bus journey, but this time well worth it.

What a joy, what an absolute privilege it was to go to this school for four years. My mother worked flat-out in order to pay the school fees, albeit in a really interesting, responsible job, as well as looking after four daughters and holding the fort at home. And what a huge home it was.

When I was ten years old, we'd moved into an elegant, three-floored Victorian house. It was situated behind a pretty park in a long row of similar houses, with ours attached either side; it

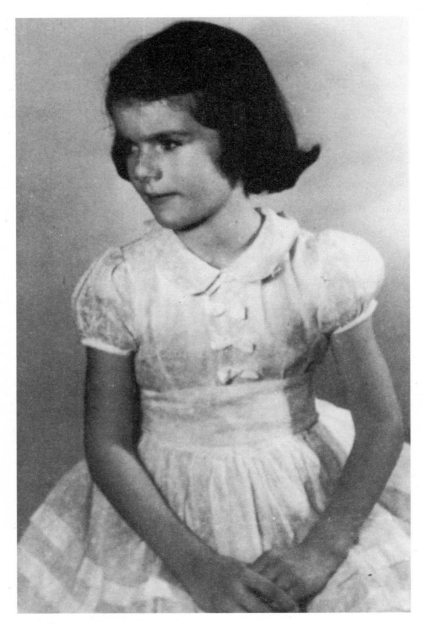

My dance dress

was a big step up from the council house on the massive estate where we'd previously lived. Pa had got a job as a computer operator and not only did he feel elevated in the workplace, he wanted his new status to be reflected where we lived. This was the high end, the top end of Barnet, the posh end. You entered our house via a grand front door with patterned ceramic tiles in the porchway. The hallway was straight, long and narrow, with an intricate black-and-white pattern on the stone floor. Halfway down the hall on the right-hand side was the first set of stairs. At the top of them, in full view from the front door, was a big photo portrait of my father in his soldier's uniform, a picture taken in his younger days during the Second World War.

At the end of the downstairs hall was the large breakfast room. As you entered, behind the open door and against the wall was an enormous, yellowing, built-in dresser with black knobs on the drawers. Propped-up plates were on display in neat rows, with knick-knacks and bills on the dresser top; the dog box for Hector, our golden Labrador, was in the wide open space underneath. Further into the room on the other side was a big boiler standing on polished dark-red tiles, set back in a recessed alcove. Opposite and almost central in the room were the table and chairs. The table could be extended with a leaf you could pull out at either end, an imaginative design I thought. Ma sat at one head, my father at the other. When we sat round it for mealtimes, I made sure I always sat in the same chair next to Ma, never the opposite end where my father sat. I couldn't sit anywhere near him. He was a terrifying and controlling figure who reacted to typical childish transgressions with cruel and sadistic punishments. Why would I want to sit next to him?

The back of the breakfast room led to a small door and a step that went down into the scullery. This was a really tiny, primitive room. The sink under the sash window had a small, wonky wooden draining board to the right with an Ascot heater above. Every time it ignited to heat up the water, it would make a loud whooshing sound. Its attached long arm swung over the butler's sink, dribbling out the hot water and taking an eternity to fill up the washing bowl. Against the side wall, by the back door, the free-standing gas cooker stood precariously on the uneven, stained, tiled floor. A small table was placed beside it so Ma had somewhere to hand to place saucepans, or for us when drying up the plates and cutlery. The tumble drier that had replaced the old wringer that we affectionately called the tub was parked by the remaining wall. When switched on, it would burst into life and judder and dance around this tiny space.

There was a pantry leading off the scullery to store the food. Shelves for all the tins, milk and butter, sugar, flour and eggs and a wired vegetable rack stood on the cold stone floor. If you looked above the door when leaving the scullery, you could see, nailed above on the door frame, a piece of history. A line of six bells mounted on a piece of wood, each with a number on it. They looked like miniature church hand bells and had a purpose; they were each connected to one of the main rooms so the maid could be summoned. A souvenir from Victorian days. We of course could manage without a maid, but what we really

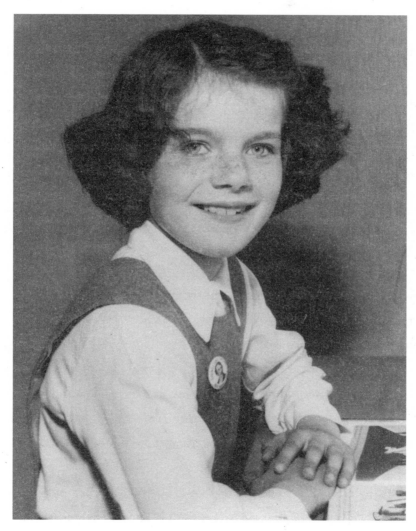

Primary school

needed, because the house was so big, was a cleaner. My mother didn't have time to clean because she was secretary to Reginald Maudling, our local M.P. His constituency office was based near Hadley Green, a good two-mile walk for Ma. She also had to cook fresh food for the family, do the shopping and washing and, after she broke her hip, it was impossible for her to physically do all the chores.

I loved my mother dearly and would do anything I could to try and ease her hugely busy and difficult life. There was one obvious answer. Cleaning. There would be no need for a card to be placed in the local shop window to advertise for a cleaner. Vacancy filled. I would see to it; cleaning would be my new role. I was already happy being the dog walker and the nipper out to the local corner shop, seeing how fast I could run back with the latest forgotten food; I could be the charlady too. This way, I could repay my mother for working so hard to pay my school fees. She was always so grateful and I was happy because I could keep her happy.

Doing all the cleaning gave me a purpose, a sense of usefulness. The scullery, no matter how much you scrubbed it, never looked good, but at least it was clean. There was brittle, mottled lino in the breakfast room under the two hessian mats that shed their hairs; I methodically swept it with the broom and occasionally washed it down. It was a big house to look after. There were two flights of stairs in total with a long landing in between, three bedrooms on the first floor, a separate loo and a bathroom with an adjoining door into my parent's bedroom. The top floor had two bedrooms and a tiny box room.

The cleaning was all very good practise for when I was a student at college. I needed to earn money to pay for rent and food to supplement my grant. I signed up for part-time work with two agencies with Min, my best friend, who I was to happily share a flat with in my third year at college. I didn't mind in the slightest that I didn't have enough money; I was experiencing freedom for the very first time in my life, total freedom away from home.

Our Victorian house was too expensive to heat and often in wintertime we wore coats and scarves to keep ourselves warm. The coal fire in the lounge didn't emit much warmth, and needed a lot of raking out and preparation, so we'd turn on all four gas taps on the cooker and heat up the breakfast room by keeping the scullery door open and sit at the table. Except my father thought this was an enormous waste of gas and money and it wasn't allowed.

Every evening at about 6.30 p.m. before his imminent arrival home from a day's work, one of us would climb up on the sofa in the bay window in the lounge and be on watch duty. You'd have to balance precariously on the padded arm of the four-seater Chesterfield sofa in order to see over the fence, but it was by far the best vantage point. As soon as there was a sighting, the spotter, usually me, would shout. Whoever was in the breakfast room rushed into the scullery to turn off the gas cooker, tell our lovely Labrador to get back in his box under the dresser, but he knew the drill anyway. If I was in the lounge I would turn off The Beatles LP blasting from the record player and we'd either scarper to our bedrooms or sit down with homework at the table and await the front door key in the lock.

When we moved up in the world to this Victorian house, my bedroom was on the first floor. I had a big old-fashioned brass double bed. The mattress was big and the softest thing, all feathers so you could leap up into this puffed-up mound and disappear. Hanging down from the ceiling behind the bed was a long, twisted, manky-looking rope. It was connected to one of the bells in the scullery. It worked. If you pulled the rope hard, the bell would ding-a-ling. You couldn't hear it ring in the bedroom because the scullery was too far away downstairs. On the rare occasions I was too ill to go to school, I'd reach through one of the brass struts and give it a tug. Up would come Ma to comfort me, clutching the jar of Vicks and a glass of lemon barley water for a stuffed nose from a cold or a bottle of calming pink calamine lotion if it was something itchy like chicken pox or measles.

When my sister moved out to board at a ballet school in Sussex, I moved up to the top floor. There were two bedrooms on this floor and a tiny box room where the maid would have slept. We were convinced the back bedroom overlooking the garden was haunted. When my second sister and I tried sleeping in it, we both had nightmares. We decided to take a friend's border collie dog up to the top floor, to see if he would react, as they are known to be very sensitive. He got to the top of the stairs and refused to move. No matter how much we enticed him, he cowered, refusing to budge, hackles up, with a quivering top lip. Something must have happened there. Was it in the back bedroom or in the maid's tiny box room or both? What an existence she must have had.

Her life must have been constantly on the move, cooking in the scullery, running up and down two flights of stairs, scrubbing and sweeping the floors, cleaning out all the ashes from the hearth. It must have kept her very fit.

And I was, too, but mine was from the fortune of choice and not just from the cleaning. Not only did I have a walk and a long bus ride to Southaw Girls' School, I had a much longer journey to get to the other end of High Barnet to catch the Green Line bus to attend Potters Bar High School. Green Line buses were country buses that didn't stop all the time, they connected country towns and villages and travelled much greater distances than the local ones. The bus stops were a distance apart and the buses less frequent. I couldn't afford to miss the early morning bus, because I had another walk the other end to get to my school in Quakers Lane. Once there, I was invariably changing straight into my ballet clothes for the first lesson of the day.

Walking long distances I'd always found enjoyable; it gave me a sense of freedom and relief. I was away from the constraints and the imprisonment imposed at home by my father. I would walk miles, often taking Rowena, my baby sister, with me, pushing her in a strange-looking unstable contraption that was balanced on three rubber wheels. It had a flimsy, light-green, canvas seat for her to sit on and a small green canvas piece to support her back. She would be seated facing me, strapped in by a thin, single belt. A long steel pole was fixed into it and I would clutch the handle with both hands to push it and steer it, or try to steer it. If I didn't get the balance right, the thing would tip up and she would be knocked backwards with her head dangerously close to the pavement. A few times the pavement struck her head, or, if I'm honest, her head struck the pavement, which wasn't surprising. How was I meant to control this stupid design going up and down high kerbs? I never told my mother of the near misses and my little sister fortunately never complained.

Probably the longest walk I did as a child was when the trolley buses went on strike. With father's work as a computer programmer, and with Ma working too, it enabled all three of us to learn ballet and go to weekly Saturday classes to Mary Honor's studio in Golders Green. Mary was a famous retired ballerina who had performed with the Sadler's Wells Ballet Company and Ma wanted us to have the very best training, something she herself had been denied by her own mother.

The large back room of Mary Honor's house had been transformed into a ballet studio and was in a suburb of Golders Green where all the houses look the same. The studio was very striking, very professional with its well-laid wooden floor, a barre all the way round three sides of the room, a piano in the corner and a tray of white resin on the floor for us to rub our ballet shoes in so we didn't slip as we danced.

The mothers would sit in the bright, glass conservatory changing room waiting for their daughter's class to finish; they'd sit knitting pink and white crossovers to go over the ballet tunics. They would chat animatedly about their daughter's latest ballet exam results. Ma fortunately escaped being a 'ballet mum' because of the long distance. It was a forty-five-minute trolley bus ride to get to Mary Honor's studio. Sometimes it would take longer if one of the two arms from the trolley bus had come away from the overhead tram lines and an inspector would be needed to guide it back on with a long wooden pole before we could continue with the journey.

One day, we couldn't get there because of the trolley bus drivers' strike. I was absolutely determined to go, even if it meant walking alone. I set off on the six-mile journey, accompanied by my shoe bag stuffed with my ballet tunic, crossover and pink ballet shoes. I made it in time, did the class and arrived back home very late in the dark. Ma must have been worried to death.

Both of the day schools I attended were very different – chalk and cheese. The pupils, too. Apart, that is, from Elaine Bickerstaff at Southaw, she was different and I'm sure she would have loved to be going to my ballet day school too. Here, in this girls' school, we were all sharing our love of dance and drama and going to school was a pleasure. What a wonderful privilege to be able to be a pupil in such a remarkable arts school in Potters Bar.

And so, it was with great relief I happily blotted out my first year at Southaw Girls' School and concentrated instead on the wonderful opportunities on offer at Potters Bar High School. My greatest joy was to make up dances and learn about putting steps and sequences to music, and because the other girls were better at performing them, I really enjoyed teaching them how to perfect the steps and sequences I couldn't do. I was chuffed when I won the school's annual choreography prize. I was also influenced by a wonderful late-night dance programme. If my father was away on business, Ma would let me stay up and watch a weekly ITV series called *Cool for Cats*. It was dancing to pop music by professional modern dancers; I remember the vivacious actress, Una Stubbs, being one of them. I found the whole show captivating, riveting and it certainly influenced my meagre attempts at choreography.

I was also lucky enough to play the violin and win a Junior Scholarship to the Guildhall School of Music & Drama. Every Saturday for five years during term time, I would clutch my violin and travel on the Underground train from High Barnet all the way to the Embankment in London, and spend all morning playing and learning the theory of music. It did wonders for my appreciation and my confidence grew sky high when I became leader of the junior orchestra at the Guildhall, albeit the second orchestra. Playing the cello, but in the first orchestra because he was that good, was an attractive, small boy with very black hair. He was called Anthony and I had my girl's eye on him. He was quite mischievous and together we struck up a good friendship, but I think it was more I fancied him than the other way around. I would seek him out and wander down the vast corridors of this imposing old-fashioned building to a cacophony of musical instruments emanating from the individual music rooms. Invariably I spied Anthony behind one of the double glass doors in the same music room with his father. He was a professor of music, a cello teacher and a performer with a string quartet, so I knew where to find him. A few times, I would see his father teaching the same pupil. She had long blonde hair and I would

Secondary school, age 15

stand mesmerized in the corridor, peering in listening to the most exquisite depth and warmth of sound she seemed to easily illicit from her cello. I learnt later her name. It was Jacqueline du Pré.

With this comprehensive musical training, coupled with my summer at the National Youth Theatre and the choreography I learnt from my ballet school, I was afforded the most won-derful opportunity to learn from the arts; for that, I am hugely grateful to my parents. It could well have been the catalyst for me wanting to give children who fail academically other oppor-tunities in the arts, so that they too can succeed.

Back in the sixties, when I did my final year's teaching practise at a borstal in Hertfordshire, I was sitting in the staff room when one of the social workers asked me a question, a question I didn't want to think about too deeply when I was about to embark upon my teaching career.

'We fall into two categories at the borstal. You're either someone who is here to do good or you're here because you need to do it. Which one are you?'

I suspect it's something to do with my father.

It can take time to unlock buried memories, but an incident, a comment, a relevant association out of the blue, can ignite a flashback. If I go back to my time at Southaw Girls' School and my desk partner for a year, is it possible I could forget who that person was because I've erased that unhappy time in my life? Well that's exactly what happened.

When I was at TV-am, a record company sent me a super new song by Elaine Paige, a huge star with a stunning voice who was well known for her wonderful musical roles on the West End stage and on Broadway. This record was called 'The Second Time'. It was the theme tune from a French film with lyrics by Tim Rice. It kept going round and round in my head as I spent time working out a flowing sequence of moves to try to reflect the mood of the song. It entered the charts, but very low down. I was really pleased with the exercises I'd put together and knew that with more airplay time it could definitely climb higher. I planned to dance to it twice more, following it up in both slots, and wondered just how big a hit it could become.

Two things happened and one of them was out of my control. One day, as I walked out of the television studio into the vestibule area, I saw Elaine Paige and Tim Rice coming towards me; they were the main sofa guests on the day's programme. When they approached, I was taken aback by the way they greeted me.

'Ah! *Dear* Lizzie,' exclaimed Elaine, while Tim proceeded to thank me for exercising to her record and helping to get it into the charts. What an accolade coming from him, *the* Sir Tim Rice. How kind of him and how very friendly it was for Elaine to greet me with such an affectionate term. I was really pleased with her response when I told her I would be exercising to it again the following week. It didn't enter my head to ask if she would join me exercising to her record, she was surely too big a star to agree to doing that. Anyway, I didn't get the chance – they were due on set and hastened into the studio.

I went into the green room later that day to read the morning papers. I skimmed through one of the more popular rags and there, looking back at me, was an advert for Elaine's record. Tim must have passed on the news to the record company that I was working out to 'The Second Time', because in big bold letters was Elaine's name, the title of her record and underneath it: *The new single out as exercised to on Breakfast* TV-am *by Lizzie*. This must have been another record the music stations hadn't put on their playlists; it must have been the TV-am viewers who were buying it and this was another way of publicising the record. Unfortunately, the following week on 21st November the TV-am technicians went on strike and the station was forced to come off air and close down. My plans to help make this beautiful song a smash hit for Elaine were completely scuppered.

One evening, decades later, I was at home watching Elaine being interviewed on television and out of absolutely nowhere I had a flashback straight back in time to my stored unhappy memories of Southaw Girls' School. Wasn't this Elaine Bickerstaff, the very same Elaine I'd sat next to at school for a year? Could it be? It was surely her. Is that why she had said, 'Ah! *Dear* Lizzie' when we met? Oh my goodness, I'm sure it is the very same Elaine.

I googled the question, 'Did Elaine Paige fail her eleven-plus?' and there was the answer – a whole feature about Elaine Bickerstaff, professionally known as Elaine Paige, at Southaw School. Mystery solved. Had she recognised me when she walked in with Sir Tim Rice? She must have thought I was being spectacularly rude!

Advert for Elaine Paige's new single

CHAPTER 10

CREATIVITY IN SPORT

In February 1983, TV-am made television history by becoming the first commercial breakfast broadcaster. They're about to make history once again, but this time, by losing their franchise. Margaret Thatcher has decreed that an auction of the commercial stations is necessary and in 1991 TV-am is outbid by GMTV. The new franchise holders aren't offering anything different, it's simply because their bid is financially the lowest. They'll undoubtedly keep the same, populist format Greg Dyke devised and so successfully implemented. Why would you want to change it? But understandably, GMTV wants to look as if they're offering something new and require different faces. Anne and Nick had already changed sofas and gone to the BBC, and instead Eamonn Holmes and Anne Davies would be occupying the presenters' sofa. Linda Lusardi, one of the glamour girls from my Page 3 week, will replace me as their fitness presenter. The final broadcast is at the end of December 1992. After nearly ten years of daily breakfast television presenting, a new phase in my life has begun.

Dougie and I decide to buy a small non-working farm-holding with a huge barn that had already been converted into a studio by a photographer. It's in the country, just outside Marlow in Buckinghamshire, a perfect place for 'Lizzie's Fitness Studio' and ideally situated for Ben, who's rowing with the GB squad and studying for a degree at Oxford Brookes University. We kit it out with a sprung wooden floor, a wall of mirrors and a ballet barre where you can look out onto the fields and smell the flowers from Dougie's stunning rose garden while stretching your hamstrings. When the sun's shining, we utilise the two vast empty paddocks for our warmup, running round the perimeters like energetic spring lambs. As you enter the building on the left side, we create a large welcoming lounge with sofas, chairs and a drinks machine. There's a mezzanine floor above the studio floor and the room below we make into a changing room with showers.

I teach two or three classes every day. It's all female – not by design, it's just how it's naturally evolved. It's an intimate, carefree time with lasting friendships made and, although it's a demanding timetable, it's an enforced but very welcome time to catch my breath after the whirlwind of everything that has previously happened. The boys' comprehensive school, the drama club, the home for adolescent kids, giving birth, the dance group, hiking in and around London to teach with my beat box slung over my shoulder, getting divorced, the stage schools, television commercials, travelling and guest teaching around the country, and no longer getting up at 3 a.m. for TV-am. The adult company is relaxing and the teaching undemanding, but after this intermission of six years, it's time to reassess.

What do I still yearn to do, what do I really want to achieve with the rest of my life? What do I feel I've been put on this planet to do, what gives me the most satisfaction? The question is rhetorical. It seems I have a gift for turning round the lives of troublesome youths, especially with fitness and dance. How can I get back into schools and teach disadvantaged children? So far in my working school life, I've been able to teach my own programmes, my own content. Where, at the start of the millennium, can I do this and how would it be looked upon by other teachers if they recognise me as 'Mad Lizzie'? And can I juggle it all while keeping my fitness classes going with all these women who have become additions to my extended family? Maybe I should close the studio and continue my fitness classes by hiring a studio in Marlow or at the Sports Centre at Bisham Abbey for just a couple of nights. One of my attendees at the studio has bought a magnificent country estate from the Queen's cousin, and offers her baronial hall for me to continue teaching during the day as her personal trainer with a handful of her friends. I will try and juggle it all.

In 2000 I complete a Return to Teaching Refresher Course at Reading University. If I'm to have any credibility going back into the classroom when I've become known as a 'face' on television, it's important that I update my qualifications. I don't want to rely on my past teaching success or to be seen as out of touch and misinformed while successive governments have innovated with their latest educational reforms. It's possible, though, that my television exposure might work to my advantage and open doors if headteachers recognise me, especially as there's been the video success with my children's fitness character called Joggy Bear. But, it could also have an adverse effect and teachers might assume I'm jumping on the tails of 'those who can do, those who can't teach'. I'm passionate about young people having the opportunity to experience the benefits of exercise, to enjoy the freedom of wide open spaces as they develop their physical skills and increase their energy levels, or benefiting from dancing and group aerobic work with the emotional and expressive interpretation that all forms of dance ignite. It's maddening that pupils in state schools don't have dance or aerobics as an option in the curriculum. Can I now use all my accumulated teaching experience and, if necessary, my 'celebrity status' to innovate and assist in the updating of physical education in the state system?

The recent commercial success of the film *Billy Elliot* has heightened the awareness of the creative stimulus and empowerment dance can engender for boys from a disadvantaged background, but there is no sign as yet that this 'revelation' is translating into an option in the PE curriculum. I had four of my own 'Billy Elliots' back in the seventies while teaching at the South London boys' comprehensive, with countless other lads performing dances in the drama club who had no intention of becoming professional dancers. The training in strength, agility and flexibility required in ballet and modern dance easily outweigh those required in many sports. And just as important are the invaluable mental health benefits. Surely a creative physical programme would be an obvious inclusion when we repeatedly see statistics that schoolchildren aren't timetabled the required amount of weekly sport and PE time? And for pupils who have little interest and lack motivation in playing games, or using indoor sports apparatus or taking part in competitive outdoor team games, there seem to be few alternatives, apart from a run round the playing field (if the school hasn't sold it off) and the school coach taking them for a swim in the local pool. Why not offer a more diverse programme and one with cultural influences that include different forms of dance, tai chi, yoga and judo? Independent schools have an even greater choice that will often include rowing, fencing and golf.

I'm going to embark on a mission and call it Creativity in Sport. For several months I've been compiling a huge collection of pictures from the sports pages of national newspapers and photos from a mountain of dance magazines and ballet programmes. By carefully juxtaposing an action shot of a sports person alongside a photo of a dancer framed in exactly the same position, it instantaneously illustrates how sport and dance require the same physicality of strength, speed and suppleness. The similarities will be conclusive evidence, and help validate my theory that forms of dance should be offered and included in physical education curriculums. I have created a vast photographic album; I'm hoping it will be my trump card.

I started by cutting out action shots of footballers. I'd become a fanatical football fan when, at the age of nine, I would go with Pa to support Barnet Football Club. They're an amateur club in the Athenian League and every Saturday we'd walk the mile and a half from our council house in Mays Lane to the football ground at Underhill. He revelled in having a daughter who shared his passion. Come rain, snow or shine, we would stand right by the side of the pitch. We'd have to get there early to bag a place behind the steel railing with supporting dodgy mesh wire; it was just about chin height for me and much more enthralling than sitting miles away in the stands. I felt safe with him at the matches and it was the only time it didn't matter that he was standing so close to me.

It was basic, muddy, oranges-at-half-time stuff and utterly absorbing – my Saturday fix. I was captivated by the grace, the masculinity and balletic physicality the players had as a team. Footballers were light on their toes with their speed and accuracy. Bobby Brown, the number nine striker, was my hero. His tinged, auburn hair clashed with the team's kit of yellow and black, but could he score goals. 'Up the Bees!' we used to shout as the team strived to rise to the top of the Athenian League. And they did. All around the ground, people would whirl their football rattlers, winding them up with a clicking sound as they went round faster and faster; it all added to the excitement, but they were too heavy for me to hold. My father enquired about buying me a junior season ticket. They were surprised, nobody had ever asked for one before, least of all for a young girl. How proud I was to become the first holder of a Junior Season Ticket at Barnet Football Club – a flimsy, pocket-sized piece of card with my name written on it. I never missed a match whenever Barnet played at home and I was ecstatic when we had tickets to go to Wembley to play against Crook Town in the FA Amateur Cup Final.

The Sunday papers are a fantastic source for the best sports pictures, especially football. So many of the action shots of the players capture bodies in exactly the same positions as dance photos and some of the accompanying text even refers to them as such. One I cut out in 2005 is captioned 'Stepping Out: Frank Lampard and John Terry in training yesterday as Chelsea prepare to face VfB Stuttgart'. The two of them are side by side, their left legs in the air at exactly the same height like a kick-line of dancers. The strap line 'Stepping Out' is a clever reference to the title of a popular West End musical.

There is one particular stand-out photo from a Sunday back page that's a flag bearer to my cause and fills the first page of my overflowing album. It's of Graeme Souness when he was manager of Blackburn Rovers around about 2003. He's on the touchline wearing a shirt and tie, trousers, shoes, and an open mac. This superb action shot is of Graham doing a fantastic high kick, his right leg straight and high in the air; it's a kick worthy of ballet dancers like Carlos Acosta or Rudolf Nureyev. Both arms are outstretched to the sides, perfect body balance. The standout thing for me is his back: it's completely straight, not rounded, he's not collapsing from lack of abdominal strength. This photo is taken way before the awareness of the importance of core strength with football training, dancers have always trained 'their centre', not footballers, not in the same way.

Fourteen years later, when I show Graham the photo, he straight away recalls the specific match. He explains he spontaneously did the kick to draw the referee's immediate attention that one of his men had just been fouled with a dangerously high kick. I doubt the offender had got anywhere near the height Graham had illustrated. I tell him about the comparison I'm making with his perfect position alongside a ballet dancer, but I'm not sure he wants to acknowledge the connection; he's never been to the ballet and I didn't do a very good job of persuading him to see for himself how balletic football is. But wait. Didn't Rio Ferdinand, the Man United and England defender turned football pundit, acknowledge in interviews he wanted to be a ballet dancer? Isn't Dion Dublin, an ex-Aston Villa player, a great ballet fan? And what about English football manager Graham Potter? When he was manager of a Swedish club he performed a dance solo in the club's own modern version of *Swan Lake.*

And they're not the only professional footballers who've acknowledged the merits of ballet training. In the late eighties, my partner Dougie and I walked into a London restaurant to be greeted loudly and warmly by a table of first-team Wimbledon football players. They were clearly TV-am viewers by the ribbing I was getting. After a brief chat, the manager announced they were doing ballet classes to improve their football skills. Bingo! Who would have expected to see hard man Vinnie Jones doing high kicks and knee bends at the ballet barre? A few months

Dance and football, dance and tennis

later, I had the opportunity of three Chelsea football players, Dennis Wise, Dave Beasant and Kenny Monkou joining me on one of my TV-am workouts. The three of them entered into the spirit of doing leg exercises in their football strip. If you look at the photo taken on set, you can see our quads are pretty well matched. It's just a pity they weren't Liverpool players!

• • •

With my album complete, I am ready to rekindle my profession as a schoolteacher. I check my DfES number registered in January 1970; it's still valid and is now called the Teacher Reference Number. Thirty years have elapsed since introducing dance to the Clapham boys' comprehensive school, but before trying to convince others, I need to prove once more to myself how the value of dance and exercising to music can stimulate even the toughest, most unlikely group of pupils. It would make sense to replicate and engineer a similar teaching environment to the one I had back in the seventies. What would be the best way forward, do I have any contacts that will be open-minded to this suggestion and help kickstart me in my quest with Creativity in Sport?

Andrew MacTavish is the recently retired headmaster of John Hampden Grammar School, a boys' school in High Wycombe, Buckinghamshire. He's continuing to use his expertise as a governor at the Royal Grammar School, another high-attaining boys' school in the same area. I was initially introduced to Andrew via his wife when she attended exercise and dance classes at 'Lizzie's Exercise Studio'. Change from this all-female environment happened in the unlikely form of a Christmas present. Some of the ladies thought it would be a novel idea to buy their husbands an all-male aerobics class as a stocking-filler, an amusing dig at their husbands' lack of fitness. But much to their amazement, it didn't have the outcome they'd envisaged. The twenty-one men who had gingerly and somewhat reluctantly turned up to this evening class enjoyed it so much it quickly became a weekly all-male class. And then, the eighteen regulars from the original stocking-filler become a twice-weekly class.

Andrew has been championing these classes from the very start and not just because of the physical improvements that he and the class are appreciatively making. I'd become accustomed to some of these grown men behaving like naughty little schoolboys, particularly those who jostled for position in the back row. They'd been unleashed from the daily constraints of their work and, for Andrew, it was clearly a role reversal. No longer a headmaster, a symbol of authority, but a delightful *Just William* character contributing to the witticisms and banter from the back row. I asked Andrew if he would be a flag-bearer for these all-male classes and arrange an introduction to the Royal Grammar School so I could try out my experiment. We both agreed we need to request the most challenging group from the school – it might encourage the headmaster to give my hypothesis a go.

Andrew organises a meeting and a somewhat bemused headmaster listens to this unexpected request. He doesn't hesitate and suggests, with a wry smile, I can try taking an aerobics class with a group of fourteen-year-old lads in place of their usual Wednesday afternoon session. And who might they be? The school's first fifteen rugby team. Well, I did ask for a challenge and I've certainly been given one. As an ardent football fan, I'm used to watching precious top players fall over clutching their shins, or any part of their body, at the slightest knock of an opponent's boot. These lads will probably overindulge in their rugged tough image. How will they take to doing dance aerobics set to music? Andrew's reaction is to also give a wry smile, he's seen me coping with overgrown boys in the studio all vying and failing to match my cardio output, quad and triceps strength. He doesn't doubt the rugby boys will equally be confronted with a challenge.

I arrive early for this guest class, which is held in the smaller of the two sports halls; I want to make sure the hall is clear and free from any obstacles and be at the ready when they all pile in. I bring with me a huge stack of mats for the floor work and pile them into a corner, place my big beat box with several CDs on a bench at the front, alongside my photographic album. I pace up and down waiting with Andrew for this melee of rugby boys to arrive; there will be at least twenty lads. A few of them pause and peer in through the windows en route to the changing room next door. We wait, listening to the raucous sound as they shout across each other, but not one of them is appearing and the clock is ticking. We sense there's an air of reluctance. Andrew decides to round them up and finds them unenthusiastically donning their kit, their body language making it clear they would rather be roughing it up and improving their training on the rugby pitch. There's a glum feeling this new training is going to be weird and of little value.

'Have you seen her? A maypole with a mop of hair on top,' a voice gleefully describes me.

'Come on gentlemen, hurry up,' urges Andrew, ignoring the comment.

'Sorry, sir,' is the respectful chorus of replies as they scramble past him into the hall where I'm waiting.

Andrew stands in the doorway as I introduce myself. Is he beginning to wonder if I've bitten off more than I can chew? Instead of me giving an account, I ask Andrew if he would do so for the Head of Games who'd been sceptical, but had bowed to the Headmaster's request.

'I had known Lizzie long enough to enjoy her impact at first meetings. The boys were big and bumptious; Lizzie stood radiating exuberant authority in the centre. She arranged them crisply in rows and began a dynamic routine. I would say within thirty seconds she had impressed the team with her personality; I'm not exaggerating, it was that fast. Within a minute and a half they all realised she was a powerhouse, was fitter than they were and had something of real value to offer them. The room was charged as if with electricity. I went away and then looked in at the end of the session. The team was uplifted by the strenuous dance exercises to the heavy beat of the music. The high morale and noisy voices showed they were looking forward to the next session.'

The next session? I didn't need any persuasion. Neither did the lads, but at the end of this exhilarating, high-energy, pulsating class, I still wanted to try out my album of photos, my trump card. I gather them round me on the floor and leaf through the pages. The juxtaposition of the photos with the footballers and the dancers elicits favourable grunts as I point out the only difference between the two is the clothes they're wearing. I turn the pages slowly to the pictures of a big, strapping rugby guy held aloft in the air by his herculean teammates, arms thrust in the air as he's about to catch the rugby ball. I'd put this cutting alongside a group of male dancers in a modern ballet lifting a dancer in exactly the same position. It goes down well with these lads and they're even more responsive on seeing the strength of one of the male dancers, holding a dancer high above his head as she sits in the palm of just one of his hands.

In the album I've pasted an atmospheric photo of two men with shaved heads sitting side by side on a concrete floor, barefoot and leaning against a wall. They're casually dressed in open-neck blue shirts and dark-blue trousers. Two young lads, about ten years old, are standing beside them. Their outfits match their sombre pose and facial expressions.

'So what do you think these guys do for a living?' I ask trying to not give any indication, any vocal nuance in my questioning.

'They're dossers, out of work,' comes back a swift reply.

'They're villains,' proffers another, which causes a general murmur of agreement.

'What gives you that impression?'

'Well, they just look it,' a loud voice bellows.

'Oh no they're not,' I laughingly reply. 'These two men are known as BalletBoyz, two ex-Royal Ballet dancers who have formed their own modern dance company. They're both married to ballerinas and the two boys standing beside them are their sons.'

Don't judge a book by its cover boys!

We're up and running. I feel I'm back where I belong.

For the next two academic terms, I take a very pleasurable weekly class with these rugby lads. Their co-ordination with the energetic aerobic routines to music improves, they pit their muscles with the squats, the biceps and triceps dips, battle with the ab work and succumb to completing the classes with the essential stretches. They're currently competing in the *Daily Mail* Schools Rugby Competition and climbing closer to the final; they're defeating every school team and brimming with confidence in our hourly class. I want to record their compliance and enthusiasm for dance aerobics for our pilot scheme, and choreograph and stage a dance routine in their rugby gear. The moves are strong and aggressive, rhythmical and totally in unison, it's worthy of a routine from *Billy Elliot*. Ben films it for me with a video camera from two different angles so that Joe, my nephew who edits *Top Gear* with the Jeremy Clarkson trio, can kindly utilise his expertise for us, so I have it all on record. The lads are converted, the sports department are converted. In Andrew I have my first and influential ally. We consider our next move.

A document is needed setting out our aims and suggestions for creative additions to existing sports curriculums. We outline a pilot scheme for schools we can present to an education authority and individual schools, quoting the current alarming growth in childhood obesity statistics. One of them we've titled 'Body Breaks' and is a concept close to my heart. Re-energising pupils and helping them to focus for the second half of the day would be such an effective addition to the school day. During my visit with the trade delegation to Japan, I'd watched a workforce in a factory in Osaka spill out during their lunch break into their backyard and, still dressed in their white boiler outfits, execute a sequence of exercises with military precision. The authorities had measured the effectiveness of these exercises on the workers' afternoon output. Such an obvious wakeup call and one that school pupils would benefit from too.

Andrew has excellent connections within the education community and suggests we contact Malcolm Peckham, the director of education for Maidenhead and Windsor, to arrange a meeting. After outlining the aims of Creativity in Sport with our document, Malcolm advises we meet with his heads of various learning departments. It soon becomes evident in the meeting that the most valuable contribution we can make is to provide a family fitness programme for young mothers and their small children.

They would like us to trial a programme for pre-school children using Joggy Bear in Bumbles Nursery School, which is based on an estate solely for army families in Dedworth, just outside Windsor. The morning will start with a forty-five minute class for twenty to thirty children as young as fourteen months old and their mums, followed by an hour's session with three- to five-year olds from the nursery school, all doing fun exercises based around my children's character Joggy Bear. In the afternoon, further down the road, I'll take two Joggy Bear classes at the local infants' school and then run an after-school dance club in the next-door primary school. This is all an excellent starting point, especially as I'd already devised and presented an ITV daytime exercise series for young children called *Work It Out*, written a children's exercise book titled *Exercise Zoo* and a collection of exercise programmes with Joggy Bear for three videos. It meant I already had a wealth of material, although it's very different doing it in person as opposed to on camera or on the written page. It also involves working with an actor appearing every week with me inside the enormous six-foot costume. This age group is not what Andrew and I had originally intended, but it was a foot in the door. Being employed by Maidenhead and Windsor Education Authority will help us to establish Creativity in Sport. Can we now use their recognition and take the ideas for our pilot scheme to the very top?

• • •

One of the many advantages of my ten years of being the producer of my own twice-daily fitness television slots was the contacts I'd made when organising guests. It was unusual for a presenter to have direct contact with a proposed guest or their agent, so I have a very good list in my address book of celebrities working in television, theatre, sport and politics. One of those names was Colin Moynihan. He'd appeared with me on one of my 'Shake Outs' at TV-am when he was Minister for Sport. When I was subsequently asked to devise a class and invite celebrity guests for the opening – attended by HRH Diana, the Princess of Wales – of a London health and fitness club, Colin – then Lord Moynihan – had entered into it with a great deal of enthusiasm. I decide to contact him regarding our pilot scheme. The meeting I subsequently have with him and his team is very positive and he assures me he will give it further thought. He suggests I put the scheme to Carole Raymond, an HMI Ofsted Inspector for School Sport and passes on her details. Meanwhile, an announcement is made in the House of Commons that couldn't be more timely.

Diana, Princess of Wales at the opening of the health club in 1998

Tessa Jowell, Culture Secretary, has just confirmed London will bid for the 2012 Olympic Games and they have two years to prepare for it. A report is being compiled looking at the feasibility of holding the Games in London and, if approved, an Olympics Minister will be appointed. I have a vision. I can see the potential for embracing the ideas we're developing with Creativity in Sport running in tandem with the Bid. We could widen the horizons beyond merely sport and use our cultural heritage, engage pupils and inspire them in the belief that London is the place to hold the Olympic Games using the arts, dance, songs, paintings. They, the future generations, should play a massive part in immersing themselves in this great opportunity and, in particular, focus on young people in areas of deprivation who can be motivated to take part in physical education. Tessa Jowell clearly thinks this too in her announcement.

> Our Olympic Bid will also rest on a growing commitment to grass-roots sports. It will be central to our efforts to increase physical activity and identify and develop talent. We want to harness the power of sport and to help address some of the key issues our nation faces – health, social inclusion, educational motivation and fighting crime.

My past teaching experience echoes all these sentiments, my photographic album endorses it and this last sentence is exactly what Andrew and I are trying to develop and install. Who to go to next? We could wait, along with countless others, to try and get a meeting with the new Olympics Minister, but our ethos is not just sports-based, it's also educational and culturally based. Would it be more beneficial for us, given the pilot we're implementing in Windsor and Maidenhead, to try and link into an educational programme with the Olympic scheme? An ambitious plan but why not try?

Estelle Morris has been Secretary of State for Education and Skills and is at this point the Minister for the Arts. Prior to her role in government she'd been a PE and humanities teacher in an inner-city school in Coventry; with her knowledge and teaching background she might have a sympathetic ear and be willing to support our innovative scheme. The minister kindly agrees to see me and listens attentively to what I have to say. She tells me to use her name when she gives me the details of an excellent contact: Sue Campbell, the CEO of the Youth Sport Trust. She is energetically enthusiastic in her response, too, and is excited by the elements devised for primary schools and the suggested link into the London Olympic Bid.

'Joggy Bear for the children! I love him, let's do it!' she enthuses.

It isn't quite that simple. The staff member in the organisation designated to liaise and implement it is already busy overseeing Youth Sport's own schemes; he has no financial powers to innovate using Joggy Bear as an introduction to physical activities for early years. But all is not lost, they're keen to liaise on some of the aspects of the London Bid, and it's agreed with their marketing director that they will work on the ideas with us. And another totally unexpected opportunity is about to come my way.

CHAPTER 11

THE LONDON 2012 BID

I'm immersed in developing ideas for London 2012, using the original ideas from Creativity in Sport's concept for a schools competition, when I get a surprise invitation from a very unexpected quarter. It's from the Great Britain women's and lightweight men's rowing coach. I've been a rowing mum for years, supporting Ben who's worked his way up through the junior ranks, the Under 21s and is now a sculler with the Great Britain Lightweight Squad. Initially it involved financing his kit and travelling to support them in their local and international competitions, cheering from the banks. The other parents and I are now adding additional cheers for the largesse from the National Lottery Fund, a wonderful grant that's enabling them to become full-time rowers.

So far I haven't met Paul Thompson, the recently appointed Australian coach. Paul has heard that Ben's mum was a fitness presenter on breakfast television and thinks it a fun, light-hearted gesture to invite me to take a guest class with the women's squad at Dorney Lake (where the Olympics will take place if London win the Bid). I'm excited, if not a little overwhelmed, and readily accept his invitation. It's another unplanned diversion in the unexpected learning curve of my career.

I'm not sure what Paul's hoping for, but I decide I'm not going to do what I've become publicly renowned for with my TV-am 'cabaret' spot. Instead, I put together a testing session for these most competitive of achievers. I focus on their core stability and include a series of abdominal and oblique exercises, plus some quad and butt work; with the amount of exercise teaching I've been doing, both past and present, I'm confident this mum is somewhat fit and can hold her own, although I'm a little daunted at the thought of teaching such well-honed bodies. Rowing is one of *the* most challenging of physical sports and their coach is renowned for his demanding discipline and dedication.

What will I wear? For the rowers who know me, it might feel slightly incongruous to be bellowed at by Ben's mum; others might view me as a fleeting 'kick your legs TV fitness presenter'. I redesign one of Ben's rowing T-shirts by cutting out the sleeves to wear with my leggings and decide to play it cool. I take Val with me as my assistant, she's been one of my stalwart evening class exercisers for years and is also a qualified fitness instructor.

The clubhouse at Dorney is big and majestic, overlooking the expansive lake with several competition lanes marked by perfectly spaced buoys that bob far into the distance in exacting straight lines. The boathouse is stacked high with row upon row of racing boats, the lengthy oars hanging symmetrically from the walls and ceiling. There is one floor above with a huge airy sports hall that houses the gym machines that have been cleared to one side to accommodate my session. There are several adjacent rooms off the hallway, treatment rooms and a big canteen. These rowers are well catered for.

The girls arrive in dribs and drabs, the hall gradually filling up; the class is going to be bigger than I expected. There's the Under 21 team as well as senior squad members, at least thirty of them in total, nearly all dressed in their GB squad kit. I've taken my beat box with me and a selection of pre-planned CDs. I ignore the fact that most of them have done their first training session earlier this morning and, after the warmup, their co-ordination is still a little bit suspect, perhaps because warmups are something to be tolerated. Plus some of the girls are taking this 'foreign' concept of doing it to music very light-heartedly. I persevere.

I do squat work with pulses before the floor work. Val scatters the mats among them and we get to work on both the adductor and abductor muscles for some leg raises. There aren't too many takers of my five kilo ankle-weights and I realise that when doing the lifts, they primarily focus on their quads and butts. Then it's time for the ab exercises. I demonstrate and after variations and several reps, leave Val out front for them to copy while I traverse the room, urging them on with my booming projected voice. I encourage them to hold the ankle-weights or a free weight in their hands for an additional challenge. I'm perplexed. Although they're clearly supremely fit, their ab work is surprisingly lacking in both quality and sustainability. Several of them lie back clutching their stomachs and, when doing the oblique work – the side waist muscles – they struggle, and neither are they faring well with the back elevations.

As they leave at the end of the class, I understand the cynicism of those who remind me they've already been training hard on the river first thing this morning before the session. Maybe one or two of the more cynical among them are a bit affronted that at my age Ben's mum can outdo them with her abs and leg raises. Others are profuse in their thanks and say they will definitely carry on and incorporate some of the exercises into their daily routine.

So this invited guest class isn't just stored in my collection of memories, Ben has also been taking photographs discreetly. I'm quietly pleased and relieved I haven't let him down and feel hugely honoured to have been given the opportunity to teach virtually the entire women's squad.

A couple of days later, I'm contacted by Alison MacGregor (now a professor). Alison tells me she is based at London's Imperial College and leading a programme of research into rowing performance, focusing on rowing kinematics and mechanisms of injury. She's been regularly testing the rowers from both the elite men's and women's squad and is inquisitive as to why so many of the girls she's just tested have sore abdominal muscles. Their reply was my guest class; they'd found the exercises challenging and pain is the result. She asks if I would consider putting my own abs to the test as part of her research programme. I hesitate, but only for a moment. If the team are struggling with my constructed set of exercises, then I should be able to cope with the tests myself, so it would be foolish not to accept such a request. Ben is bemused I've accepted; he has prior knowledge and experience of the challenging task facing me. He vaguely prepares me with a paucity of words, apparently it's all about resistance.

I meet Alison in her laboratory. She looks so young; she must surely be wondering what on earth I'm doing here. I survey the tiny room, crammed with huge, torturous-looking machines. I'm beginning to feel daunted. The first testing machine looks the most awesome and cumbersome, the most onerous of all. But first, she has to weigh me to adjust the machine weights. I must surely be one of the lightest 'victims' she's ever tested, well, apart from maybe a cox or two for the eights boat.

Alison clamps me into humungous, long, heavy steel plates, one on my front and one on my back. They engulf my torso. She tells me it will give an exact measurement of the strength of my abdominals. Really? I'm thinking – how? I can't see me being able to even move. You have to bend forward and downwards and then, with a rounded back, push up against the resistance. We have a practice run first, but first Alison reminds me to have some restraint and reserve my strength. Restraint? I can barely lean forward. Did she really get my weight details correct? Because, no thanks, I don't want the same resistance applied to these steel weights as Katherine Grainger, Steve Redgrave or James Cracknell.

I do the test once. I can only describe it as slightly less torturous than knowing another contraction is coming when you're in labour and then the relief when it's over. Alison utters sounds of both surprise and pleasure and asks if she can increase the weights. My utterances are both silent and congratulatory to myself. Maybe I shouldn't have pushed so hard with this torturous machine. Torturous?

'Didn't Ben tell you the rowers call this "the machine of death"?'

I heave away as she increases it a further two or three times (I'm too delirious to remember how many) with each time requiring a greater, extra monumental push, until, exhausted, I can push up no more. Phew! But I can tell she's surprised. It seems I've passed the test with flying colours. As she unclamps me and I stagger away, she's now wanting to test my obliques. Maybe I can come back another day? What a relief, it's just an ultra-scan, I can lie down and recover. When noting my sizeable muscles showing on the screen, I hear more uttered surprise. I'm chuffed.

In fact, the results are so good and Paul is so pleased, it's the start of a very happy and intense working relationship with both Paul and Alison. We combine her biodynamic and musculoskeletal expertise and regular testing with my practical core stability and leg programmes, and together we devise the trunk programme for the women's squad. Alison doesn't want to call it a core stability programme, she says it's the whole trunk area that's going to give the force the rowers need, so the trunk programme it is.

For two years I teach the exercises in a weekly and sometimes twice-weekly hour-long class at either Dorney or Bisham Abbey. It isn't always easy for either of us. Paul is a very hard taskmaster – it's how he works. To achieve results, the medals, he pushes them to strive to their absolute limit. I'm similar in my approach, having taught and achieved success with my boys and then with stage-school students. It's not always a popular approach and doesn't suit everybody, but it's often only after they've achieved their ultimate success, when they've gone way beyond their own expectations, that they comprehend our method and reasoning and are grateful. Of course we know it isn't easy for these rowers when they arrive for the hour session either before or after a heavy training session on the river, but nearly all of these winning medallists including Olympians Katherine Grainger, Debbie Flood, Alison Mowbray, Elise Laverick, Rebecca Romero and Fran Houghton are an absolute pleasure to teach. Sometimes, living so close to the Leander Club in Henley-on-Thames, I'll take additional sessions and be joined by other gold-winning male Olympians, including Steve Williams and Mark Hunter, and Ben will loyally tag along too.

I'm initially paid to do the first half-dozen classes at the beginning of my collaboration with Alison, but the Amateur Rowing Association doesn't want to continue any further payments as they've enough staff on their books. Paul feels it's absolutely vital to continue with our programme, Alison's ongoing tests and results are proving it since we've introduced them. I am more than happy to continue. It's an honour to contribute to their huge success at the Athens Olympic Games in 2004.

It isn't only with Alison I enjoy a happy working relationship. It's while teaching the squad that I meet and get to know Debbie Flood. She and I talk one morning after the class and discuss her ambition to work with vulnerable and disadvantaged young people. In her spare time, she's a volunteer at a local boys' juvenile prison. When I share my own past teaching experiences with her, we both know that one day we will work together.

Time passes. On 14 May 2003, Tessa Jowell announces in Parliament they have two years to get the London Bid in place and Sebastian Coe will lead from the front. This could be the very opening we need to showcase our ideas. Seb had been a guest at TV-am a couple of times, discussing his illustrious career as an athlete. I decide to contact him about Creativity in Sport's scheme with suggestions of how it can be merged and embedded into the principles of the London Bid. In September 2004 I send him an email, reminding him of how we'd met at TV-am and detailing the purpose of the pilot scheme, how to involve arts in sport and the competition we'd already devised that could easily be transferred to the Bid; and most importantly how 'this would present a unique opportunity to show the world how nationwide our schoolchildren are all participating in helping to bring the Olympic Games to London.'

I receive a reply the following month from Kathryn McColl, the Education Officer. My email to Sebastian has been passed to her, she's extremely interested in the ideas and wants to arrange a meeting. Excellent. I get in touch with her straight away to see how we can become involved with her department. We arrange to meet for a coffee in the River Room at the Savoy Hotel, which I suggested because it's a quiet, comfortable place for a meeting with deep sofas you can sink into and, of course, I have very happy memories of my boys dancing for the boxing promoter's black-tie event in that very room. I soon discover there isn't an education department, but just one sole person, Kathryn. She'd been seconded from the Department for Culture, Media and Sport (DCMS).

I discuss in detail my concept of aligning sport and the Olympic Games to the arts and our cultural heritage. As I leaf through the pages of my two bulging albums with the photographs and newspaper pictures, I point out the numerous alignments, the similarities between dance and sport; how we can engage non-sporting pupils to be a part of the competition by using traditional rhymes such as 'London Bridge', to translate them to the proposed Olympic venues using song and dance; how there could be painting competitions of contending sports personalities and game shows based on fitness and past Olympic winners. For the little ones in primary school, they could explore different sports and related exercises and be inspired by Joggy Bear and his own Bear Olympics. It might sound like I get carried away with my enthusiasm, but it has an effect; Kathryn looks thoughtful and taken aback. Aligning the arts and sports is something she hadn't thought of. I propose running a nation-wide competition for both primary and secondary schools. Yes, but Kathryn has no money, no funds available to do anything new, or indeed anything at all. She's been given an empty pot.

Andrew and I attend a meeting at the Olympic headquarters at the London Athletics stadium in Stratford, East London, which at this stage is looking like one gigantic bulldozed building site.

Sebastian Coe is showing a visitor round, and as we gaze down at the huge expanse of work being done, he glances over and nods his head and smiles in recognition of my presence. I hope it will be possible to speak with him later, to run through the ideas I'd sent him, but when the time comes he's nowhere to be found.

The meeting, organised by Kathryn, includes a representative from the Department for Culture and Sport (DCMS), one from the Youth Sport Trust (YST), Andrew, Kathryn and myself. The representative for the YST agrees they can get involved in the distribution of the competition details. They will also investigate along with the DCMS to see if they can donate a small amount of money to enable a pilot to be put in place. The reward for each of the participating schools would be an allocation of tickets to a venue, that's if we win the Bid. Hurrah! It's moving forward, but we leave knowing that probably little money, if any, will materialise. Kathryn gives us the go-ahead in an email a few days later and Andrew and I prepare for the hard work ahead.

I set about formatting the competition ideas for both primary and secondary schools and call it the *Go! London 2012* competition. Ben registers the website with the same title and designs the artwork. The YST introduce us to Derek Peaple, a dynamic headteacher of a school in Newbury that's been designated Sports College status. We establish a wonderful working relationship with him and although it entails a lot of travelling, I'm delighted to do so as Derek is able to link us up with at least six local primary schools. We arrange for me to visit six schools, plus two specialist schools, the Mary Hare School for the deaf and the

Castle School, a school for children with complex disabilities. Derek's school is going to host the final so that all their artistic works, stories, songs and dances can be displayed and performed in their vast hall. Redroofs Theatre School in Maidenhead agree to supply Martin Clark, an experienced actor who is just the right size; he has to fit Joggy Bear's six-foot costume and join me exercising on some of my school visits. Andrew and I also make a similar arrangement with three primary schools and one secondary school in the High Wycombe area. We are ecstatic at seeing our plans coming to fruition, but we need to acquire a financial structure for the future.

I'm happy to supplement my own travel, teaching and organisation for this competition to make it work, but it's imperative we find a sponsor for when we complete the piloting to roll the competition out nationwide. No sponsors have been forthcoming from further meetings with the DCMS and Kathryn herself is drawing a blank. None of the official sponsors are interested in supporting our venture, clearly we will have to go it alone and try and find one ourselves. Could we engage any big commercial companies when the official channels have failed?

Once again Andrew comes up trumps. He has a contact on the governing board of the Royal Grammar School in High Wycombe who has a contact with Tesco's. In November, a meeting is arranged at their headquarters with their marketing director. I come away from that meeting somewhat deflated at his response; he didn't think there was any hope of London getting the Bid. I wrote to John Madejski, the owner of Reading

Football Club, and the reply from his PA is ambivalent, too. He saw our scheme is such a long way off and not at the bottom-line stage, so wouldn't be supporting it. Fair enough. Kathryn is also getting the same feedback. It's so disappointing, it seems that nobody has any faith in London winning the Bid, and certainly is not interested in investing in an innovative competition that aimed to engage all schoolchildren whether they are already active in sport or not. I remind myself of Lord Coe's projected statistics for 2010, which was that one in four of the adult population would be obese. If we don't do something now with this massive opportunity, whatever would the state of the nation's health be in 2020?

I go ahead with the competition. Any setbacks were far outweighed by the enthusiasm and motivation the competition inspires in the primary schools. We firmly believe this could be a turning point in physical education, that we would embrace a new era of sport taught in schools, giving young people the opportunity to explore a more relevant modern curriculum, to inspire them to want to participate, to enjoy taking a vested interest in looking after their health and becoming physically fit.

With every visit to each of the schools, I'm buoyed up by the remarkable creativity they're producing. The younger ones have the title of 'Bear Olympics' and Joggy Bear as their mascot. I'd written three stories about Joggy Bear so I could read to them when visiting. Each book contains their own specific set of exercises relevant to the storyline. Ben drew the most remarkable illustrations and action pictures of Joggy Bear with such clarity they're easy for the teachers and pupils to follow. He also made a big poster of the words of the Joggy Bear song with the actions they perform in lesson time. The Youth Sport Trust donated a grant to enable these books and posters to be printed and left with each school; the resulting work it inspired was way beyond anything Andrew or I had envisaged.

One school creates a whole frieze of bears exercising around London, which they display right round the children's cloakroom, mounted above their coat pegs. Another school makes a six foot by six foot mural on a stand that can be wheeled around to different classes. They used different materials to depict important London landmarks with lots of colourful bears exercising among them. The River Thames is made out of blue plastic, delicate pieces of foil to create the London Eye and pinned flags on the painted Tower of London.

The older pupils have a more difficult task. I asked them to research the venues in London where the different sports would take place and set their names to the music of a traditional folk song such as 'Oranges and Lemons', 'Three Blind Mice' or 'London Bridge is Falling Down' and mime the actions. They could also choose to choreograph and stage either an opening or closing ceremony, miming a variety of sports and doing traditional dances from the competing countries. During my weekly visits to each of the schools, the staff and pupils need little help from me.

The competition culminates in the most magnificent celebration at Derek's school, Park House School in Newbury. BBC South covers the event as their lead news story, as does the ITV regional news. Presenter Wesley Smith from Central TV picks up the story, too, along with the local newspapers. The hall is packed with children from all the competing schools, their imaginative, colourful artwork of paintings and masks mounted and displayed. Each school performs their vibrant songs and dances, their staged opening ceremonies. Olympic rower Debbie Flood, accompanied by Steve Williams, our constant supportive gold-winning Olympic rowing medallist, also take part, inspiring the children to look forward to London hopefully winning the Bid. The *Go! London 2012* regional competition proved to be a winner. It was ready to roll out nationwide.

In December 2004, I receive an email from Kathryn. She'd forgotten to mention they were trying to get some examples of school projects in time for the International Olympic Committee (IOC) visit, would we display our creative school's competition work as other schools have been traditionally curriculum-based so far? They would need it by the middle of January in an A3 or A4 booklet.

As you can imagine, I have the most extraordinary amount of creative work at my disposal, among them the awesome six-foot-square mural. On film, singing rhymes to 'London Bridge' with the appropriate mimed sports, choreographed singing sequences for venues to 'Oranges and Lemons', staged opening ceremonies enacted to the 'Eye of the Tiger' and a host of photos and the BBC footage. Clearly, London 2012 needs to impress the IOC with something other than the mundane and we had creativity in bundles, but an A3/A4 booklet?

Ben suggests a brilliant solution. We could make a brochure that reflects our competition entries and set it against a background of famous London landmarks. For copyright reasons, he'd spend a day in London photographing them with Rowley Douglas, a talented photographer and a gold-winning Olympic medallist from the 2000 Sydney Games. I, meanwhile, would contact as many helpful friends and acquaintances as possible, some that I'd previously worked with, who might lend some supportive words to our nationwide competition. We'd been allowed to continue using the title 'London 2012' when no other charity or commercial organisation is able to do so. What a privilege and what a recognition for the competition. Maybe we should consider another title, just in case they change their minds. It's agreed, to be safe, we call it something else in the future, like 'Creative Champtions'.

I ask around and get a great response. My friend Min asks her son Matthew and his future wife Keeley and actor David Oyelowo who are all in the popular television series *Spooks*, and they kindly send words of encouragement with their photos; as do Nicholas Serota, director of Tate Modern Art Gallery, ballerina Darcey Bussell and the Duchess of Kent, to name just a few. And my Clapham boys offer their expertise as guest dance teachers for the winners.

I'm overwhelmed with all their support.

There's one particular photo I want for the brochure that will encapsulate the very essence of the Olympic Bid. I approach Lowbrook Primary School in Maidenhead who were so enthusiastic and supportive and dress two Year 6 pupils in Ben's Olympic tracksuit kit and his London 2012 promotional T-shirt. They're far too big for both of them, but that's the whole essence of the message. I ask them to imagine being the Olympic stars of the future, and what a picture we get!

When designing the layout for the brochure, Ben frames these two pupils in his picture of the London Eye with the caption 'Making their dreams come true' underneath. We position it on the opening page of the brochure, next to the foreword Steve Redgrave, our greatest Olympian, has kindly written for us, to inspire the stars of the future. For the eye-catching cover Ben transforms the colours of the Union Jack into the five colours of the Olympic rings. It takes hours of Ben's expertise, hours of his patience to do the artwork; there's a lot of cooking, washing and ironing done for him in return. I had the better deal.

Another friend kindly organises the payment for five hundred brochures to be printed; it meant we not only have it sorted in time for the impending, all-important IOC visit, but enough for upscaling the competition for the national version. We miraculously delivered our brochure to Kathryn on time and she makes sure copies are placed on the table for the IOC members.

The Bid is soon to be announced.

Sebastian Coe takes thirty schoolchildren with the Bid team to Singapore for the final lobbying, a visual reminder they could be the Olympic stars of the next generation. It would have been a timely acknowledgement if he'd included the two schoolchildren dreaming of being winning athletes in our *Go! London*

2012 competition brochure. It's been stated in a review of the Bid that, besides the presence of these multicultural children, a video called 'Inspiration' was also featured that focused on inspiring and encouraging the next generation to take up sport, and might have swung a few votes.

In 2011, organisations in the charity sector were invited to apply for the '2012 Inspire Mark', it was to be a celebration of winning the London Bid and for promoting exercise and engaging young people in physical activities for the future. I send in an application for Creativity in Sport, thinking it would be a perfect reward for all our efforts in devising and organising a very successful regional competition to support the London Bid. I also look forward to all the schools that had participated so generously and successfully in our competition receiving their allocation of free tickets to one of the Olympic days at Dorney Lake. The tickets, much to my huge embarrassment, never materialise (but neither, it transpires, did they for the Inspire organisers. I presume it was just a lack of organisation).

I email Kathryn in October in the hope that she would recognise our contribution and our organisation could be awarded a coveted 2012 Inspire Mark. She did indeed remember me and suggests the official channel I should go through.

We apply and, after a visit from the South East regional co-ordinator, we achieve the Inspire Mark. With the London 2012 Olympic Games about to begin, the organisers are hoping for some congratulatory publicity, so we organise a wonderful launch for them. Paul, the GB rowing coach, is overwhelmingly supportive, interrupting his intense training schedule and bringing twelve of his finest elite squad rowers to be taught, with his blessing, by our 'Body Rocks' apprentices, a project I was implementing at the time. What an experience for them. Several adults from my regular evening exercise classes swell the numbers and the interaction between them all encapsulates the very spirit of the impending London Games. BBC Radio Berkshire did live inserts, their presenter relaying some of the exercises our lads were teaching the Olympic rowing team. All the local and regional press covered the story. It was a glorious recognition regionally for Creativity in Sport and of the support from so many wonderful people, including Andrew MacTavish, headteacher Derek Peaple, and the countless staff and pupils from all the participating schools, and my wonderful son.

Later, as an extension of the London Legacy celebrations, we are invited by our London Inspire organiser to give a practical demonstration to Sir Keith Mills, deputy chairman of the London Olympic Games. It will enable us to showcase our 'Body Rocks' apprenticeship training scheme for disadvantaged and vulnerable young people. We readily accept the invitation and felt extremely honoured to be selected from over one hundred South East Inspire organisations. The apprentices did a magnificent presentation, skilfully teaching choreographed aerobic routines to a supporting cast from my supremely fit evening exercisers. Sir Keith Mills appreciates the work we're trying to innovate and congratulates the inspiring apprentices for their contribution in marking the start of the London legacy.

We learn much later from our supportive South East games organiser that our application for the London 2012 Inspire Mark Award had been turned down. She'd retrieved it from the pile marked 'Applications Rejected'.

CHAPTER 12

WHY ARE YOU TEACHING SCUM LIKE US?

I'm standing in a car park gazing up at the rolls of razor wire embedded in a high fence. It surrounds the perimeter, the formidable steel gates and the buildings that house over two hundred juvenile prisoners. Boys aged fifteen to eighteen, boys whose lives have gone astray. I've been to prisons before while visiting ex-Henry Thornton pupil Timmy in the seventies at Latchmere and Ashford remand homes. As I survey this one, the empty feelings of sadness at this solitary desolation haven't diminished. How, at the tender age of fifteen, can you end up in a place like this?

But I'm not here for the inmates. Déjà vu has happened. I have an invitation to take another guest class, but this time it's not come from an international rowing coach, but from a prison gym boss. Would I take a fitness class one Saturday morning with the officers who work in the gym at Huntercombe Juvenile Prison? Huntercombe is situated just outside Henley-on-Thames, a Thames Valley town steeped in history and renowned for its annual rowing regatta. Debbie Flood is a regular volunteer in the gym and mentioned in passing that 'Mad Lizzie' was currently training the Great Britain Women's Squad with her fitness programme. So here I am in the car park, with my beat box slung over my shoulder, staring once again at razor wire.

It's a cold Saturday morning. I walk past a long, snaking queue of hushed adults, parents, siblings in pushchairs, relatives, girlfriends, waiting with passes for the gates to open. I sign in at the visitors' reception area that resembles a wartime barracks hut. I'm searched, my belongings checked. The head of gym escorts me down long bare-walled corridors, past two boys who are sporadically mopping the floor. We walk through two wings, sets of iron gates are unlocked and locked, more corridors, more unlocking and locking, until finally we reach the sports block. It's impressive. There's a massive sports hall, a large, well-equipped gym, changing rooms and an area with washing machines. A few lads are milling around in grey tracksuit bottoms and T-shirts, boys without visitors who've earnt precious gym time. This is the place these incarcerated boys want to frequent, but space and time are at a premium.

The class I'm taking is with a dozen prison officers. Nearly all of them look musclebound, presumably from utilising their hours supervising and working out with the boys in the gym. No wonder they're priority staff when trouble flares on the wings.

I've meticulously planned my class and hope these officers, like the rowers, are in for a surprise. I will give them a class that challenges their stamina and then use a variety of softly padded wrist- and ankle-weights. (They only keep soft padded ones in the sports hall, presumably safer to use than heavy steel weights.) The officers don't hide their surprise or their pleasure at being taught a completely new approach to fitness and, at the end, request a repeat class the following Sunday, and the next, then the next, which I obligingly do. And then it dawns on me. If I'm volunteering to do this for an already fit gym staff, why aren't I doing it for the boys?

I make an appointment to see the deputy governor. It's not easy to find a space in his diary teeming with meetings and events, but they find one. I expect to be greeted by a gruff, almost dismissive, authoritarian figure. Instead, I sit with a quiet, caring man, whose empathic concern for his charges is endearing and impressive. He looks beyond my television persona, and discusses my previous teaching experience and understands my willing-ness to teach aerobics and strength-training to the lads. He isn't optimistic they will be overly enthusiastic and will entrust me with boys from the long-stay wing. The long-stay wing, at the age of fifteen? He tells me that once a boy has been in prison for more than thirteen months, the chances are he will become institutionalised. I'm compelled to start straight away.

Taking the sessions with the gym staff has, on reflection, been a good initiation. I've learnt to utilise this exceptionally large sports hall and extend a warmup I'd originally devised for the High Wycombe grammar school boys. It combines running a couple of laps around the perimeter, stopping in a corner with light co-ordinated aerobic exercises, and repeating it with a change of exercise in all four corners. I'm confident the lads will enjoy it and that my quads and abs will prove to be stronger than theirs; it'll help gain some respect, if not their irritation. And if I tell them the gym staff could be outdone with some of the challenges, I think they'll be up for it.

The lads jostle noisily outside the hall. About twenty-five have volunteered to give my first session a go, but they look and sound remarkably half-hearted. Wearing my son's blue Great Britain Athens Olympic T-shirt and loose blue tracksuit bottoms, I set up my beat box. In my bag is my standby, my photo album with the press pictures of sports stars and dancers. The boys are ushered in by two officers who suggest they stay. I suggest they don't. If I'm to get these lads exercising to music, I suspect it's not something they would be willing to do in front of the staff who lock them up. Other boys are peering in through the door window, banging on it to create a distraction. The staff would be better utilised keeping them away and keeping an eye from a distance. They agree, show me the panic button on the wall and leave me to it. Am I nervous? A little apprehensive, perhaps, but I'm confident my past experience will help. The fights I've broken up at the boys' school using my thundering vocal projection, the confrontation when left alone teaching a lad who threatened me with a saw at the home in Isleworth, the tactical persuasive techniques used to win over cynical schoolboys. I've been told these lads have football and basketball coaching, so I'll tell them how my aerobic routines will enhance their required skills, how remembering the routines will vastly improve muscle memory and get them thinking like lightning on their feet. Running round with them doing my four corners sets the tone of the class. They accept me as the boss.

We finish the energetic session with the cool-down stretches. A voice speaks out:

'I wish you'd come before. This is really good; I'm leaving prison on Tuesday so I can't keep doing it.'

'Where's home for you?' I enquire.

'Reading.'

'Well that's local to me. If I start any classes in Reading, I'll let you know.'

I happily agree with the rest of the lads to extend this weekly weekend class to ninety minutes. It'll probably vary between Saturdays and Sundays because of visiting passes and restrictions, but I'm happy to oblige. I also make a note to keep my promise to the lad from Reading.

I continue going every weekend. Some of the lads from the first class have chosen to spend their time in the gym, but I've still got a big class. Six of the lads are showing a real interest in teaching exercise to music. I add a mid-week evening class for these lads. There's Jim, a quiet, slim, laid-back boy. As I watch him dancing, he beams at the freedom and fluidity of his movement to the music. It's incongruous that this boy has the longest ASBO given by any magistrate's court for confronting shopkeepers and causing havoc on the streets. Then there's Robert, an unlikely-looking lad for the group. He's got the stocky, muscular build of a rugby player. He tells me he's got two left feet so I'm not convinced he will master the aerobic sections. A day after his six-teenth birthday, he started a three-year sentence to serve thirteen months. It's his first offence. He'd stashed a fake gun in his trouser pocket at a robbery with his schoolmates; it stayed in his trousers, but was deemed intent.

James reminds me of one of the grammar school boys in both looks and behaviour. Softly spoken, well-mannered, there's a refinement about him that stands out from the rest. He tells me he's been given a two-year sentence to serve twelve months for Grievous Bodily Harm. The other three that make up the group also want to take their NVQ2 for teaching exercise to music classes when they leave prison. Debbie is doing the paperwork to establish the prison as an exercise-to-music examination centre. It's a first for the prison; inmates haven't previously shown an aptitude for dance and aerobics, but then there's been no one to teach it. And they're loving it.

I blast out the music from the latest *Now* compilation CD as I run and jump around the massive hall, encouraging the lads to do the same, not that they need encouragement. They love the freedom of this huge open space. They look like little boys, running by the sea as if fresh air is blowing in their faces and ruffling their hair. (And who would have guessed that Boris Becker, a three-time Wimbledon tennis champion, would be exercising in this very same hall thirteen years later?) We repeat the aerobic dance routines, practise and practise and practise. One by one, they come out to the front to teach and lead the rest of the group. The classes are having an impact on their self-esteem with the regular six inmates intent on mastering cueing in the music, the required coaching points, staying cool and learning to control their temper when they make mistakes. For some, like Robert, getting him to control his emotions is a huge part of the learning process. We line up against a wall and do the timed held squats and banter as I'm always the last man standing, or rather squatting. They use ankle-weights for leg raises and after the exhaustion of it all, sit in a circle on chairs and just talk for an hour, discussing their coping mechanisms for being confined alone in their cells, their hopes, their fears for the future and what will happen to them when they go back to the environment that's causing some of their problems. They unanimously agree they are never coming back here. It's all become so much more than a fitness class. I'm in loco parentis. They call me their 'prison mum', well that's very generous of them, more like their 'prison granny'.

With the deputy governor's blessing, I maintain regular contact by phone with their parents; it's always with their mums. When visiting, the parent will come separately or with their new partner. If either the parent or boys request I join them in their monthly visits in the visiting room, I do, sometimes observing and sometimes mediating out of necessity.

I get into a routine of one three-hour class at the weekend and a two-hour Wednesday evening session, that's if time permits;

sometimes there aren't enough staff to collect and escort them all. They're a caring lot, the gym staff. I've been given my own set of prison keys. I keep them secure in a zipped pouch that's attached to a belt around my waist. It gets in the way of exercising, annoyingly bouncing up and down. The keys allow me to roam the wings in my own time as well as the sports block, to play table tennis in the recreational area and to sit and talk with the lads. One Saturday I'm waiting outside the sports hall for the lads to arrive. They noisily appear in dribs and drabs from the changing room. I'm about to enter the sports hall when Robert kindly picks up my bag and beat box and carries them into the hall.

'Why are you teaching scum like us?' he asks.

The question stops me in my tracks. I turn and look at him. I can see by his expression it's genuine, he wants to know. Why the question? Why now?

'You're not scum, why on earth do you think that?'

'Cos that's what my Dad asked me. He saw you in the visitors' room on Sunday and says you're famous and been on television. So why are you teaching us?'

I'd asked the deputy governor and staff not to mention I'd been a presenter for ten years on breakfast television during the eighties and early nineties; it was irrelevant. And anyway, most of these lads would still have been in nappies, they wouldn't have seen me.

My head is scrambled. How can a dad say these words to his own son? He's been severely punished; he's apologised to both his parents and accepted his own stupidity. Instead of exercising, I sit the lads in a circle on chairs to talk; this was important. It pains me to think that Robert sits alone in his cell and has even less self-worth than when he started his three-year sentence. He's already told the group his parents had an acrimonious divorce; they make sure they never visit him in prison at the same time and he's left stranded between the two of them. Robert's escape from his warring parents was to hang out on the streets with his mates. He has little contact with his youth offending team; travelling from Kent to Henley isn't happening when they're short-staffed.

'Why, just because I've been on television, wouldn't I want to teach you?'

He grins and looks chuffed. 'I dunno, why are you doing it?'

As usual, I'm not about to give an honest answer. It's the question I'm still avoiding. In my heart I think I know; I just haven't formulated it into words and heard myself articulate it. I have complete faith in the lads who are on this long-stay wing, many of them considered to be serious violent offenders, who can explode and trash their cells. As volunteers, we're given training in self-defence. I'm not sure if something did happen, I'd be able to put any of it into practice. If something unexpected does occur, the other lads' automatic response would, I feel sure, be to protect me.

I think I'm getting to understand their lives a bit better, but I'm far removed from the type of violence they're experiencing. They're brought up in an area that requires being constantly on the lookout and fighting, just to exist. It seems an unimaginable way of life. James says living in his part of London in 2006 means you need a bike. If you unintentionally cycle into a road that's the territory of another ruling gang, it's imperative for a quick getaway. They have to learn to take care of themselves at an early age to survive. James was regularly beaten up after school. He says his mum encouraged him to fight back, smash the bully in his face or she'd do it for him.

'I only hit him once,' James says quietly in one of our chats on the chairs. 'I knocked him out. Nobody touched me after that; I was top dog.'

As for the amenable, very likeable Frankie, his actions in class sum it up. It's his turn to stand out in front of the others and teach. I'm training his group in the power of vocal projection while giving dance instructions over the music.

'Shout Frankie, we can't hear you, project your voice.' Frankie issues the same instruction, but still we can't hear. I urge him to repeat it again, louder, really shout.

'I can't shout,' he says, 'I don't raise my voice.'

'Oh come on, I'm sure you do,' I remonstrate. 'What do you do in an argument? You must shout.'

'No, I don't,' says Frankie, 'I *never* shout.'

'What! Well what do you do then?' I reply sounding a little cynical and at the same time mystified; at some point everybody has an argument and raises their voice.

'I just do this,' he says quietly. He stands in silence and punches his right fist into the palm of his left hand a few times.

'That's what I do.'

I should probably have worked it out. In one of our group discussions he'd told us he's not too popular at his local police station because when he was arrested, it needed four officers to hold him down.

I need to progress their presentation skills, help them understand the need for vocal projection and clarity, how to use their individual personalities that will turn them into exceptional trainers. Val and Roger, who attend my evening fitness classes, plus the owner of the stunning estate where I'm personal training, have kindly become weekend 'guest' class members in the sports hall. It seems quite incongruous that in holiday time, I'm teaching the sons and daughters of the ladies I'm personal training on the estate, including Rosie, who went on to marry Prince William's best friend, and Will, a Great Britain junior fencer, who has since become a team doctor with Everton, the Premier League football club.

Much to the genuine surprise of the lads, the guest volunteers are all extremely competent energetic exercisers; they expected these 'oldies' to lag behind them while running round the hall and huff and puff their way through their high-energy routines. The volunteers gain even more respect when we tell them the four of us have done lots of half marathons and two years ago I ran all the way in the London Marathon. It raises their level of teaching and gives these lads a much-needed confidence boost that 'posh' people are willing to give up their time for them.

I arrange a demonstration in the sports hall for the deputy governor so he can see what these lads are achieving; it's also to thank him for the faith he's showing in me, for the freedom he's given me to prove to myself that, yet again, the arts have a huge role to play in our education system. My big sister is immersed in the ballet world at the Royal Opera House, and accepts an invitation to attend the demonstration to observe Jim perform a dance that expresses his laidback character. Jim says his family will need persuading this is something worthwhile for him to pursue, especially when he's failed at everything else. In the prison this has been the motivation that Jim's been needing. I think back to the Clapham school. All that talent on display on the stage, but not one of the parents of the dance group ever came to see them perform.

When this cheeky, cheerful lad serves his time and leaves, I maintain close contact, visiting his home and regularly phoning. His mum happily travels with him to my Saturday fitness classes in Marlow so he can polish his teaching skills. The continuity of the 'guest' classes at the prison and also knowing four of the lads released from the prison are also travelling to Marlow is boosting his confidence. His mum comes with him and takes part in the classes. She's bowled over by his natural ability and his coaching skills, and it's gratifying to see her interest and involvement, but it's a long way for them to keep travelling. My sister arranges for him to become a member of a private health club not far from his home; he's too embarrassed for his mates to know what he's doing, it's not part of their world. His mum encourages him, but his attendance is sporadic.

And once again, Jim gets into trouble, he's gone back into an environment he doesn't seem able to escape. And once again,

I become Mad Lizzie. In September 2007, I went with Jim's diligent youth worker to his next court appearance. At the magistrate's court we walk slowly through the security beepers, and the officer does a double take.

'What are you doing here Mad Lizzie?' he asks quizzically with a smile.

'Just popping down to the cells,' I cheerfully reply as I disappear down the steep, concrete stairs to the tiny, cramped cell below the courts.

I fear, and in my heart know, that Jim isn't going to manage to break his habit, his revolving door of crime.

• • •

One really small lad seeks my attention in the sports block by banging and kicking the hall door. They're thick double doors, but we can still hear the rumpus over the music. This repeat behaviour results in the gym officers banning him; and no sooner is he allowed back, he's banging on the doors again. He repeats this cycle of self-sabotage on the long-stay wing in his cell. If your behaviour is good, you move up to the next floor and get given privileges, if you get moved to the top floor, you're given positions of responsibility. He never moves from the ground floor.

Every week, without fail, this small lad completely trashes his cell. He's fifteen and disowned by his family. Was he, as a child, ever owned by anyone? I was told he has no visitors apart from an aunt who occasionally travels to see him. I track him down on the long-stay wing. He's unable to read. This is not a case of

'How did this boy go through primary school unable to read?' This boy hadn't even attended school. I sit with him in a tiny glass room in the recreational area and teach him phonics, but he can't focus for long, he isn't used to sitting for any length of time. I'm making headway, albeit small, but in terms of this boy it's big steps. He tells me he has only one interest, one passion: Luton Town Football Club. A thought occurs. I know someone who can possibly help break his cycle of destructive behaviour in his cell. It's Nick Owen, the presenter from my TV-am days.

Nick has been a lifelong supporter of Luton Town Football Club and is soon to become their chairman. I get in touch, explain the situation and, without hesitation, he sends a package with signed photos from the players and club posters that can be stuck on the cell walls. There they stay. It means a lot to this little lad, but he has to put up with ribbing from the older lads; they aren't signed photos from the likes of Alan Shearer or Stevie Gerrard and, after a while, he carefully takes them down and stashes them under his bed.

The inmates approaching eighteen are getting shipped out to young offenders' prisons due to overcrowding. It necessitates interrupting the education of those studying in the education block for their GCSEs, or training with me in the sports hall, but there's no alternative. There's always a turnover at Huntercombe. Lads like Jim, who the staff know when they bid him farewell that it won't be long before they see him again. I am, though, not too disappointed to see Rickie when he returns. He's very much a loner and the weekend fitness sessions were bringing him out of his shell and giving him a sense of belonging to something, to at least talk and interact in the chats with our group. He'd been done for stealing and he'd got stern words from me when he told us he'd stolen mobile phones from locker rooms at his local gym. I'm playing table tennis when he walks in sporting a huge black eye. He looks worn out, run down. He's been involved in several fights being the junior in the young offenders' prison; the black eye had come from being stabbed with a snooker cue. When he leaves prison, he attends my Saturday classes in Marlow. I suggest it might be a good idea if he comes directly to the studio and avoids going into the changing rooms. I know it will appeal to his sense of humour, but it's also a gentle reminder that I'm putting my trust in him.

Huntercombe, too, is becoming more violent, and the perimeter fence regularly patrolled because of the insidious rise of drugs entering the prison, often having been lobbed over the fence. Lads will go to great lengths to hide their incriminating evidence. A new inmate secreted a phone up his backside. Staff are bemused during the strip search, not because it was discovered in the most unimaginable place, but because he'd forgotten to turn it off before putting it there. When the alarm goes, and it happens a few times during my time, duty gym staff immediately down their weights, don their riot gear and rush to the wing where the trouble's flared. One evening, a few lads climb onto the roof and steadfastly refuse to come back down. It necessitates a complete lockdown. Nobody, but nobody, is allowed in or out of the prison. You can be there for twenty-four hours or for however long it takes. Fortunately the deputy governor is able to let me out just in the nick of time.

I've written endless reports for the boys I'm training. Sometimes it's for a release on temporary licence (ROTL), or they've done their time and a reference is required or it's a character reference in support of yet another court appearance. One of my reports for James sums him up.

This is the shortest report I have written so far for a pupil at Huntercombe as there is nothing to write concerning his progress, he has been an exemplary pupil from the start. His conduct, his attitude and the quality of his work have made him a pleasure to teach and his quiet but authoritative manner has been an excellent influence within the group.

I still phone James's and Robert's mums to keep up to date with how the boys are doing. They're both thirty-four, both excellent parents and both in employment.

This 'prison granny' has been sent pictures of all their major milestones. How do they look back at the twelve and fifteen months their boys spent in prison?

James's mum
I was so frightened, really scared when he went to prison. The family had never had any contact or dealings with the police before, nobody had been in trouble. It was a

Debbie Flood, my co-director

HMP Huntercombe cartoon, 2008

Ooer!, I tell you what, you go to Lizzie Webb's Fit Club – I'll go to Freddy's Fat Club

6/30.

All the best Martin

Dante teaching, 2013

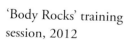

'Body Rocks' training
session, 2012

A demonstration at our Slough premises attended
by HRH Sophie, Countess of Wessex, 2014

Dante skating

Garry inside the costume, cartwheeling

Joggy and Flossie Bear

A Joggy Bear hug,
1991

With Dougie winning the England Senior Amateur Golf Trophy, 2017

My sister Ro, Ma and me, 2017

Gotcha Oscar, 1992

A reunion at the filming of Peter Kay's *500 miles* video for Comic Relief in 2007 with (T) Sonia and *Coronation Street* stars Michael Le Vell and Sally Dynevor, and (B) Rainbow and Timmy Mallett

The boys from Henry Thornton School, Clapham. Standing L to R: Patrick, Jeff and Floyd. Kneeling: Garry and Rupert

Reunion in 2000, celebrating the start of the school Drama Club twenty-eight years ago. L to R: Garry, me, Patrick, Rupert, Jeff and Andy

Reunion with Garry and Jeff, 2020

difficult time; his dad left when he was young and James has never wanted anything to do with him. But prison worked for James. It taught him he wasn't untouchable; it's helped make him what he is today. He proved to himself he can achieve, without going inside, I don't like to think what would have happened with him living here. He's gone to the gym every day ever since he's been out and teaches his mates 'Body Rocks' in his own time. His girlfriend stuck by him, they have a lovely son who starts primary school soon, he's a great caring dad. I'm so proud of him now. Creativity in Sport changed his life, he knows the difference it made to him and to all of us, it changed our family.

Robert's mum

I still worry that the relationship between his dad and me really affected his life. He'd been at private school until the age of eleven, but when we got divorced we couldn't afford to carry on educating him privately. It was a massive change for him to go to a big secondary state school. He was in large classes with kids, some who didn't want to learn. He'd been used to a class with just ten in it at the most and teachers that wouldn't let the pupils get away with not learning and not doing their homework. He started hanging out on the streets with the wrong crowd. His girlfriend's mother was on drugs and she was the one that encouraged them to do the robbery because she wanted drug money. I didn't know that until it was too late, before he was sentenced, it will haunt me for the rest of my life. I don't know how we all got through it. He's done so well since, and now I'm really proud of the man he's become, I don't like to look back. And yes, after all the classes we came to in Marlow, he did teach 'Body Rocks' for a while at the local fitness centre, but his friends goaded him, so it was easier for him to just stop.

When Robert leaves Huntercombe, he gives me a card; it's embossed with a teapot, a cup and a plate of cakes, a homely-looking card. He apologises that it doesn't say 'thank you' on the card; he had to buy it in the prison shop.

Dear Lizzie

I just want you to know how much I really appreciate what you have done for me. I now have better confidence in myself and I have a good future all thanks to you. I am looking forward to doing the real thing out there, I can't wait to get started! Also thanks for everything with my parents – or should I say children?!

Love Robert

CHAPTER 13

'BODY ROCKS'

I'm standing in the small dark basement of a large office building opposite Reading station. Looking around at the kids, they show no fear. Some are sitting sprawled on chairs, others are lounging around, chatting in small groups. There are fifteen kids from six secondary schools with at least six staff sitting among them, and yet you get this tangible feeling the place could erupt at any time. It seems absurd. The kids know they hold the cards, they rule, they learnt their collective power at a very early age; all of them have multiple school exclusions and several have complex behavioural problems.

I'm here to try and encourage them to take part in 'Body Rocks', our fitness course, but holding their attention for forty minutes during this introductory talk is going to need all my accumulated experience from teaching in sink schools and a borstal. This generation of challenging kids need fast-moving images or their sixty-second attention span is gone. To further complicate the situation, the sexual energy is tangible. This is about the lads wanting to impress the girls, it's not 'cool' to be seen to be too enthusiastic, about anything.

I'll liven up the introductory talks with a few gimmicks that I know will get a response. A high kick, the splits and then a challenging leg test for the quads that I've performed live with top sportsmen on TV-am, it creates interest because it looks so easy. Once demonstrated, I select a lad who volunteers to do the strength test; he cockily considers it's a doddle and swaggers out to try it in front of his cheering mates. With each attempt he falls over, encouraging other clamouring lads to have a go too. And, as predicted, they also fall over.

'Respect bruv.' Maybe this old girl knows a thing or two about exercise after all.

I produce my prison belt. I ask them if anybody knows what it is, what might it be used for? A few guesses, a purse belt, an exercise/running belt, a decoration belt. On hearing it's *my* prison belt, there's a look of complete astonishment. There's a hushed silence. I tell them about my sixteen months' experience of teaching aerobics in Huntercombe Juvenile Prison. They listen intently as I describe what life is like inside the prison and it isn't long before one of the lads asks if I've taught one of his mates there, but as there are over three hundred and fifty inmates with a fast turnover (well, for some) the odds of recognising the name of his mate aren't too high. I suggest, instead, that he doesn't follow him in there. I tell them how I taught some of these boys to become teachers with my fitness programme called 'Body

Rocks', and I could teach them to do the same if they want to give it a go.

I'm concerned at the number of withdrawn pupils staring expressionlessly into space. I want to make contact with them, give them the chance to communicate, to have a voice in what should be a safe, controlled environment that's clearly dominated by the loudest, foul-mouthed individuals. I request from the leader of this organisation, which is called Cred, that the frightened individuals who had said 'No' to a taster session, presumably for fear of being ridiculed, have a separate, timetabled 'non-exercise' session with me.

The suggestion works. Once separated, I sit chatting with them, and a lad called Jim starts gaining confidence. He eloquently describes how he'd been threatened with a knife and had decided to join a gym. He lifts up his T-shirt and there, on display, is this wonderfully toned torso which he's been concealing under his sagging posture and drab, baggy clothing. But in spite of this, he's still too untrusting and intimidated to come and exercise in front of the others. I learn later, when talking in our little group of two in the 'non-exercise' session, that his mum's boyfriend, who was an ex-army officer and a fitness fanatic, terrorises and beats up his mum as well as physically threatening him and his younger brother. It's Jim's intention to physically pump himself up so one day he can square up to him, protect his mother and also have an answer to those knife-carriers on the streets who've been threatening him.

The other lad sat next to him is an utter delight, smiling now with such ease it is heart-breaking to hear he's suffered from bullying and depression as a result of being groomed by a teacher at his secondary school. I just hope he will survive learning in the Cred environment and that we might be able to give this sensitive soul some sense of freedom and security. The two of them ask to do the fitness course in isolation from the others and I assure them we will make this happen and call them a 'collage group' instead. We base our timetable not around their fitness ability, but around the group friendships established in this introductory session, and in order to gain their confidence, decide with the staff to extend the taster sessions for a further week. We can do this because Debbie and I have formalised Creativity in Sport and it's now registered as a Community Interest Company. It's great news, it means we can develop our own programmes and apply for grants. Terri, the head of learning at the prison, is a Rotarian, and has been a great flag-bearer for us since attending one of our presentations for the prison authorities. She suggested that if our fitness concept can be this successful with boys on the inside, then we should be reaching the boys on the outside, especially ones who are permanently excluded or in pupil referral units. Now it's the start of the new academic year 2008–9, the perfect time to introduce 'Body Rocks' to the kids.

We've been really fortunate in being able to hire a magnificent thirteenth-century church for these sessions. It's bang in the middle of Reading town centre, at the back of Marks & Spencer and next to the town hall. From the outside, it looks like a sedate ecclesiastical church with a majestic tower, but turn the ornate heavy black handle of the door, and you enter another world. A lengthy, cavernous space reaching down to the altar and not a pew in sight.

The interior has been cleverly designed. The ground floor is a sprung wooden floor, an exercise instructor's dream, and extends from the front door all the way down to the ornate nave and the altar. On the left side, there are two loos, entered by large, stainless steel doors which are encased in a wooden frame. It continues down to a kitchen area with proper cooking facilities and an open hatch. Beyond that is a long table with chairs round it. This whole area is separated from the rest of the church by intermittently spaced original stone pillars. On the opposite side, spread out all the way down the wall, are five comfortable sofas – and all this comes with underfloor heating.

The mezzanine floor looks like something out of Tate Modern. A combination of circular glass rooms of stainless steel and light wood. One of these is the vicar's office directly above the church entrance. Follow the gallery round, and there's another circular glass meeting room, a snooker table, a table-tennis table and huge speakers for a sound system.

The church has been adapted for weekday use as a youth club and for hire during the day for groups like us. What a concept and what an incredible place for us to be working in. And what a coincidence that Debbie, my co-director, is the Christian representative for rowing in sport. This wonderful hideaway is the perfect venue for us to initiate and develop our project, and the Reverend Chris Russell, the street-cred vicar in charge, is kindly discounting rates for charities like ourselves to hire this remarkable venue.

First Session

The first group of five lads who've shown a glimmer of interest in starting the course arrive at the church and immediately jostle with each other as they noisily make a beeline for the sofas. They sit slouched, with their hands thrust deep in their pockets, headphones on, either silently nodding their heads, or with heads bowed as their thumbs, with great dexterity, tap out text messages on their mobile phones. I have deliberately placed my upright wooden chair opposite the sofas to retain an air of authority, in a position where I can see them all. I make a start trying to vocally instil some enthusiasm and energy for the exercises we are about to do, but their body language is showing a complete disinterest and resistance as they continue to 'thumb away'. And this is meant to be the enthusiastic group.

They stay rooted to the sofas, some with their hoodies still up. In one of the introductory talks, four of them had sat throughout my entire talk with their heads covered and faces hidden, but staff had either accepted it as their normal dress code, or wanted to avoid a confrontation. Now, I decide, is not the time to remonstrate with them. If I can get them to have a go at some exercises, their hoods will surely have to come down, won't they?

With the music playing, and at my request, they reluctantly stand up and form a ragged line. They stare back at me motionless and expressionless as I vigorously march on the spot, then energetically jog up and down, encouraging them to participate in the warmup. 'I ain't doing that,' says a voice as lifeless as the body it's come from, the lone voice quite clearly speaking up for the other non-compliant bodies. I sit them back down. Just as well I've taught in so many different institutions, otherwise I'd feel defeated, totally powerless and ask them to shoot me there and then to put me out of my misery. Ah! But don't pull the trigger yet.

By the end of this introductory chat to the class, after realising a) I'm not fazed by the music they're initially listening to on their mobile phones and b) I will ignore and not react to their endless flow of swear words and c) that I can also communicate in their Jamaican patois (learnt in the seventies while teaching in the boys' comprehensive school in Clapham) they start to pay attention. Strike while the iron is hot, it's time to impress and win them over. How? Challenge them.

They are unable to compete with my strength in lifting free weights. This is apparent with the help of a reluctant lad who has confidently volunteered to sit on a chair beside me and demonstrate the bicep exercises. 'I lift weights much heavier than these,' he mocks … then struggles to keep up with the triple pulses I'm doing. The six pack, time to pit their abs against mine – for those who said they could knock out one hundred sit ups, I'm doing a series of controlled ab and oblique work; they lie back groaning and clutching their stomachs and I keep going. And finally. 'A fiver to anyone that thinks their legs are stronger than mine.' No takers – they'd seen at the introductory talk it was no competition.

I've passed the test. And they've even taken their hoods down.

There's this strange thing about teaching kids. You have that one, initial chance to prove yourself. It's like an initiation ceremony, unspoken among themselves, where you're either ok and cool, or your life thereafter as a teacher is going to be hell. I think after all these years I'm close to bottling how to achieve success in winning this battle. With experience, you learn just how far to push, how far to *appear* to be one of them and how much to let them *think* they are the ones in control. But pity the poor history or science teacher – fitness is my weapon.

Their body language is shifting, the eyes beginning to reflect a gleam of interest. This teacher isn't as weak as she looks. While we do some exercises, I keep emphasising that their football will be vastly improved. Well, as long as they keep doing them. We manage to finish the session with more than a monosyllabic grunt as they cheerfully shuffle out, agreeing to turn up the following week. I've earned their respect and they leave feeling they've achieved something. They're even adhering to the two rules I'm insisting upon. Raise your finger when speaking, so it's not just the one who shouts the loudest who's going to be heard, and no mobile phones. Can this really last?

The girls, much to my surprise, are easier to interest and generate more initial enthusiasm and congeniality when they saunter into the church for their first class. Well, in comparison to the lads they seem more congenial and they show a bit more tolerance as I keep saying 'Pardon' while looking blank at their utterances. It's not just that they mutter, but they talk to each other in their own 'text' language, their lips seemingly not moving and their phrases always ending with the word 'innit'. We sway and move about to the music as we put together an exercise routine with an occasional move suggested by them. It's important to include any of their proffered suggestions no matter how inappropriate to the style, and they do actually seem interested. It helps when Sushi, one of the most vocal of the girls, announces, 'I've known your friend Debbie for years; she looks after me and goes to the same church as my foster parents.' This puts me in an ok category with the others, and things stay calm.

Amazingly, all three groups of girls from the first taster week are the same in attitude, keen to develop the routine and be better than the previous group. The segregation of the girls from the boys is working. Bingo! Will it last? I soon find out that girls are so much more difficult to teach.

Next Stage

I finish the end of the second week victorious. The centre manager at Cred timetables the twenty-four enthusiastic pupils into small groups, so I'll be teaching three whole mornings a week, with each group having two full weekly sessions. The lads, surprisingly, are remembering all they've been taught – accurately naming muscles, how they work in pairs, how to progress an exercise, the coaching points, but they're still all adamant they are never going to exercise to music.

There's something wonderfully incongruous about these non-conformist lads running energetically and perfectly in line behind me, circling round and round the church, then after a few laps running into a corner to do high-impact work and then repeating the system until all four corners have been completed. After a quick water break standing at the church kitchen bar, we slow the session down while they calmly lift heavy free weights, focusing on technique (and how quickly they can grow their biceps for reasons I do not have to ask) before spreading out the mats for the floor work and a cool down.

I'm sure God's looking down on the church, smiling and giving his seal of approval. Far better the church space is put to good use than left empty six days of the week.

Quotes from the first weeks

Amy: (shouting out when going wrong)
'Oh! Fucking hell!' followed by a quick glance up at the vicar's office and then hastily saying 'Sorry vicar,' as she does the sign of the cross.

Gloria: 'You're really posh Lizzie. Bet you live in a big house with bay windows.'

Antony: (looking at the lectern) 'Is that bird [eagle] real gold?' then quickly adding, 'I'd *never* rob a church.'

Alex: (to me while doing squats) 'This is fucking hard. What you on … crack?'

Me: 'Anyone got any favourite CDs they want to bring to exercise to?' (silence)

'Well you must have some – don't you buy any?'

Tasha: 'We don't *buy* them … we download them on the mobile.'

Me: 'I've forgotten my watch – what's the time – any one got a watch on?'

Claire: 'We don't *do* watches' (of course not, silly me again, what's a mobile for?).

'Body Rocks' is the initial vehicle for communicating with these kids. Sometimes they just want a voice, a platform to be heard, to express their opinions and, with gentle coaxing, their feelings. This can last for anything from thirty to ninety minutes. And invariably, enlightening details of their lives become group experiences discussed and shared, with moral guidance from Debbie and myself when certain subjects are raised. For example in one discussion about honesty, they're incredulous and probably think we're telling fibs when we say if we found a bulging wallet with cash on the pavement, we wouldn't pocket it, but hand it in to a police station.

Talking of which …

This morning, while sitting in a circle on chairs with the girls, who are holding light weights and rhythmically doing bicep curls, Gloria, with no connection to any previous conversation, suddenly announces she was arrested in Primark on Saturday. Gloria can be extremely volatile and proclaims she felt a great sense of injustice had been done to her when her long-term feuding neighbour had appeared in the same shop. She'd unfairly and deliberately picked a fight in order, so Gloria thought, to make her lose her temper. After thumping and brawling on the shop floor, she was arrested by security and the police were called.

'If only you'd stuck to trying on the bargain-priced clothes instead,' I say.

'What's the point?' is the reply. 'I was banned two months previously from entering the shop anyway.'

She's to report to the police station on 16 December.

In the lads' next session, Jordan didn't physically have to go to the police station because they came to the church for him. A policeman appears in the doorway just as we are completing our stretches at the end of the session. I have no idea why he's come as he stands patiently watching us. I call out, 'I won't be long, we've nearly finished,' and notice Jordan, who's seated on the sofa due to an injury or laziness, agitatedly looking at the door. I finish the class. Jordan is the first to leave and then the commotion starts.

It turns out that four other policemen have been patiently waiting outside for us to finish the class. My head is scrambled, what has Jordan done that there are five policemen queuing up for him?

Oh how they must have wished they'd waited inside, because as Jordan saunters out of the church, as soon as they do a name check and attempt to handcuff him, he literally bolts as if in training to smash Usain Bolt's 100 metre record at the 2009 Olympics – and this from a lad who's sat watching the class because he'd said he had a bad back.

It was only when Antony ran outside, saw what was happening and shouted back to me that Jordan has fled and the police are giving chase, that I realise why the police have come to the church. I run as fast as I can out of the church, turn right and down the High Street. I can see the direction Jordan has run from the way the gathering crowds are facing; so down Friar Street I run and there, on the corner, is a stationary police van. I bang on the driver's window assuming Jordan's inside, but the officer shakes her head at me, sounds the siren and speeds off; the chase is on for little Jordan.

Jordan turns up to our next class later that week and proudly announces he'd run for at least a mile before being pinned down by five puffing police officers. How they must question our fitness classes at the church: get fit at 'Body Rocks' in case you have to go on the run.

And is there a law that says you cannot make an arrest in a church?

He, too, is to report to the police station on 16 December.

Help! 16 December is the demonstration day for our providers. We've already invited an audience of our supporters, including Charles Brims, high sheriff of Berkshire, and his wife

Patricia, plus Lady Stevenson, another of our invaluable supporters and a trustee of the Berkshire Community Foundation. At
this rate we'll have no pupils to demonstrate our work! Maybe
we should hold it *at* the police station and devise a course for
the kids *with* the police. After all, Jordan has proved to be a very
good advert for our 'Body Rocks' course with his cardio escape
and Gloria with her swinging bicep punches.

A couple of weeks later, my partner and I go Christmas
shopping in Reading. As we walk over the bridge, the water
below looks as freezing as the numb fingertips thrust deep inside
our pockets. Running clumsily towards us are three boys, two
are lanky teenagers, the one behind them I can't see. They're
clearly having difficulty bump-starting a very flash-looking
cross-country motorbike while steering it as fast as they can on
the narrow pavement. It looks decidedly shady. As they pass us
trying to control this spluttering machine, the third figure turns
around grinning.

'Hi!' he says cheerfully to us as he continues walking
backwards.

'Hi Jordan,' I say, trying to sound reproachful.

Note to self. I must remember when term starts in January
to ask about 'his' bike. It turns out Jordan is well-known to the
police as a prolific burglar. Hopefully the bike was returned to
its rightful owner.

The second time the police appear during an exercise session
is to arrest a lad who's already on tag and been sent to 'Body
Rocks' by the Reading Youth Offending team. This time they

don't wait for me to finish the fitness session but come in, and stand inside the doorway watching, ready to make the arrest. Unbelievably, the guilty lad in question whispers to the lad next to him to make a run for the door. Fortunately I hear and tell this lad in no uncertain terms not to be so silly, in any case they're getting wise to these 'Body Rocks' lads and have probably sent the fittest of their force to make a safe arrest.

After a third visit by the police, I ask the vicar what the situation is regarding making an arrest in church. Apparently, they can do so, but *not* if it's by the altar. I don't think I will be imparting that information to our Cred students.

Debbie and I think it would be a great idea to set up a fitness challenge with the Thames Valley Police Force. With all these arrests happening, it'll be a good way of introducing them to each other. One Saturday morning, the church has ten of the finest from the Thames Valley Police Force in their T-shirts and shorts preparing to battle it out against ten of our finest 'Body Rocks' participants. Looking at their intimidating bulging biceps and humungous thighs, these police must be spending all their off-duty time in the gym. Comparing them against some of our skinny, puny lads, there doesn't seem much hope of us winning. As they line up to shake hands and introduce themselves to each other, it isn't long before one of the lads recognises his arresting officer and, with smiles all round, the challenge is on.

Together they cover the length of the church running up and down, lap after lap, hopping and jumping, skipping and galloping, calling out the number of scissors and squat jumps as they leap in the air with each team trying, very good naturedly, to outdo the other. Our lads are holding up well with this first aerobic challenge.

Next the strength work. I confess I had deliberately based the tests around the ones I'd devised for the GB Women's Rowing Squad and the gym staff at Huntercombe Boys' Juvenile Prison, which our 'Body Rocks' team are now expert at doing. These include side leg raises and knee dips with added 5lb ankle-weights, pulses in sumo squats for the adductor muscles and a series of ab holds which I know are not the usual gym exercises the police force would be used to doing. Fair play to us, our team is only little.

The way the police interact with these lads as they contest the fast-paced cardio session, a timed race on the ergo machine which Debbie supervises, plus the weights session where clearly our lads are having the upper hand, is really heart-warming. As each side is awarded points for winning their respective tests, the cheers echoing round the church come from a motley mix of supporting local youths, policemen's wives and volunteers from my evening exercise classes in Marlow who'd arrived laden with sandwiches and homemade cakes. And who won the challenge? Diplomatically, it's a draw – and it doesn't hinder future arrests.

The girls from Cred are now restless and don't have the same focus in their weekly sessions as the boys and they need a change from their exercise routine. They're not expressing any interest in doing another type of exercise session either and often end up squabbling with each other over some minor detail. They usually arrive early at the tail end of the boys' session and stand huddled in the doorway. They can see how enthusiastic the boys have become, but their disengagement and lethargic approach is unsettling.

'Why don't we do a line dance?' suggests Marsha.

'Yeah I reckon I'd be good at that,' chimes in Gloria. There's a glimmer of hope.

A line dance is not something I've ever done before, but I've seen clips on TV and if it's going to keep them motivated to regularly attend and they make a decent attempt to learn it, then a line dance it will be. I make up my own quite complex version, inspired by a country and western record by The Woolpackers. And who are the ones who end up practising and perfecting the moves in every 'Body Rocks' session, proudly performing it to our grant supporters at our next demonstration? The boys, the five boys who several weeks ago were adamant they wouldn't ever be dancing to music. They love the feeling of moving as a unit, and rehearse it endlessly so they can perform it with military precision. With their enthusiasm and dedication I get even more ambitious with the choreography. During the instrumental break of this toe-tapping music, I put them in two lines with alternate spaces between them so they can perform a moving square round each other. Looking like soldiers on parade they reverse the square to advance forward into one long line. They proudly perform it for our grant supporters, looking good enough for the Edinburgh Military Tattoo.

After my son's filmed and edited their performance in the church, they watch it back over and over again and behave as if they've won the World Cup. It'll probably be their finest achievement during their time at Cred. And they've ignited an idea for an apprenticeship scheme. This 'Famous Five' from the line dance, could, in the not too distant future, become assistants in inspiring other young people at risk of permanent exclusions, just like themselves. It seems the logical progression in this very steep learning curve. Would it be an impossible task, a mountain too far with the challenges they're already coping with both at home and within their communities?

CHAPTER 14

HOW DO THEY SURVIVE?

When I first started teaching in 1970, we didn't get any information from the heads of years about the boys whose welfare was at risk, we could only guess by their behaviour. The system then, or lack of it, was very different, so I tried to give the boys in my socio-drama improvisations the tools to cope and, with Andy's help, the boys in the drama club a continuity of support. But we questioned ourselves at the time: how many more boys in this huge comprehensive school are we missing? And were these boys having to contend with the often unimaginable appalling backgrounds that Debbie and I are now currently coping with in our 'Body Rocks' courses? I'm astounded how some of these children survive. But some never do. Here's my story about Rick.

In 2012, Rick is assigned to our 'Body Rocks' fitness and behaviour management course as a result of countless exclusions and lack of attendance. The school want him to attend for two half-days a week and it's agreed they'll phone me at 8.45 a.m. every session to check he's arrived. Well, that's a bit of an anomaly. When he does turn up at school, it seems they can't get him to stay there because he signs in and goes straight back out again via the playing fields.

Rick is thirteen years old and comes from the most indescribably violent background. His real dad is living in another town and witnesses three men butchering his dad's friend to death in his flat. Rick's really scared when he goes to visit him, because of the two warring families, but he wants to keep in contact with his dad. At home, Rick sleeps on the floor because his uncle has his bed; their house is overcrowded. His mum has suffered from mental health problems, and Rick tells me he tries to play the man about the house because no other male is taking responsibility.

There's something very endearing about Rick. He looks so scrawny and vulnerable. He's come wanting to learn, but he can't even read. His school's suggested he's dyslexic, but nobody – not even his primary school – has ever tested him. Maybe his attendance was erratic at that school too; how could he have been so invisible? Given all this background, the few times he does go to his secondary school, is he going to sit at a desk and concentrate?

I take him to WHSmith and he chooses books about animals and motorbikes, books that will hopefully motivate him to read. He stays behind when other course pupils leave and we go right back to basics and phonically, step by step, we're getting there. When we can't use the church, we go round to the café next door and sit at a corner table with two older lads and one from our Jobcentre course. They take it in turns, helping each other to read out loud from the *Daily Mail* sports pages. Rick's quizzical. How can an ex-gang leader at the age of twenty-three with six kids to look after not be able to read? And *I'm* quizzical too.

How did all these boys go right through primary school not being able to read?

Rick can see that this big man, in spite of his embarrassment, wants to learn too and it spurs him on. We read passages together from *A Street Cat Named Bob* by busker James Bowen. Rick asks to take home a copy, he identifies with James's situation, his bonding with his cat. Within twelve weeks Rick has learnt how to read.

The 'Body Rocks' programmes are now officially recognised as a Level 1 and Level 2 fitness qualification. Level 2 is a teaching qualification and is one of our proudest achievements, enabling us to train young people on our 'Body Rocks' and Jobcentre Plus courses to become qualified exercise-to-music instructors. If we have enough grant money, we can train some of them to become our apprentices, but we'll need money to pay them. An apprenticeship is now Rick's goal, and it's mine to help him achieve it, but it might be a bridge too far. I make sure he turns up on time by giving him an alarm call at 7.45 a.m. so he can catch the bus in time for the agreed phone call I have to make to the school. Only twice is he a few minutes late, and that's because he's had to take his little brother to school. With the other course participants spurring him on, we help him to believe in himself, how to teach 'Body Rocks', but it takes a long time before any of us can hear his instruction, he's so quietly spoken and his gestures limp and timid. And yet by all accounts he's prone to fighting, fearlessly standing up for himself when necessary. He's making great strides learning to write, too, patiently learning and even works on the spellings I set him for homework. He's closer to achieving his goal. The vicar, when he works in the church, regularly walks past us and smiles; he can see Rick's progress.

But I can't get him to attend school on a regular basis. The school threaten to stop him coming to 'Body Rocks'. It blackmails him into attending and it works, but only for a time. I go to the school for a meeting with his mum, the Year leaders, the school welfare officer and a child education psychologist. A lengthy report written by one of his teachers is read out, and it's as if I'm hearing about a totally different boy. When he turns up to this class, he's been calling his teacher a 'bean head' and tells him he'll do all his work if he tells the class Rick is stronger than him, switches the lights on and off, clambers over the tables and intimidates the teacher by squaring up to him. He has no concern that this pattern of complete disruption is interrupting the rest of the class wanting to learn and neither does he turn up to any of the dozens of detentions this teacher has set. Rick looks at me throughout with embarrassment. It reveals so much about how troubled he is. A plan and a future assessment are put in place. I'm asked if I could attend some lessons with him; I readily agree.

I leave Julie, my assistant, in charge of five exceptionally challenging pupils from the referral units for the three-hour 'Body Rocks' session at the church. I meet Rick outside the school and I sit with him in class, being careful not to undermine the teacher who had written the report, and establish with the rest of the pupils I am assisting Rick with his work. He sits quietly, making the effort to understand and answer the questions the teacher has distributed to the class, questions that are impossible for him to answer as he hasn't attended any of the lessons, but together we quietly try. Walking round the school during break time, it seems like all thirteen hundred pupils are rushing at us in the corridor; I can feel Rick wanting to escape. We go to an empty pre-arranged room and continue the written work we've been doing for the Level 2 examination.

Back at the church, Julie is coping with a volatile confrontation. It's between Jaz, an excluded school pupil and now one of our potential apprentices, and Sharon, who regularly barricades herself in the classroom at her referral unit. She's provoking Jaz with racist comments, deliberately picking a fight, egging him on, slyly hoping he will lose control and thus his apprenticeship. He keeps himself in check and stays seated. Sharon, in her frustration and fury, picks up two glasses full of water and hurls them against one of the church walls. Fortunately, nobody is hurt by the shattered, broken shards of glass. I can't attend any more classes with Rick.

We're running out of the grant money that supplements the low fees we have to charge schools for the excluded school pupils and pupil referral units. I invite Charles Brims, high sheriff of Berkshire and a keen supporter of our work, to talk with Rick and to watch him teach other course members. He sees his potential, listens to the incredible personal struggles he's having to overcome and makes a personal donation to ensure Rick can continue his studies two mornings a week with us. As far as I'm concerned, instead of wandering the streets on the other days, Rick can come and join us and attend the other courses and, if necessary, I'll argue his case with the education authorities.

After two years' hard work, Rick is blossoming, his confidence is sky high, we all applaud him, he revels in his achievements. He's on the point of passing his Level 2, but in one fell swoop, it all comes crashing down. A large company that's amalgamated with the Careers Office offers his school an alternative provision for their pupils because they've been given an enormous grant. They promise the school they can turn things around for Rick and it won't cost the school a penny; they can offer it all for free. He comes to the church and excitedly tells us they've said forget Level 2; he can get his Level 3 with them. It's the other side of town, a long bus ride away for him, but they have brand-new premises on a business park estate with fantastic facilities, including a state-of-the-art music recording studio. He can join the other kids about to go away for a week's holiday too and they'll allow him to take forty cigarettes and smoke. They've promised him outcomes that I know are going to be impossible for him to achieve. He ticks their grant form boxes and we have no alternative but to let him go. He very quickly establishes himself as a 'waster'. Getting up in the mornings to take a bus ride to the business park estate was never realistically going to happen and when he does make an appearance, his work output is negligible. He walks away with absolutely nothing, it destroys everything he's achieved with us.

When Rick finally comes back to see us to tell us what's happened, he apologises, but sorry was not for him to say; I apologise to Rick on behalf of their organisation. It isn't too late to pick up the pieces, but during his months of absence, things have changed for us. We're in the process of moving to Slough, and only running a 'Body Rocks' course once a week to enable us to expand our curriculum in Berkshire. We've been given a magnificent office space on the Slough Business Park Estate, all for free, a dream come true. Their business director had attended a gathering of social enterprises like ourselves to meet local companies, and we'd been invited to give a talk about our work, followed by a practical demonstration. We took two permanently excluded school lads and one recently released young-adult ex-offender. One by one, they'd graphically detailed their extraordinary life stories and then, with drilled precision, performed a choreographed energetic aerobic dance routine taught by Simon, an excluded school pupil, out front. The business director was so impressed he asked us what we needed to establish our organisation in Slough. We're now in a position to expand from these wonderful premises and introduce 'Body Rocks' to schools in another area of the county. We're also focusing on teaching early learning years in primary schools with Joggy Bear, my children's character.

We keep in constant touch with Rick, and he supports us whenever we need help. One evening he comes with Jaz to talk to business grant funders, to the mayor of Wokingham and invited

VIP guests about our work, and the positive impact it can have on pupils and lads like themselves. Talking about himself to these strangers doesn't come naturally to Rick, but he overcomes his shyness and wins them over with his charm and enthusiasm. And when we need someone to operate the CD player for our demonstration in Slough attended by HRH the Countess of Wessex, he learns all the music cues for the singing primary schoolchildren and for the exercises with Joggy Bear. He makes sure he's reliable and, with his help, it all goes without a hitch.

At the end of this exciting day that's rounded off with a wonderful buffet, I drive him back to his family's temporary B&B accommodation, temporary because his house has burnt down. Rick carefully balances platefuls of the exquisite left-over petit fours on his lap to give to his mum, a typically thoughtful Rick gesture. His kindness and caring have never left him. Our faith in him and the support from Charles Brims and the Berkshire Community Foundation has not been wasted.

. . .

Rebecca is in her third year at a girls' secondary school. Her learning mentor is hoping that if she attends the 'Body Rocks' fitness and behaviour management course, it might enable Rebecca to turn her life around. I attend a meeting at the school to learn more about her background. She's on a child protection plan and several social workers are involved with the family. There are six sisters, all with different dads, and one brother. Rebecca hasn't seen her dad since she was two years old; her stepdad, with whom she has a good relationship, is serving a two-year prison sentence for drug dealing; her mum is an alcoholic. She doesn't live at home because her mum tried to drown her when she was twelve years old. Living with her brother became problematic when he burnt her hand in a fit of temper and she now stays with a sister who has multiple issues. Her attendance at school is sporadic, and when she does appear, her behaviour can be defiant and disruptive.

When Rebecca arrives at 'Body Rocks', she's adamant she doesn't want to do anything physical in front of the boys and I assure her there will be no need for her to participate in any of the exercise sessions. I've assigned Julie as her personal trainer. Rebecca is small in stature, slight in build and a fragile teenager. Her brightly coloured head of blue hair, the metal piercings in her nose and tongue make her clearly visible. The others ignore her. We sit with them around the huge table by the kitchen; she's steely eyed, and doesn't say a word. Julie takes her upstairs, where she's cocooned in one of the round glass booths, while downstairs I contain the ongoing challenges with the permanently excluded boys and girls from the pupil referral unit.

Rebecca needs time and, after a hesitant, reluctant start, the real Rebecca starts to emerge. She gains confidence, enough for us to suggest she starts exercising with the rest of the pupils. I give her a pair of trainers and her Ugg boots come off. She contributes in the discussion groups and is perceptive in her understanding of the others' negative attitudes towards authority, perhaps seeing herself mirrored in their resistance. Gradually, she lets the protective wall she's built around herself down and places her trust in us. I arrive half an hour early before each morning session, knowing she will be patiently standing outside in the wind, rain and snow, waiting for me to unlock the church door. The attention and reassurance she's been craving is in the safety of the church, where she can unleash her thoughts and feelings. She tells me that living with her sister she feels like she's 'treated like a dog' and that her sister gives her nothing, that Annie, her school mentor, has kept her alive, caring for her, even providing her with money for sanitary wear. In spite of several meetings that take place with social workers, Rebecca says everything stays the same. There is no acceptance of her situation, no self-pity, only a determination to resolve it by changing it for herself.

Rebecca becomes part of our apprenticeship team. We invite Annie to come and see her teach a group of 'Body Rocks' pupils, all of whom are on the cusp of permanent exclusion. This is what Annie wrote about Rebecca:

'Low in self-esteem and lacking in confidence, we hoped this course would bring out the best in this student. A year and a half later I witness a completed 360-degree change. I witnessed her (I must add, full of pride) taking a fitness class brimming with confidence and I was amazed at her now outstanding leadership skills, being proud and loud in a positive way, it was awesome.'

Rebecca has no idea what she wants to do for a job, but she knows she's going to get one, to prove to herself and to her mum that she's capable of achieving and she can exist by herself. She attempts some GCSEs, but hasn't attended enough schooling to pass, but at least she turns up for the exams and tries. She thinks she might like to work with old people. I take her to the plush private home my mother is cared for in a mansion on the banks of the River Thames. At tea time she hands round the cups and cakes and they listen attentively, close to tears as she recounts her life. But she decides she's too young and lacking in patience to work with elderly people and thinks again.

She's never been to London. I decide to take her for a visit, first class so she can travel in style for her first train journey. We meet Julie at Paddington station and stroll around a buzzing, colourful Chinatown and a bustling Covent Garden, packed with people and mime artists. We have tea at Patisserie Valerie and head for the Royal Opera House to see a performance of 'The Nutcracker'. My sister has arranged front row seats in the grand tier and after a magical first act we drink champagne during the interval. Rebecca leaves hers; the scars haven't healed from the experiences with her mum. She absorbs the day's adventure and travels home with happy memories to think again.

We do some cooking in the church kitchen with two of the adult ex-offenders. They help her cook some pasta and it ignites an interest in catering. Rebecca can enrol on a cookery course at the local college while studying English and maths. I'm not sure why the education authorities think that by resitting these exams at college she'll start attending lessons and miraculously catch up on all the years she's missed, but it's a new ruling and choosing a practical subject like catering could be really useful.

Rebecca attends the catering course, ignores the academic subjects and achieves a Level 2 in catering. But she doesn't see herself having the patience or the character to work in a kitchen day after day and thinks again. She leaves college. Her determination to be self-sufficient and prove the doubters wrong ensures she achieves her goal. The blue hair's gone, the metal studs are out.

Rebecca is now twenty-four. After leaving college, she worked for two years at Poundworld, followed by eighteen months at McDonalds, a year at a drive-in motorway branch at KFC and is currently a crew trainer for employees at a local burger chain. We keep in constant touch by phone and meet regularly. She and her partner have been in a solid relationship for six years and are the proud parents of a delightful two-year-old little girl.

● ● ●

Like Rick, Ashley came to 'Body Rocks' at the age of thirteen, but I'm going to relate his story differently; you will understand my reason when you reach the end.

Ashley is twenty-three years old. He's sitting alone, in silence, staring at the walls of his Sheffield flat. Time to reflect. Too much time.

Ashley has recently moved from Reading to Sheffield to be with Lysander, his best mate, so he can make a fresh start, try again, learn from all his mistakes. He's too close to being in trouble with the law again and mixing with the wrong crowd. Lysander has known him for fifteen years. They're so very different in looks and background, but so very alike in thought. They once walked for four hours round the block, just walking and talking, talking and walking, walking and talking, sharing their similarities and their differences. Lysander is studying art and is in his second year at Sheffield Hallam University. Ashley is stacking shelves at Tesco.

Ashley is twenty-two years old, sitting alone, in silence, staring at the Tesco walls. Time to reflect. Too much time.

When Ashley joined 'Body Rocks' in 2008, we were the school's last gasp of hope.

He arrived having had several school exclusions, playing the fool, it was how people defined him, so naturally he assumed being the clown was the role that was expected of him. The entertainer, the leader of the pack. Lysander knew the real Ashley. He says Ashley felt he'd never shown the world the *real* Ashley, so people couldn't help but make judgements and underestimate him. It took me some time to realise that Ashley was no fool. Prior to his joining us, the school in their report commented upon his totally inappropriate behaviour, his lack of attendance and when he did bother to appear, nearly all his time was spent in the isolation room. An isolation room is best described as a large room, smaller than the average classroom but with lots of tiny wooden divisions enclosing portioned-off units – and that's your space.

Ashley is fifteen years old, sitting alone, in silence, staring at the walls of his wooden cell.

All day, nearly every day, all through lesson time, during break time, during lunch time, isolation, until it's the end of the school day. At least, that's what he was supposed to do. Ashley didn't always wait for home time. He'd break out as soon as he could and, being so thin, was able to squeeze through the window and flee his cell. Ashley was ever the clown. There were numerous occasions we'd be sitting round the kitchen table focusing on the 'Body Rocks' Level 2 written theory, never the group's favourite task. Suddenly, there would be an explosion of noise interrupting the imposed silence. It was Ashley hee-hawing or whooping or cackling. He'd then look up, grinning from ear to ear as the kids convulsed with laughter. His vibrant personality was like a magnet to these kids. He was a lanky-looking lad with the thinnest legs and arms, but when he opened his mouth to teach, wow, where did that come from? This rich, deep, commanding, booming voice, full of authority, would echo around the church and had the potential to stop even the toughest of kids in their tracks. He was a male vocal version of me. And so Ashley progressed, and after passing his Level 2, he joined our expanding team of apprentices, developing and increasing his teaching skills, not that he had much to work on: he was a born teacher. He became a pivotal, invaluable member of our team, helping to inspire the next generation of excluded school pupils.

We ran weekly fitness classes for the over fifties at the YMCA in Tilehurst. Every Monday afternoon, twenty-two ladies would come and pay £5 for their one hour. It helped to swell our coffers while giving our apprentices invaluable teaching experience. What an unlikely mix it was. If these ladies saw our lads in the street on a dark night, they would have hurried across the road to avoid them. Equally, the lads probably wouldn't have given these 'posh' people the time of day if they hadn't been teaching them. It did, though, work wonderfully well. Great bonds were forged and these very correct, beautifully spoken women, made the effort to come every week to this grotty YMCA hall, to lend their support. This was social inclusion as its very best. They adored Ashley. He would place all the ladies in a huge circle each holding onto the back of a chair.

'Right then, squats,' this booming voice instructed, 'get them legs apart, hold onto the back of the chair, bend 'em a little bit, down a bit more, a bit more. Hoooold it and up yer come.' Ashley had found his vocation with his voice. He was both the performer and teacher with a huge heart.

One Monday afternoon, I was sitting in our pick-up place in the car park opposite Reading Prison. It was the usual arranged time to drive these apprentices to teach their Monday class. Simon arrived, Jermaine arrived, but no Ashley. I phoned his mobile but it just rang out. I waited and waited until we finally had to leave, otherwise we'd arrive far too late to set up the chairs, weights and mats to start the class on time.

'I don't understand, where is he, anyone had a message from him?' I agitatedly enquired, looking in my driving mirror at the faces of the boys on the back seat. Simon looked uncomfortable and muttered:

'It's his birthday today.'

'Yes, but what's that got to do with it?'

It had everything to do with it. The little devil had bunked off for the day with his mates to Thorpe Park to celebrate his sixteenth birthday and everyone knew, except me. My turn to make a sudden explosion of noise. One day, Ashley introduced Lysander to us. He said he had a friend who was interested in teaching 'Body Rocks' and he'd like to train and become an apprentice. But there was a problem. His time would, of necessity, be limited because Lysander actually attended school. So I shouldn't have been surprised when Lysander arrived. Of course he was the exact antithesis of Ashley. Quietly spoken, thoughtful and undemanding, Lysander was clearly going to be an enormous asset to our team of apprentices when he was able to attend and hopefully impact on Ashley's impulsive behaviour. Hurrah. But how come these two are such close buddies?

'Ashley has uncontrolled, reckless energy. School isn't able to manage that energy, it can't contain it. "Body Rocks" allows him to channel that energy, it gives him a focus, a goal, something he's always lacked.'

Such wise words from someone so young and what a great influence and friend he was to Ashley. They would meet in each other's houses and enjoy choreographing routines to music. They'd take everything on board I'd taught them about constructing dances to music, how to mirror image, how to cue and correct. They were really impressive when team-teaching their own routines, sharing their dual role like a Morecombe and Wise, an Ant and Dec. We had a grant to teach in another converted church in a place called Finchampstead. It was beautifully constructed for a thriving arts community in an economically challenged area and was a perfect setting for holding our weekly evening dance class for twenty teenage girls. Ashley and Lysander choreographed a routine to 'DJ Got Us Fallin' in Love' by Usher. I proudly learnt with the girls, staying at the back as these two accomplished lads taught their routine section by section. A stage school would have been proud of them, they had reached new heights.

We won three awards during the time Ashley was with us. The first, in 2009, was the Philip Lawrence Award. What a huge honour. We'd made a written submission to their selection panel and, as a result, we were asked to submit a short film about 'Body Rocks'. We chose five lads to front it. They watched a film the panel had sent and point blank refused to do something similar. The consensus of the group was that they weren't going to stand there and say, 'We are "Body Rocks" and this is what we do.' I couldn't see anything contentious in the statement, but they were adamant 'it looks rank'. I eventually get their approval by getting Ben to shoot it from above so the camera was looking down on them from the mezzanine gallery. He filmed a huge variety of material and did a wonderful job of editing them dancing and exercising with weights and teaching aerobics in one of our Saturday family sessions. We headed the film with interviews from each of the lads giving a potted version of why they were at 'Body Rocks'. Simon sported a huge black eye having been in one of his regular fights, but hey, that's our reality.

The evening award ceremony was held at BAFTA in Piccadilly in the Princess Anne Theatre. Our film was being shown with all the other winners and a trophy presented. Trevor

McDonald, the ITN news reader and broadcaster, was the presenter and Alan Johnson, the then Home Secretary, was guest speaker. We were allowed to take seven lads and one parent, so Antony's mum, who'd also spoken in our film, accompanied us in the hired minibus. Antony was good friends with Ashley. Antony could be very sensible and a great asset to the team, but at other times a mischievous leader; it was a bit of a gamble to take him, but as his mum was also going we'd get the more mature Antony.

A few of the lads had nothing suitable to wear, so we took them to Primark and kitted them out in suits, shirts and ties. By the time we'd finished, they looked like a young Mafia. They loved their new image, so much so that when it came to photos at BAFTA with the official photographer, none of them would smile, no matter how much I implored them. All eight of them stood tight lipped, looking menacingly into the camera in their newly found Mafia roles, courtesy of Primark. Ashley was in his element as he posed, the theatricality of it all appealed to him; it held a much greater thrill than when he made a parachute to float down out of the isolation room at school.

What should have been a relaxing, exciting and rewarding occasion turned out to be a confrontational nightmare as the lads were let loose in this beautiful London theatre. They were surrounded by all the other winners, who were, unfortunately, mainly girls. The hormones took over and the 'Body Rocks' lads sat in our row of plush velvet seats, excitedly chatting up the girls in the row behind. These girls were very well spoken and well behaved, but that just encouraged Antony and the others all the more. Their voices grew louder and their gesticulations wilder as they tried to impress.

'Posh totties like a bad boy,' Antony whispered, his eyes darting with excitement.

I left Antony's mum in charge while I went to see the organisers who asked me to nominate one lad to say a few words on stage before our film was shown, then our 'Body Rocks' boys were to line up on the side steps, file on the stage and receive their award from the Home Secretary. With all the shenanigans going on, who on earth could I rely on to be sensible and speak? The only quiet one not trying to impress in his Mafia suit was Sean. I pleaded with him to do it, wrote out a few words, and returned to our row to find Antony's mum in tears. Antony, Brendon and Jim had said they were going to the loo, but instead had gone to loiter outside the building with a couple of girls from the row behind to have a cigarette.

When the time came for the speeches and presentation, they quietened down as their nerves kicked in. When the 'Body Rocks' film was shown and they could see themselves performing on the big screen, they were so chuffed, they gave a little cheer. As their names were called, they shuffled down the steps in an orderly line onto the stage, dutifully shook hands with the Home Secretary and proudly accepted the award. Sean did really well with his words. And so it was, with great relief, Antony's mum and I rounded up the lads and herded them back into the coach before they could swap any more phone numbers with the girls. After a boisterous journey home, we arrived back at the church. I collapsed at home with a large glass of wine and

Antony and his mum didn't speak to each other for two days. The Philip Lawrence panel kept sending me emails requesting all their award winners keep in touch by Facebook so they could continue sharing experiences and build up a fraternity of winners. A great idea, but not one I was prepared to risk; they would have turned it into their Mafia dating agency.

When we won the 2011 Sports Award with Wokingham Borough Council, I kept the numbers attending the evening ceremony to just three to avoid a potential repeat of the London ceremony. Debbie and I asked Ashley, because of his love of performance, Lysander, because his behaviour would be impeccable, and Liam who, like Lysander, would make *this* ceremony enjoyable and hassle-free. It was a far less formal occasion, so I suggested they were 'smart casual' in their appearance. I should have known better. I met them, as arranged, at our Reading car park. Liam was the first to arrive, looking his usual neat and tidy self, then I spotted Lysander walking towards us with Ashley. Lysander looked as if he'd spent the last hour grooming himself in the mirror but there, walking alongside him was Ashley, tieless, with his shirt tails hanging out. Apparently, Lysander had tried to smarten him up and get him to tuck them in, but to no avail. I didn't even bother. This was another statement from Ashley.

It was at this stage that Debbie and I were experiencing the complexities and issues raised from combining the participants from the lone parents' returning-to-work course with our young apprentices. It was about to have a detrimental effect on Ashley.

He was already feeling unstable and overreacting to situations because his girlfriend was two-timing him. We would try and pacify him and offer advice but he was not to be consoled. The smokers in break time would congregate outside the church for fifteen minutes. They were out of my sight as I needed to supervise the pupils inside, but clearly Ashley was being influenced by Jayden, one of the lone parents who had been trusted to keep an eye on them. She'd achieved so much with her course that she, like three other lone parents, had passed her Level 2 and joined us as a paid assistant with the apprentices. Her teaching was exemplary, her communication with girls on our behaviour courses empathic and her shared life experiences with them really useful. So much so, we had successfully nominated her for an achievement award, but she subsequently arrived to accept her award at the black-tie dinner stoned.

But, and it became a big but, she had the most volatile, screaming temper. Ashley would take great pleasure in her occasional emotional outbursts, which would turn into personal attacks on me. My tactic with these outbursts was to talk quietly and to try and reason with her. The group tossed aside my rational, calming attempts to explain how they would understand my system when they left 'Body Rocks' and taught in the outside world. I was aware that Jayden was used to physically fighting. In the juvenile prison, I always knew that should a lad become violent, the other lads would protect me. In this situation, with Jayden aiming a punch at me, I wasn't so sure that the same protection would apply.

The final time it happened we were sitting around the kitchen table. The vicar, on hearing the abusive commotion, came down from his office upstairs and walked, very slowly and deliberately, down the centre of the church to the altar. It was hugely comforting for me, but made not a jot of difference to Jayden. She stood up glaring at me demanding more money for the apprentices. She could not comprehend that because of the lack of grant money and low fees we had to charge schools for our courses, Debbie and I were earning the same amount of teaching money as they were and working for free the rest of the time. Ashley, who had been gleefully egging her on and echoing her words, dramatically stood up and together, they made for the door. I tried to metaphorically pull him back, to disentangle him from Jayden, calling out as a last resort 'Ashley, if you leave now, you're never coming back'. He left the church with Jayden. It was the last time I saw Ashley.

In October 2017 I had an urgent message from Lysander asking me to phone him. Ashley had gone to Sheffield, telling his distraught girlfriend the only way he could reassess his life and make a fresh start was to make a complete change and leave Reading. He needed to break the negative cycle. Lysander and Ashley were planning how they could make exercise and dance videos for YouTube. They'd contacted an organisation about becoming personal trainers and had decided to seek my advice about teaching dance and 'Body Rocks'. He told Lysander he'd thrown away his chance to do the thing that he loved doing the most. It didn't happen. He didn't contact me. He'd already decided it was all too late.

Ashley, at twenty-three years old, sat alone, in silence, staring at the walls of his Sheffield flat.

Debbie made sure she was with me at his funeral. The church in Tilehurst was so packed she and I stood outside listening to the service with the rest of his friends. We could see the video screen they'd set up and watched the compilation of photos Lysander had put together. Seeing Ashley clutching his 'Body Rocks' awards, his one achievement in his too short life, was difficult to comprehend. The eulogy Lysander gave at his funeral was beyond remarkable. For twenty minutes he recounted his friendship, relayed stories and spoke with quiet maturity and clarity on behalf of Ashley's parents – and he made sure the congregation heard about the *real* Ashley.

Lysander didn't return to Sheffield. With the support of the university, he completed his art degree and continued to pursue their dream. It didn't take him long. He is now an aerobics teacher and a personal trainer. Until Covid struck, I regularly attended his Monday evening aerobics class with thirty other exercisers. The warmth of his personality, his clarity and inspirational teaching and choreography, it's all there. As I joined in with the grapevines, leg routines and dance steps he'd learnt way back in the Reading church, I glowed; but it was tinged with sadness. I had taught Lysander and, with his absence, Ashley has taught me.

Lysander achieved what they'd set out to do together and Ashley would be so proud of him. I wouldn't have been the only one congratulating Lysander at the end of the classes.

'Yeah boy,' I can hear Ashley saying to Lysander, 'you smashed it.'

We had so many successes, but there are always failures. I console myself with the vicar's words, 'Lizzie, you don't know what seeds you've sown,' and I know I let Ashley down.

CHAPTER 15

APPRENTICES

We have a request. A local person living in Berkshire would like to visit our organisation. He wants to see a variety of charities and community interest companies in his area and we fit the bill. Andrew, the CEO of the Berkshire Community Foundation, knows how important it is to spread the word about Creativity in Sport, and without the support of the Berkshire Community Foundation we could never have survived financially. Andrew will be accompanying our visitor, James Middleton, and we suggest that our kids aren't told anything about him or his background; we don't want them getting over-excited. Of course it was possible that the boys weren't that interested in the recent Royal Wedding with William and Kate, or aware of the resulting global interest in this now hugely famous Berkshire family. But we impress upon the boys that this visit was just as important as all our other demonstrations, and being such a perceptive lot, they probably notice that Debbie and I are more cautious than usual with their choice of music. The current list for choregraph-ing their routines includes 'Haven't Met You Yet' by Michael Bublé and 'I Gotta Feeling' by the Black Eyed Peas. I dispense with one of their favourites, 'I Kissed a Girl' by Katy Perry for James Middleton's visit, just in case they bellow out something inappropriate. We're ready and well prepared.

The ornate black handle of the church door turns and Andrew and our visitor enter. He stands quietly, admiring the impressive surroundings. He's casually dressed, smart and wearing jeans, perfectly understated. After my introduction to this charming, softly spoken gentleman, they sit on the sofa we've previously positioned against the wall so they can observe the exercise teaching from the front. No background info needs to be exchanged; Andrew will have filled him in about our appren-ticeship scheme. I join the class at the back, it's my vantage point for keeping my eye on the boys and to operate the beat box. I've asked Antony to lead the warmup; he's our first qualified apprentice and the most experienced. He goes to the front of the class as the rest of the lads scatter around the church and wait in readiness as he cues in the music. There's a slight hint of nerv-ousness in the air, but once we start, they enthusiastically give it their all. After a few minutes, James beckons me over. I stop the music and he asks if he can join in. I'm taken aback; it's totally unexpected, but of course he can.

I watch James quickly walk to the far end of the front line, acknowledging the lads as he passes, but I become slightly con-cerned. His jeans look extremely, worryingly tight. Antony restarts the warmup, and sets the standard by giving excellent instructions, which is then followed by Mac's energetic aerobic routine. And what I'm seeing completely takes me by surprise. Not only does James follow the warmup, he also follows Mac's dance instructions to the beat and executes it all with excellent co-ordination and fluidity of movement. And he grins throughout! He genuinely looks as if he's enjoying himself. But, deep breaths, I know the lesson plan. Aaron is about to teach the sumo squats.

The sumo squat is my fun name for the exercise; it's the same as a ballet plié out in second position, different to a quad squat in that the legs are quite wide apart and the feet and legs are turned out. As you bend down and up, the insides of the thighs known as the adductor muscles are the ones being targeted. When you stay down in this deep low position and add a few sets of six little rhythmic pulse lifts before pushing all the way back up, it's tough, really tough. And even tougher if you also add heel raises in that held position which is in our lesson plan. He could, just like the prison officers, not exercise his inner thighs as much as his quads so I can just imagine some of the lads calling out 'Chicken' or something far more unrepeatable if he gives up and stops. But that's not my main concern right now, which is whether his very skinny tight jeans will withstand these sumo squats without splitting at the crotch. Fearing the worst, I tell Aaron I'll lead the sumo squats, that way if his jeans do rip, I can control whatever happens.

I shouldn't have been concerned about the sumo squats because James performs them with effortless ease; it's the lads who are beginning to groan and, one by one, give up, James and

I are the only ones keeping going. I don't attempt to hide my surprise and pleasure as I banter across the room with him. The competition is on. With the lads encouraging James, I increase the number of pulses and reps, but he can't be outdone. And my thighs are burning. For the first time I've been exercising in this church with a class of lads, I am beaten, outdone.

'Respect bruv,' rings out around the church.

James grins. He must have known all along he could do it because of the tough competitive cross-country skiing and challenging triathlons he and his sisters do. And there was me thinking he was being polite when requesting to join in. And yes, miraculously his jeans stay fully intact.

After the stretches, the class finishes and James stays to chat to the boys. Thirteen of us squeeze round the long table in front of the kitchen area while Debbie and Andrew make the tea. Antony is sitting directly opposite James. There's a fresh, deep, slashed knife wound right down the side of his face and a heavily stitched pink scar all the way down his upper right arm. He was stabbed recently and rushed to Stoke Mandeville Hospital, their transport speed negating possible plastic surgery on his face. Although he no longer lives in Reading and it's not feasible for him to continue as an apprentice, I've invited him to take part today because he deserves acknowledgement for being the inspiration for the apprenticeship scheme.

James isn't fazed and is sensitive in his questioning. He listens intently while they describe their day-to-day lives, their permanent school exclusions, their hopes for the future. As I wrap up the session with thanks to our delightful, gracious guest, I get the impression he would happily have stayed for the rest of the day. One by one the boys shake him by the hand and thank him for coming. As they're about to leave, I can't help wondering if he's ever had any contact with lads like ours before. Andrew quietly tells me that, at James's request, they'd recently visited the Reading Young Offenders Institute, the prison down the road.

Debbie and I feel a huge sense of relief when they've gone. It wouldn't take much for visits like these to go horribly wrong, but everything's gone according to plan and we congratulate the lads on their impressive teaching and impeccable behaviour. We tell them they've just been exercising and teaching the brother of the future queen of England. They erupt. The noise of their incredulity and excitement is palpable. They jump up and down in disbelief and can't wait to go home to tell all and sundry who they've just been teaching.

'Now, let's get it right, who is he?' they keep asking as they head for the door, 'he's the brother of the king of England?'

'No,' I keep replying, 'he's the brother of the future queen of England.'

'He's a good geezer,' Antony calls out at the door. 'Bet he's loaded.'

• • •

Antony started the 'Body Rocks' course when he was fourteen years old. He's from a travellers' background, quite stocky but not a physically imposing lad, with short black hair, olive skin and darting brown eyes. He oozes charm and a guile that belies his age and he's clearly used to manipulating situations to his advantage. He learnt very early on that this iron-fist-in-the-velvet-glove teacher had taught too many pupils in her time to be gullible, and neither could she be charmed into changing her mind. I think he quietly respects me for that.

The current course for the Cred students and future apprentices is three mornings a week. Getting up for all three morning sessions is not something these kids are used to, it's only Antony who manages to arrive on time and attend all three. His commitment is all the more remarkable because of his 'loads of exclusions' from his secondary school. He takes these training sessions very seriously. He's got good leadership skills and the influence he has with the other Cred pupils is invaluable; if it's good enough for Antony, then it's good enough for them, they just need to get up in time for all three of the sessions. When Antony's interested in something, he focuses intently and if he's not, he'll playfully enjoy distracting others, particularly when doing the required written theory work. When it involves the understanding of the functioning and mechanics of the body, Antony thinks he knows it all because he's had plenty of practical experience with his numerous girlfriends. Neither his divorced parents nor his grandparents have ever worked, so breaking the cycle is going to be a significant task. I visit his home many times and forge a good relationship with his mum, so much so she asks if she too can attend 'Body Rocks' and get qualified with the Level 1. She's never achieved any qualification.

What a great advancement it could be with our original plan, mums joining in and studying with their sons, sons that had caused havoc in their secondary schools. We give it a try, and of course it's not all plain sailing. It can often end in tears when their unforgiving arguments at home spill into the morning session, and it isn't always easy to mediate. A couple of times Simon, who's a very easy-going lad, soon has his mum in tears of both frustration and despair; Simon 'won't see sense and enjoys arguing and scoring points'. But having the mums learn alongside their sons unquestionably improves their relationship. Simon's on yet another learning curve without his mum, when he gets some teaching practice with a lower ability band at a local secondary school.

'I never really liked school, so I never used to go. They kicked me out, I went to Cred and I then had the option to come to "Body Rocks", so I chose that, because I thought I'd be better than you at it (exercises) but obviously I can't. But it was when I was teaching at a secondary school, like it was with a fresh new group, they wasn't listening, they were just mucking about so I couldn't really teach. I was just getting angry. But I was worse than that, that's why I feel a bit sorry for my teachers, how I used to act, cos I was ten times worse than that.'

Maybe teachers should give their pupils the opportunity to teach a lesson – and the teachers behave like the pupils!

We want to raise the aspirations of these apprentices beyond the confines of just their teaching practise and I know the very person who can do it. Jeff's producing a new BBC Saturday evening show called *So You Think You Can Dance* with Cat Deeley as the presenter. It's a highly successful series on the Fox channel in America and Jeff's back in England supervising the first series. He offers us tickets to take some apprentices to sit in the audience and watch a recording at the Television Centre in Shepherd's Bush. Debbie and I think carefully about who to take and Antony and the two lads from the college group, the two who were so intimidated at the introductory talk and now our latest apprentices, are excited at the prospect. Garry, one of the Clapham dancers, comes too, that'll be two inspirational adults for them to speak to.

How rewarding it is to sit in the studio audience with Garry and the current boys I'm teaching and watch Jeff working on the studio floor. I shouldn't be surprised at his calm authority as he cues in the dancers and organises the dance panel. Between takes, he chats with the panel of judges, one of whom is Arlene Phillips. That's now three of the Clapham boys who've had the opportunity to work with the celebrated Arlene. All three are now choreographers, producers and theatre directors in charge of other dancers, but they'll always be 'my boys'.

After the recording, Jeff takes us to the staff canteen and sits talking with the lads while they eat. He gently lectures them, telling them not to waste the chances they've been given and to grab the 'Body Rocks' opportunity. He tells them if he and Garry can do it, so can they. As we leave, Jeff turns to me and says, 'You've come full circle Lizzie.'

Garry's now the resident theatre director for *Cabaret*, the musical in the Strand Theatre in London's West End and he too offers us tickets. This time Debbie and I allow time for a walk about London on a hot summer's evening. The only time any of the three lads have been to London is when we took them to Jeff's show. We walk with the lads alongside the River Thames so they can have a good view of the House of Commons, the London Eye and then it's over Westminster Bridge to Trafalgar Square. As we weave our way through the narrow streets of Covent Garden, office workers are spilling out onto the pavements from the many pubs and stand chatting and drinking in big groups, blocking the pavements. Antony's amazed. 'If they did that where we live, there'd be trouble, fights and a lot of nicking going on.'

We arrive at the theatre and Garry takes us backstage. The boys stand quietly at the side of the stage observing the set, before we take our seats in the auditorium. They're absorbed in the show. Antony purchases binoculars from the seat in front and trains them on the scantily dressed dancers throughout the entire rendition of 'Mein Herr'; his reasoning being that he can concentrate and view the dancing and choreography much better with the binoculars. I, without binoculars, keep glancing across at Garry. He's sitting alone in one of the boxes making notes on the cast's performance. Is this really the same boy from Henry Thornton who I had to keep cajoling out of the back row to make him believe in his own performance?

Seeing Jeff and Garry again is also a reminder that my personal relationship with Dougie needs attention; he needs my support too. I've made the mistake before of becoming too involved and totally absorbed in my world of teaching, resulting in a divorce; it's a salutary reminder. Dougie's an exceptionally good amateur golfer and his present goal is to make the England Senior Amateur team. I know very little about golf, and sports psychologist is certainly a more apt title when I caddy for him in his major competitions. Dougie's about to compete in the English Senior Golf Championship and this year the competition is being held in Saunton in Devon. It'll entail me going away with him for a few days.

We're currently successfully teaching our Joggy Bear programmes for the early learning years in several primary schools and Julie, my reliable, able assistant is team-teaching with myself and Jaz, our apprentice. The children really enjoy exercising with Jaz, and he's exceptionally gifted at teaching children with special needs. I decide, and they readily agree, that I should go and support Dougie. I leave the two of them with the lesson plans sorted for each of the schools, the travel arrangements for when, where and what time the two of them will meet as I won't be around to give them a lift. I confidently leave them with everything meticulously planned. It's all very straightforward, I can't imagine anything going wrong. My imagination doesn't stretch far enough.

After a very good early morning first round, we're sitting in the clubhouse when I see a series of text messages on my phone from Julie asking me if I can please phone her when I get a moment. Something can't be right as Julie wouldn't be apologising for persistently texting me. I text her back and her response is to call as soon as I can. I leave the clubhouse, timing the call so it's in the school's lunch hour.

'Is everything alright Julie? I couldn't answer you straight away because we were on the golf course.'

Julie politely asks how Dougie is doing, but I speed her on so I can answer what might be a question to do with a school's timetable or has something happened to a child and she needs advice?

'I'm so sorry, I didn't want to call you, but it's Jaz. I waited for him as planned at the railway station, but he didn't turn up. I was just about to give up and go on to the school otherwise I'd be late when I get a call from him from the police station. He was arrested last night, kept in a cell and they won't release him.'

Why do these things happen when I'm not there?

'He insisted and argued with the police that the one call he was allowed to make had to be to me, he knew I'd be waiting,' said Julie.

Given the dire circumstances, it was responsible of Jaz to ensure that Julie wasn't left waiting for him at the station and could get to the school on time. Whatever he's been arrested for, he wasn't telling Julie. I know how embarrassed and fraught he will be, and although I have no further details, I decide to keep in constant touch with Julie for any further news, sort it all out when I get home, stay put and caddy for Dougie. I put this calamitous incident to the back of my mind, caddy for Dougie for the next two days followed by a nerve-wracking play-off. He wins the title and makes the England team.

• • •

We have to expect setbacks with these lads; it's too easy to forget how far they all come while on the course. When Jaz arrived at 'Body Rocks', he'd come with a dreadful reputation. He was on the cusp of permanent exclusion due to his disruptive and aggressive anti-social behaviour, with much of it directed towards the staff. His head of special educational needs at the comprehensive school did everything in her power to avoid sending him to a special school. Jaz loves sport, particularly football, and it was with this in mind she felt we had a good chance of turning around his challenging behaviour with the 'Body Rocks' physical activities and behaviour programme.

Except when he starts attending, Jaz's behaviour doesn't need much turning around. He soon realises he can't get away with things if he wants to stay on the course, respect is quickly gained, and respect on both sides, mainly due to his love of exercise. He can't outdo me with several of the strength exercises, which irks him, in the nicest possible way. He loves the challenge of competing against me, particularly with free weights. He's mystified as to how I can compete with his muscular strength, but then I never let on I know exactly which exercises I can impress with and how best to execute them in order to win the challenge.

Like all these lads, top of the body comes first and is about honing the torso, shaping the deltoids, bulking the biceps, building up the lats and traps, not forgetting the all-important brick-hard six pack. As for the legs, I've never been quite sure of the psychology. Is it that the quads and other leg muscles are only seen in the summer in their shorts and they take second place to working the torso? Or is it that squaring up, butting each other in the chests before swinging a punch or two, doesn't involve the legs? Either way, it's easy to do squats and pulses with 10kg weights (especially for the adductor muscles with ankle-weights on) and watch Jaz looking out of the corner of his eye to see when he can stop because I have. As for the running, it's the least favourite part of the exercise programme, so he isn't too bothered if he's not able to keep up with the rest of the class running behind me. As a practising apprentice, he likes teaching and being in charge of this part of the programme. He can just stand in the middle of the enormous circle and shout encouraging words while we do all the running, lapping several times around the perimeter of the church. All he has to do is occasionally jog a little, so it looks like he's making the effort to run around with us. He has his own reasons of course for only doing just that. He says God wouldn't want him speeding round the church: it might look very disrespectful. I'm not so sure. I think it's far more to do with the fact that no able-bodied young person can possibly walk as slowly as Jaz, inside or outside of the church. He's never, ever in a hurry to get anywhere and yet somehow, he manages to always arrive on time. It's nothing to do with walking while reading and texting messages, avoiding people who are walking and texting like the rest of these kids do. Maybe it goes back to living as a child in a very hot, sunny country where people are laid back and seemingly nobody's in a rush.

Jaz's mum is a night worker at the local hospital, she's been there for years since coming to England for a better life. Jaz remained in Jamaica with the rest of a very large family until she sent for him to live with her when he was eight and a half. That's why when Jaz first started with 'Body Rocks', it took me straight back to the seventies and my time at Henry Thornton School. I'd had many discussions with lads like Samuel, Rupert and Len about school life for pupils in Jamaica in the sixties and seventies. They said it was the same for all of them: the harshest of disciplines, miserable and unbelievably strict. For Jaz, it meant that not only was he physically punished at school for the slightest misdemeanour in class or for not learning and retaining information, he was also heavily regimented at home. 'It was,' he said, 'an accepted way of life, that's how it was.' But alas, the polarity of the situation was too much for him that when he arrived in England, life for Jaz, he says, became in one word 'Freedom'. No more ruler-thumping from the teacher if you couldn't remember facts from previous lessons and no more getting beaten across the buttocks for daring to talk back to the teacher or show any signs of insolence at home. So, when he arrived at his school here, Jaz decided, to the detriment of all his stressed-out teachers and the pupils trying to learn, to have fun by self-sabotaging and causing absolute havoc in the classroom, which escalated when he went to secondary school. Until 'Body Rocks'. And two years later, after passing his teaching exam and learning to control himself with challenging pupils, as in the case of the glass-throwing pupil from the referral unit, he's become one of our prized apprentices, respected by primary school teachers for his professional approach and his teaching skills.

Will spending a night in the police cell and a subsequent court case keep Jaz out of further trouble?

• • •

Everything to do with the courses and the apprenticeship scheme is progressing well. Three secondary schools in the Reading borough have sent pupils who are struggling to regularly attend their schools and over thirty gain their Level 1 with us. The combined numbers of the school referrals and the Jobcentre Plus referrals swells the number of passes in the Level 2, and currently reaches thirty-two, a great achievement. I've also been able to keep the promise I made to Sean when he left Huntercombe Juvenile Prison, and tell him I've not only started 'Body Rocks' classes, we now have a teaching qualification, too. He starts attending and James comes too, once a week he's travelling all the way from the other side of London so he can continue the training we'd started at the prison. These two seem very different to the current lads we're teaching; prison life's given them a maturity and combining the participants from all these different programmes leads to shared life experiences. The single parents from the Jobcentre make invaluable contributions to the intensive long discussions; they listen and learn together and empathise with each other's very personal issues. The safety and intimacy of the church surroundings, the seating of the sofas in a circle encourages informality and can result in some unexpected, unsolicited subjects evolving from the combining of their challenging background experiences and these different age groups. Sometimes I find it emotionally draining.

At one of the sessions, one of the lone parents who'd passed her teaching qualification and is now one of our adult apprentices, tells the story of her mother's suicide. Slowly, hesitatingly and very quietly, two of the more reticent school participants share their own experiences of attempted suicide. There is a hushed togetherness. And I, too, soon find myself in a position where I'm unexpectedly sharing something deep and very personal.

I've been invited to attend a talk at the Cred Centre. An education psychologist is addressing staff about the difficult issues that might arise when working with permanently excluded school pupils in a referral unit. It's an optional event for alternative provision providers such as ourselves. We sit in a big circle and at the start of her talk, she says she will ask each one of us at the end of the session to answer in one short sentence why we have specifically chosen to work with these children. Panic sets in. This is the one question I've been avoiding; now I have to confront it and do so in front of other teachers. I formulate and practise the answer in my head throughout her talk. The end of the talk approaches. She starts going round the circle. As it's getting closer to my turn, I'm ready. 'After doing my final teacher training in a borstal, I realised I wanted to help children coping with complex problems.' My turn comes. I open my mouth to say these words. Instead, I hear myself saying. 'When I was a child I wished I'd had someone like me to talk to.' So that's what this has all been about. In that one, unplanned sentence, I'd found my answer, the one I'd been avoiding for decades.

Hearing myself articulate these words and recognising my reasons for the work I'm so passionately doing is a huge relief. I didn't mean it to sound in any way self-congratulatory when I gave that answer. I think I'm recognising that if I'd had the sympathetic ear of an adult, someone who would help me understand why I was living in such an atmosphere of fear while growing up, someone who I could share and offload to what was happening, it might have made a difference.

A weight had been taken off me. I could go forward with even more enthusiasm. My dear friend Min placated me, saying, 'You can't change the world, Lizzie.' I know, but at least I can try, and given what's just happened to Jaz, there's one more challenge for 'Body Rocks'.

CHAPTER 16

DANTE

Why don't we offer our fitness teaching qualification to recently released adult ex-offenders? They will have lived similar life experiences to some of our most challenging course pupils and therefore make the ideal mentors, and have some hard-hitting stories that could have a great impact on the behaviour of both our young apprentices and the 'Body Rocks' course referrals. And it will give the ex-offenders a qualification with potential job prospects for the future. It seems an obvious synergy, the perfect preventative measure. Are we being too idealistic?

Things have had to change with Creativity in Sport; our financial circumstances have enforced it. Debbie's completed training as a prison officer and is now working full time at Huntercombe Juvenile Boys' Prison. It's out of necessity; we don't have enough funding to pay for her involvement. All our outgoings are adding up, but Debbie will still meet regularly for planning meetings and keep the accounts. I'm confident that with the help of Julie, my dependable and streetwise assistant, this new initiative can have the same impact and contribute to halting the 'revolving door of crime'. We must give it a try and apply for funding to trial this initiative. And once again, it's the Berkshire Community Foundation who put their faith in us. They award us a small grant to put this concept into practice. Lady Stevenson, a trustee, has scrutinised our accounts. 'What you and Debbie are doing really is a labour of love.'

We set about notifying the relevant probation services, but will there be any takers? The London Probation Service immediately respond with a list of clients who fit our requirements. There are five names on the list. It's a start, but we aren't overly optimistic because nearly all of them live on the other side of London. Travelling to Reading and Slough will necessitate a level of commitment that realistically we can't envisage any of them sustaining. One returned form stands out from the rest. He's written his reasons for volunteering. 'I want to start a career in helping challenging and socially excluded groups of young people, who like me need a second chance in life.' This lad's also had previous experience working in youth clubs for the Prince's Trust and been interviewed on camera by the actor Idris Elba. Could this twenty-three-year old lad called Dante prove to be an ideal candidate?

He's the first to arrive at our Slough base and doesn't fail to make an immediate impression. He looks quite terrifying in size. His massive wide shoulders, expansive chest, muscular torso and bulging biceps would pack a powerful punch as a sparring partner for Lennox Lewis or Anthony Joshua. He has a round, boyish, fresh-looking face that's dotted with freckles, his beaming smile accompanied by an infectious chuckle and laughing eyes. His dark brown hair is neatly cropped. He isn't overly tall. He tilts his head upwards while speaking, his chin jutting forward, so his stance appears even more threatening and commanding. His whole aura appears to be one of power and aggression. It says, 'I'm in charge, don't mess with me'. But you've learnt, Lizzie:

Don't judge a book by its cover – and this cover is big.

Several years ago, Dante started up the notorious and infamous Tottenham Hotspur youth football gang. He's already served two years in HMP Wormwood Scrubs for inciting violence and fighting another football gang in a pre-arranged battle before the kick-off at the stadium. They'd caused havoc on the streets of Brighton. It's just one of the many ferocious battles Dante's fixed with rival Premier League football club gang leaders. He's the 'Mr Fixer' for the Spurs youth football gang. Dante gives me a book he's been writing and I get a real insight into his childhood background, his searing account of football violence and his thoughts about prison sentencing. He gives an honest appraisal of his involvement and an almost clinical account of the effects of the violence on those around him. Now I realise why he's so smart and immaculately dressed and takes such pride in his appearance. I learn that a badge of affiliation among the football supporters is the designer clothes they wear on the terraces. It's upmarket wear, it defines them. It's not the image I have in my head of a dressed football hooligan. Here's an extract, written in 'football speak' for his thousands of admirers.

I'm a member of Tottenham's Firm the Yids and I've been rowing at football since I was fourteen years old. I was brought up on the Suttons estate in Ladbroke Grove, West London. The manor I grew up on was a staunch QPR stronghold but had the old mouthy Chelsea mackerel and I think that is where my hatred of them began. Living in a manor like Ladbroke Grove I was exposed to gangs, drugs and violence from a young age on the local estates. By the time I was thirteen years old I was a criminal and learning the craft of the street very fast.

At around the same time my uncle T was taking me to Spurs every other week, he was an ex-Tottenham hooligan from the eighties and we would go to the pubs the thugs would use. They would all be dressed in smart clothes like Armani, Paul and Shark, Stone Island, Aquascutum, CP Company and Ralph. I used to think they look the absolute nuts and one day I wanted to dress like that and get involved at football. They used to talk about rows they had and it use to get me excited. The week after Tottenham had run Chelsea's mob at Edgware Road/ Marble Arch the olders were talking about the exploits of the turnout and it sent tingles threw my spine. I wanted in. The first taste I got of football violence was by the Park

Lane away end and it kicked off one year between Spurs and the Gooners. I was young and stuck in-between it and if I'm honest I was very afraid of the old bill.

In fact, giving prison terms out at football only deepens the level of criminality that a football bod is involved in. A lot of football bods are hard-working men with legitimate jobs, by sending them to prison for a few years for just simply throwing a few punches then puts them out of employment, hinders their ability to regain employment massively and draws them into a deeper world of crime. In reality it is just a few punches with likeminded people being traded! Why not give them help? Why not make the lads give back to the community on the weekends? Why not actually deliver real help to stop these addictions?

These are all arguments put forward in the last chapter and something as lads we should all feel passionately about whether retired or not because we are all the same at the end of the day, we are a subculture and a targeted one at that. If you are a professional or just a regular member of society reading and have thought wow this world is violent. Then I ask you to look at the bigger picture and remember it's a punch up between likeminded people. We are not attacking some random man with his boy like street gangs do, or picking on the weak like gangs and rapists do or running communities with drugs. Do you really think the treatment we receive is fair? Some lads get involved for a few years in their teens and end up with football-banning orders well into their twenties. Is that fair?

We have several discussions about the book and whether it should be published. I'm concerned the glorification and excitement of the football violence that's coming across and his thrill and lust for fighting could be detrimental to his future. Debbie and I feel the same about a TV production company who've approached him to feature in a documentary about football gang leaders. They want Dante to play a prominent part, one of three gang leaders the hour will centre around; it's scheduled to be aired on the BBC. We're getting to know what a thoughtful, caring young man he is: reliable, punctual and with the makings of a very good teacher. What will the advantages be if he takes part? Will the programme give a responsible insight into the minds of the protagonists? Will he be portrayed as the person we've come to know, or be the football hooligan that will forever define him? I'm too aware from my own television experiences how edited footage can completely skew the content and shape a viewer's perception. But Dante's choice is to go ahead.

It's not surprising Dante has several years of banning orders to adhere to from the Football Banning Orders Authority. He shows me the orders and the constraints imposed upon him when Tottenham or England are playing. For Dante, a passionate Spurs supporter whose allegiance to the club and the players is second to none, well, that is apart from the Clapham school lad I was teaching in the seventies who was adamant his name was his goal-scoring Spurs hero. For Dante, it's a prison sentence in itself not to see his beloved football team in action. Football is his religion, his escape, his whole being is living and breathing Tottenham Hotspur.

As an ardent football fan myself, I'm inquisitive about these football gangs and their violence, I wasn't aware the gang violence of the sixties and seventies was still continuing. I learn how these rival football gang leaders travel and meet way ahead of their scheduled matches and collude with each other to set up fights against each other's 'firm'. I've always had enormous sympathy for the police having to control the levels of violence in order to protect the public and to try to pre-empt where these ferocious battles might take place. I thought the carnage, the vicious clashes in town centres, the vandalising of supporters' trains was a thing of the past. Now these clashes are secretly arranged so they don't have to worry about the old bill and they can all satisfy their lust for violence and metaphorically shake hands afterwards. And now we're hearing in 2022 it's back on the terraces with not just alcohol fuelling the violence, but also cocaine. Dante chooses his words carefully, sparing me the gory, brutal details. Phrases like 'a lot of claret on the floor' and 'the mobs, we stamp on their heads' are not part of my own vocabulary. And I find it hard to digest and really question his assertion that not all the members of these gangs are 'thugs' and Neets (not in education, employment or training). He assures me, noting my incredulity, some really are from 'respected' professions, including teachers and businessmen. It, too, is their Saturday fix.

There is far more to Dante than his Saturday fix. Studying and passing his Level 2 is his goal with us and something he's clearly going to master very quickly. Some of the theory to do with the skeletal frame, the understanding of how muscles work (and how to pack a good punch) he's already acquired while training in the gym at Wormwood Scrubs. The leadership skills and qualities that make an outstanding teacher he has in abundance. He's a natural communicator with the intelligence to go with it, little wonder he was so good at organising his Tottenham firm.

I learn some really interesting and useful methods that psychologists and prison staff use for rehabilitating offenders. They'd clearly recognised his effective leadership skills and used them to their advantage. They'd trained him in the techniques of delivering these methods and programmes to his fellow prisoners. Now I've become the beneficiary of his prison sentence.

We sit round the table after our pupil referrals have gone home and work out how to adapt these concepts for our own 'Body Rocks' courses. I have an overflowing folder full of our combined ideas, all creative, all really useful, but too many to mention here. One of them is called 'Locked In'. We've printed a huge, enlarged picture of handcuffs on a piece of A4 paper for each pupil. In the left link circle, we ask participants to write their worst actions (crimes if appropriate) and how they felt about them when they did them. And in the right handcuff circle, express in words how they feel about them now. One of the 'Body Rocks' course pupils has written in the left handcuff: *Drug dealing, fraud, fighting, swearing, stealing* and in the right handcuff *making money, feeling happy, angry, big, fun,* then underneath, a single word *stupid.*

Another lad's written in the left handcuff: *hit a member of staff in the leg and then got put in handcuffs and leg straps, not arrested sorted.* In the right: *didn't care at all* and underneath, *don't care about it still.* He'd also drawn a gun.

We follow up these examples with Dante expertly leading an informative discussion, basing it around their written answers. They listen to his knowledge and experience as he reads through each of their personal responses, knowing and accepting they are but little fish in his big pond. He's lived some of their illustrative experiences and paid the price for it in prison. He forcefully points out that he never ever expected he would end up in jail.

Dante is making a huge impression and so are the four committed ex-offenders that have joined the programme. We've had several more recently released additions, most have fallen by the wayside and a couple want to continue, but cannot afford to stay and live with our basic apprenticeship wage. Is our thinking and concept going to be proved right? Can Dante and the other four ex-offenders help change the mindset of these kids? Are we putting too much faith in them? And have these adult ex-offenders, including Dante, completely turned their own lives around?

In Slough, we're running a weekly half-day course for fifteen pupils from an autistic unit that's attached to a very large, local mixed comprehensive school. Dante's adept in supervising our other volunteer ex-offenders in working with these young people. It's such a success with the school, we're asked by the Berkshire Community Foundation to hold a session for an invited audience interested in the rehabilitation of ex-offenders. Debbie and I are delighted, we're keen to demonstrate just how successful this ex-offenders programme is in both Reading and Slough, and send out invitations to as many esteemed people as we can.

The list of acceptances is impressive. Fiona Mactaggart, MP for Slough, the chief inspector for Thames Valley Police, the police responsible for the area and the police and crime commissioner for the whole of the Thames Valley Police. They've all accepted. Debbie changes her shift at the prison to ensure she too can participate.

The demonstration with the fifteen enthusiastic pupils from the autistic unit is meticulously planned and lasts an hour. The teaching of the four corners is shared among four of the most competent ex-offenders. When it's Jaz's turn, our young apprentice from Reading, he expertly teaches his choreographed dance routine, and our esteemed invited guests, without any persuasion, are out of their seats. They enter into it in the back row with great enthusiasm and humour, their smart polished uniforms complimenting the regimented dance steps. What a fabulous contrast for these ex-offenders whose sole experience of the police is one of arrest. Here they are with a Member of Parliament and VIP police all having a fun time dancing alongside the infectious enthusiasm of the pupils from the specialist unit.

While they sit and recover, we listen intently to Dante delivering a masterclass in motivating the pupils to make the most of their time at school, not to worry if they aren't any good at academia, but to grasp all the opportunities their school has to offer. It's a mature display of Dante's own lessons learnt in life. The demonstration spurs us on, the adult ex-offenders are making an impact on the lives of the next generation. Debbie and I still keep a look out for any other grants advertised. As fortune has it, the next opportunity comes directly to us via our links with the courses we're running for Reading Jobcentre Plus.

The Conservative government are about to introduce their 'Troubled Families' initiative. The aim is to bring together all the different agencies working with members of the same family and their numerous, challenging social issues. West Berkshire invites us to apply to run one of our fitness and behaviour-management courses. It's a trialled scheme and we're keen to be involved. It will entail a twenty-mile journey and we can only afford to have one other working alongside me for the length of the initiative. The obvious assistant is Dante and although it will necessitate him travelling quite a distance, he's keen to work on this new project. He's currently living at the other end of the Buckinghamshire county. It'll require three trains, but the length of the journey time isn't going to deter him, he's still appreciating his freedom.

I think it's the third time I'm walking through the ticket barrier at Reading station that I become aware of station staff 'clocking' me. I'm used to people staring at me thinking they recognise my face or smiling in acknowledgement at 'Mad Lizzie from the telly', but this feels different. There's a sense of urgency as they look at me and speak knowingly to each other or into their walkie talkies. I think I'm being followed by the transport police. And they're following, watching from a discreet distance when I greet Dante on the platform. And then it dawns on me. No wonder they're concerned. We've been assigned to run our weekly project at Thatcham Town Football Club; they've given it to us as a base for this new project. Oh the irony given Dante's background and his years of football-banning orders. They must wonder what he's trying to fix with supporters from this lowly non-league football club. Dante, of course, is easy to spot, he stands out from the crowd with his overpowering size. When he travels on public transport, he wears his tight-fitting extra-large white T-shirt, the words Creativity in Sport and 'Body Rocks' emblazoned across his ever-expanding ripped torso. With short sleeves defining his bulging biceps, it would be easy to pick him out, even at the height of the rush hour. Proud though we are of everything he's achieving, what if he's recognised by a rival group of football supporters? He quietly obliges when I explain the predicament and duly travels on public transport in a plain T-shirt.

We put this base in Thatcham to good use and include football practice on the big field behind the clubhouse. It's a great way for the kids to let off steam in the lunch break. Some of them come alone and are dropped off by car by their worker; occasionally a family member participates. One stocky little secondary school lad has a plethora of complex problems. His attendance is intermittent at our weekly sessions and when he does arrive, it's like a tornado raging into the bar room in the clubhouse where we hold our sessions. One afternoon he arrives early. I sit alone with him, his eyes untrusting as he shifts around on the bench next to me, keeping his distance. I'm aware of his background and understand his pain and rage. I judge the moment, it's one of the few occasions I decide to talk about myself. His circumstances resonate with me, so I tell him that I too find it difficult if someone sits too close to me and why. He stares at me intently, his eyes soften: he identifies with my story, he shares his. A bond is forged and from now on, when he attends the meetings, he sits next to me. But it's hard, it's difficult because I know this is a short course and I won't be able to continue giving him the same unspoken understanding, the extra support he so desperately needs from an adult. The distance is too great, our team too small and he will need constant supervision.

Dante is fast becoming another dependable, trusted, savvy assistant, another adult like Julie with whom I can share the load. Each time we go to interviews for grants and presentations to Corporate Social Responsibility Teams, I'll remind him, 'Dante, when I forget to say something really pivotal to the conversation, just butt in or introduce it.' He is adept at handling these occasions and remembers to ask the pertinent questions. He' s confident in his own skin and the courtesy he shows me is a reflection of his relationship with his mum. We arrange to visit her with a view to teaching 'Body Rocks' at the Ladbroke

Road Youth Centre where she's working. Dante and I walk down Kensal Rise in the hot summer sunshine. It feels like I'm accompanying a boxing champion. Lads are stopping to shake him by the hand and briefly chat, while others drive past honking their car horns, their passengers hanging out of the windows calling out, 'Hey Dante, you alright mate?' They seem desperate to acknowledge him, so he will acknowledge them back.

'You know how easy it is to get a gun round here?'

'No Dante I don't.'

I don't think his intention is to shock me, it's his way of saying this is the territory I grew up in. I decide to leave this territory to his mum.

Creativity in Sport is moving forward fast. We're now teaching in several primary schools and able to focus on this age group, the ages that we know will benefit the most from our 'Learning on the Move' and socialisation programmes. We should be working with these children with our alternative learning programmes when they are young, impressionable and at the start of their school journey. But Dante's preference is to work with a much older age group. He's now a proud dad in need of full-time employment; unfortunately, it's not something we can offer, we just don't have the financial resources for full-time employment for any of our ex-offenders. But it's typical of Dante that he delays leaving us so he can support us when HRH the Countess of Wessex pays a visit to our wonderful Slough base. It's been organised by the Berkshire Community Foundation to enable us once again to showcase Creativity in Sport and this time with the added draw of royalty.

Dante enters into the spirit of this hugely important occasion for us as he exercises with Joggy Bear, our six-foot children's character, and team-leads a fun exercise session with an invited class of nursery children and five-year-olds from local schools. This is followed by a 'Guess the Sport' section for the now seated little ones who are invited to watch a mimed sport by each of the four participating ex-offenders. The invited audience and HRH cannot contain themselves at what they are seeing when Dante mimes his, and stifle their giggles and rapidly applaud with delight. With his enormous torso squeezed into his white 'Body Rocks' T-shirt that's neatly tucked into his black shorts, he performs slow arabesques gliding around the room, his heavily bulging biceps and tattooed arms elegantly outstretched. He then slowly, very slowly pirouettes round and round on tiptoes with his arms classically rounded over his head. It's a sight to behold – and of course the little ones quickly guess he's an ice skater.

Later that month, we have a long-standing date in the diary for a meeting with Fiona Mactaggart, the local Slough MP. We were initially introduced to Fiona when Creativity in Sport was offered a massive area of empty office space, rent free, in the Bath Road on the Slough Business Park Estate. Fiona was also present at the presentation we did for HRH the Countess of Wessex and at the demonstration for the police. She'd spent some time at the end of that morning quizzing the lads about the importance of the work we were doing with them. She's particularly interested as she's recently put forward a proposal to the Professional Football Association that training offenders in prison to become football referees for grass-roots football would be a very constructive and worthwhile qualification for them to pursue. It's an exciting proposal because she's looking to link up with our organisation and to use 'Body Rocks' as an extra qualification. Debbie and I are enthusiastic, perhaps our lads can help deliver the whole scheme, it might encourage Dante to stay with us and we can confidently suggest he can help organise the whole project. A meeting is arranged. I ask Dante to come with me, it's another ironic situation when you consider his lengthy football ban. I wonder if she knows about it?

Dante is quiet when we meet, he isn't in his usual PR mode and neither is he showing much enthusiasm for her proposals in the meeting, in fact he's a little on edge throughout. I feel a bit aggrieved; I want others to see him in the light he deserves, or I think he deserves. There's something wrong, so I'm pleased when the meeting finishes; he suggests we go to the station café for a chat before he catches the train home. He's clearly nervous and looking utterly miserable as he stares into his teacup. Is he about to tell me he's seriously ill? When he does clear his throat to speak, it absolutely takes my breath away. He explains that two days earlier, having consumed several beers in a pub with his prospective father-in-law, it was suggested they go with their mates to Wembley Football Stadium so they can 'soak up the atmosphere outside' as they don't have any tickets to this all-important Champions League Final with Tottenham Hotspur.

Soak up the atmosphere!! Whatever was this man thinking? He knows Dante's background; he knows his banning orders.

It doesn't take much working out that the police are going to recognise this big, excitable, inebriated hulk, whose mugshot they're all too familiar with. I try and keep calm as he tells me they only got as far as within striking distance of the stadium. What doing? Verbally abusing the long-suffering police and being arrested. Arrested for what exactly? Dante tells me he was trying to pacify the situation; their group had got into a bit of an argument with some football supporters (obviously not Spurs) and he'd 'thrown a protective punch'. My television persona, Mad Lizzie, is beginning to take on a new meaning.

There is no point in me admonishing him, I don't need to, he knows exactly what he's done, he's put his whole future in jeopardy and he can't turn back the clock. No wonder he'd been monosyllabic in the meeting, he must have been sitting there searching for the words to tell me about this disaster. He's badly let himself down and he knows he's let us down too. At least he's turned up for the meeting, probably feeling acutely ashamed and knowing he's inevitably about to face another prison sentence. What a waste of his second chance. We depart with me trying to sound optimistic. I tell him I will see what I can do, while inwardly seething at his father-in-law.

I write a report for the court, but Dante has sealed his own fate; he's broken his banning order and back he goes to Wormwood Scrubs – minus his 'Body Rocks' T-shirt. His loss, our loss, but more importantly, what about the kids and the families from Thatcham, the excluded kids from the schools and referral units in Reading and Slough who absolutely revere him?

It's their loss too. And when they ask where he is, do I tell them the truth, that he's gone back inside?

Dante struggles with his second sentence, another six months in Wormwood Scrubs. His letter to us says as much.

'I'm still in Scrubs, they tried to ship me out to Highpoint (prison) but as I went down with my bags the move was cancelled. I'm on a high-risk wing in a single cell, that is the only plus side. Gym is a rare thing and you get about thirty minutes out of the cell, so it's twenty-three and a half hours banged up. The wing is full of people who should be in Broadmoor mental institution in all.

Even though this sentence is small, it's been ten times harder than my previous jail time mentally. I think this is down to the lock up of gym. The first month my head was a bit all over the place with stuff at home but through December I've been training like mad to get in shape. Every so often the screws come and take my water bottles off me (I use these for weights). That gets me angry but I've kept my cool.

Glad to hear everything is going well at 'Body Rocks', I look forward to coming back, although I'll need my fitness to get back up a bit my abs will be ok will be as strong as ever. Tell everyone I said hello and keep up the good work.'

When Dante comes out of prison, he seems changed and very positive. He's clearly been reflecting upon his situation and the responsibility he is feeling towards his girlfriend and his daughter. He's had enough of doing time; prison has worked for him this time round.

'I can handle it,' he says, 'but being away from family is a prison sentence in itself.'

We're really pleased to see him and ready to resume working with him, but I sense there's no going back now we're fully committed to working in primary schools. He leaves knowing our door will always be open. We have much to thank Dante for. Throughout the three years he was with us, there are many young people whose lives he influenced, young people on the cusp of a revolving life of crime, teenagers and youngsters coming from a world of chaos. They saw in this huge, masculine frame of Dante that it's alright to show you can be caring and sensitive, to share previously unspoken feelings. They've listened, and hopefully, if they too learn from his mistakes, then this challenge will have been worthwhile.

CHAPTER 17

TIME FOR CHANGE

I open the door and enter the back of a Year 2 classroom. It's a cacophony of children roaming around while the teacher's attention is with a pupil at the front. A seven-year-old boy is standing at a desk by the door. He scowls as he angrily flicks through the pages of a book. He glances up at me as I pause and walk past.

'You're old,' he shouts with a defiant look.

'I'm not old,' I immediately retort.

A triumphant expression spreads across his face.

'I'm not old,' I repeat, 'I'm *very* old,' as I continue walking to the front of the class.

He quickly bows his head and quietly carries on with his book. Is this another Samuel Brown from the Clapham school situation? He's not violently kicking down theatre doors, but is this a child who feels he's been wronged by an adult and in return, is trying to undermine a new teacher by being rude?

For the last six years, I've been teaching in numerous infants and primary schools; I'm on a quest to understand why so many children begin their secondary school education without the necessary literacy skills. *How can it be acceptable for so many children to go through primary school unable to read?* It stems from my baffling experience in 1970 when I first started teaching English in a comprehensive school to pupils like Rupert and Martin, and I'm finding decades later, I'm still asking the same question. Debbie and I have learnt that if we're trying to be a voice for change in this whole learning process for disadvantaged pupils, we have to start at the very beginning of their educational journey. If we're to enrich the lives of the many socially disaffected and disadvantaged young people who live in areas of deprivation, if we're to socially mobilise them with the power of learning and knowledge, we've been focusing our energies at the wrong end of the spectrum.

We've witnessed that poor school performance and chaotic behaviour can result in a huge percentage of illiterate young people being detained in prison, often locked in a revolving door of crime. Can this cycle of illiteracy be broken? I haven't taught one young person attending our Creativity in Sport programmes who hasn't regretted wasting their time at school. Every single one of them, whether they be an excluded secondary school pupil, in a pupil referral unit or a juvenile prison, an ex-offender, a young adult not in education, employment or training, all of them would value and appreciate a second opportunity with their education.

The hours, the months, the years of teaching in Reading and Slough have not been lost. The effectiveness of learning academically and maturing with physical programmes of expression, the behaviour management programmes, the 'Body Rocks' courses encompassing socio-drama, the achievements, they have all been recognised. And there must be many more untapped methods and alternative creative learning programmes that can be devised and explored to embrace the thousands of children who need additional support. Children who need greater nurturing and encouragement at the start of their school journey, children who too quickly become disengaged and lacking in confidence in their learning ability, children who would benefit from programmes that are an alternative to ordinary learning methods. Some of the children arrive on their first day with a huge range of lived experiences that are incomprehensibly inhuman. It's little wonder their behaviour patterns become chaotic. Our purpose for the last six years has been to try and develop a more holistic and alternative approach to learning for these children, using a set of physical skills to learn how to read, count and multiply in the classroom.

Had I not been 'Mad Lizzie', I might never have been offered so many invaluable opportunities to try and contribute to creating new concepts. I've met several teachers and headteachers who have fond memories of growing up with me on TV-am and exercising with Joggy Bear. A successful two-year evaluation by educational and neuro-educational psychologists was completed in 2019 with the Joggy Bear Learning Programmes, by Oxford Brookes University. And just when evidence was also needed for the success of the 'Learning on the Move Multiplication Programme' that would be provided by the compulsory multiplication electronic time-testing for Year 6, Covid struck. In spring 2020 my teaching in primary schools came to an abrupt end.

When I look back on the decades of teaching pupils and young adults, I realise how much I've learnt and how my understanding and abilities and failures grew from each of the many sectors I had the opportunity to teach in. In the seventies, so many of the pupils at the Clapham school increased their life chances with dance, socio-drama and exercise giving them the much needed tools to express themselves, to cope with their lived experiences. And it's even more imperative in today's uncertain times that young people also have these opportunities. The arts and sport are undoubtedly essential to a child's personal development.

'You're so good doing all the wonderful work with the boys in the comprehensive school, with excluded school pupils and ex-offenders,' people say, but I absolutely loved it. It's a cliché to say it's so rewarding, but it really is. I was in the privileged position of being able to create opportunities that I myself had the good fortune to experience when I was young. Had I not been there to offer the boys similar opportunities, they might never have scaled the great heights and reached their monumental achievements. I was able to put the good things, the positives that had happened to me in my childhood, to the benefit of these youngsters. The excitement of seeing pupils achieve from my teaching is immeasurable. It ranges from children like Rupert, Rick, Jaz and an ex-gang leader learning at a late age how to read, to helping boys like Samuel turn their lives around having survived a traumatic period, and training others to dance and act. And the shared experience of teaching a host of adults in my fitness classes, who then willingly gave up their time to become pupils for training apprentices in prison and pupil referral units.

But I know it's much more than that. Once I'd heard myself articulate my reasons for teaching and recognising my need to do it, I took the opportunity to discuss it with Ma. We had a long discussion about my father. I'd instinctively known as a young child that realistically there was nothing Ma could do about his frightening coercive behaviour; you don't forget that feeling of fear being pulled out of her protective arms from the earliest of ages to be taken upstairs and uncontrollably thrashed. She'd explained several times to me that as a family we'd have been split up and put in homes. She was powerless, and I, through my endless days of uncontrollable crying throughout my teenage years, knew I was utterly powerless too. So I thanked her for all the amazing opportunities she'd given me. It had enabled me to express myself away from the rigid conformity and fear imposed upon me, it had given me the much needed outlet to survive; and given me the tools and the power to help try and better other young people's life experiences. I also told her that had my father not treated me the way he did, I might never have been so inextricably driven and intent on trying to be available for vulnerable young people in need of a voice and a listening ear. And neither would I have experienced the pure joy and the personal satisfaction derived from guiding and developing others to fulfil their potential, to pass on to the next generation all the skills that I myself had the good fortune to learn. Ma and I agreed, we both understood.

I have the most wonderful extended family thanks to all my teaching experiences. I'm hugely grateful to all the boys who have been on that journey with me, and to those who have allowed me to share their stories. There have, sadly, been failures, but great successes too.

The Clapham Boys

Jeff rose through the ranks of television dancer, choreographer and producer at the BBC to become an award-winning producer and head of music programming at London Weekend Television. His shows included a series of *An Audience With* starring the Bee Gees, Diana Ross and Ricky Martin. He became an executive producer for the *Royal Variety Performance*.

At the end of the show in 2003, Her Majesty the Queen went backstage to thank all the performing artistes and was filmed being introduced to the line-up of stars. I was sitting at home and did a double take. Who was I looking at speaking and introducing the stars to Her Majesty in his role as executive producer? Jeff. He was going down the line, introducing the Queen to each one of the stars. This was Her Majesty playing Ma's role, except all these artistes were bowing. Jeff used to line up the boys before curtain-up at our Clapham plays and introduce each one to Ma, not that I ever asked him to. Ma was tickled pink when she heard she'd been the Queen's understudy.

I had another opportunity to work with Jeff while he was executive producer at London Weekend Television. It was for a show called *Eighties Mania* fronted by Anita Dobson and Leslie Grantham, two of the lead actors from the original cast of *Eastenders*. Jeff, in his role as producer, invited me to be part of the programme and sat me in the audience to be interviewed by Leslie, who chatted to me on camera about my ten years as 'Mad Lizzie' on TV-am. This time it was a straightforward invitation from Jeff and not a Noel Edmonds Gotcha Oscar.

Since 2005, Jeff has been working in Los Angeles as executive producer with Nigel Lythgoe for Fox television. They're currently on the seventeenth season of the hugely successful USA television series *So You Think You Can Dance*. Jeff also travels the world overseeing the production of the show's format in other countries.

He's renowned for nurturing the talent and well-being of each and every one of the show's dancers. It's not something he's acquired; his caring side was always evident when helping me teach at the boys' comprehensive school.

'When dancers ask me how and where I trained, you just can't explain it.'

Garry went on to dance in numerous television shows (and often with Jeff) including *The Two Ronnies*, *Little and Large* and *The Stanley Baxter Show*. He performed in eight musicals and I had the pleasure of sitting in the audience during these West End shows that included *Chicago*, *West Side Story*, *Saturday Night*

Fever, Starlight Express and *They're Playing Our Song*. He's been assistant director and resident director for Arlene Phillips, a West End Theatre and Resident Director for numerous productions both here and abroad, choreographed commercials and is a guest dance teacher in some of the schools I taught in – Italia Conti, Sylvia Young, the London Studio Centre – as well as teaching in many others. What a list. He's also a personal trainer and fitness instructor.

'As a fifth former I watched one of the drama club productions and realised that dancing and acting is what I wanted to do. Having joined the club and your dance classes, I learnt so much about myself and performing. It's given me a career I never thought possible. I used to hide in the back row in our dance classes and you always brought me to the front. The confidence you gave me back then, I try to instil in the performers in my auditions and the pupils I'm teaching. People don't believe I learnt to dance in a boys' comprehensive school.'

It was far simpler for Garry to write on his CV that he trained at Italia Conti.

Patrick: After our dance group Spider came to an end, Patrick successfully auditioned and trained at the Rambert Ballet School. He then joined the Royal Swedish Ballet and went on to become the first black dancer to join the English National Ballet Company.

When he became a soloist, Jeff, Garry, Andy and I sat in the audience watching and applauding Patrick. What an achievement! Like Jeff and Garry, he went on to become a choreographer. The company commissioned him to create several ballets for them. Since retiring as a dancer, Patrick has been teaching at the Royal Opera House Covent Garden on the 'Chance to Dance' scheme for underprivileged children. He also teaches at the Royal Academy of Dance. Patrick, like me, has 'gone full circle'.

'I was back in Clapham recently and stood staring at the old school building. It all seemed so unreal. How has this happened, how did I end up where I am?'

Rupert owned his own garage and, after decades of hard work, sold it and considered retiring. He's invested in property and financially doesn't need to work, but he chooses to do so as he wants to continue educating himself. He enjoys helping people and works at a busy mainline London station, supporting families and travellers with their problems. When he reflects back upon his school days, he's critical of the system.

'My parents were always arguing, my father violent towards my mother. We didn't talk, we didn't have books in my house so I was never read to. And at school the teachers just read to us to keep us quiet – we didn't work. The secondary school was violent, teachers couldn't keep control, it was common to have fighting in class. The drama club saved me, it made going to school worthwhile, it gave me a purpose and I learnt how to read. How did you manage to keep control so we always did whatever you asked us to do?'

Floyd: After performing every week on *Top of the Pops*, Floyd became one of the original dancers in Arlene Phillips' 'Hot Gossip' group, featuring in the hugely popular television BBC entertainment series *The Kenny Everett Show*. The last we heard, he was auditioning and choreographing fashion shows and television commercials.

Terry: When I was doing a live radio chat show in the early nineties, callers were invited to phone in with questions. Terry called to let me know that since Andy and I had last seen him in prison, he was now a Seventh-Day Adventist priest helping others.

Martin: In 1995, Dougie and I went to the FA Cup final at Wembley Stadium, between Liverpool and Manchester United. At the end of the match, we joined the massive throng of supporters trying to make their way out of the stadium. A voice could be heard shouting above the rowdy crowd, 'Miss Beveridge, Miss Beveridge!' It was Martin Chivers, or rather Martin Jones, who cheerfully introduced me to his two grown-up sons. I was puzzled, though, Tottenham Hotspur weren't playing. He was there because his sons support Manchester United.

The TV-am *Boys*

Take That disbanded in 1996 and their popularity waned. There was a documentary about them in 2005 that was to become the forerunner of them getting back together the following year. In it was a clip of them singing and dancing as they covered themselves in grease, and – we are told by the mocking voice-over – earning their living performing in schools and gay clubs. It was cynical and not complimentary. It was immediately followed by a clip of the boys dancing with me. Of course it wasn't representative of what we actually did, it only showed us at the very beginning shaking out our arms and legs. Every generation has their decade of TV shows and documentaries that gets sent up and so often watching and looking back on the programmes, you can see why it can all look very dated. Fair play to these particular programme makers. If they thought we deserved to be sent up, maybe some viewers were thinking it too, but I don't think Nicki Chapman from RCA Records would have been too worried about that at the time.

P.S. *Judy Boucher*: 'Can't Be With You Tonight', her beautiful, memorable song that made such an impact in the early and late 'Shake Out' morning slots in 1989, has a video of the song on YouTube in 2011. It's already accrued over twenty million views, and another, posted in 2014, has over fourteen million views, with many recent comments that suggest it will continue to reach an enormous worldwide audience.

The Later Boys

Rick is twenty-one, now taller than me, just as slim, his hair longer and with a neat quiff. He's still finding his way.

'I don't think I've achieved anything in life, I feel like I'm slipping down my Dad's path. What have I got to lose if I go to prison? Apart from my Mum, I've got nothing. Things haven't got better, they've got worse, I feel like my whole body's shut down, I don't feel, I'm just numb. There's too much anger in me. I'm twenty-one, but I still don't know how to react when people praise me. I feel like I'm in a washing machine going round and round and it won't stop, I want someone to press the button. Looking on the outside now sitting here, it feels like I've been put in the middle of a family I'm not part of. I can see it, like I'm standing looking in, but I can't move on.'

That was two years ago. These days he has something that has changed his whole outlook. He's found a purpose, a reason to get up in the mornings, to go to work. Rick's created his own family and is the proud father of a little boy.

Lysander is a very successful assistant manager at a flourishing commercial gym chain. He teaches several times a week and enjoys choreographing routines for his popular classes. He's thoughtful about what happened to Ashley and ensures that he is never forgotten. In 2021, he was invited by the BBC to take part in a documentary about young men committing suicide.

Jaz went to prison as a result of his arrest. He sent a card to Julie and me, it was a Mothers' Day thank you card, timed for us to receive it on that day. In it, he'd written his heartfelt thanks to Julie for her support and helping him to organise his travelling arrangements and apologised for not being able to teach with her. And he thanked me, his 'white mum' for the things he's learnt and his early morning phone calls to get him out of bed. He was also appreciative of my attendance at his court appearance. He returned to teach with Julie and me at one of our schools with the blessing of the headteacher. Since then, he's joined a company manufacturing food and drink for local shops.

> 'I can't say it was anything to do with home. Everything happens for a reason, so make the best of it. You've got to turn the "L's" into "W's", losses into wins, I'm trying to do that.'

Dante has always been keen on boxing and has successfully taken up MMA fighting (Mixed Martial Arts). It's the perfect outlet for channelling any buzz and aggression he's missing from the powerful drug of football violence. His first fight was in 2015. Hundreds of fans from the Tottenham Youth filed into Milton Keynes to support him. During the opening bout, a fight broke out among the crowd. Dante, microphone in hand, used his influence from the ring to take control and break it up. They stopped fighting. In their eyes, he's still their founder and leader in spite of his non-attendance at any Spurs football matches. And he hasn't published the book he wrote, the one we felt would define him as a football hooligan, and not the Dante we had come to know and work with. He's only lost one of his four MMA fights so far and kept up his rigid training programme throughout the pandemic restrictions. He's stayed out of any further trouble, is a responsible father of two children and fast becoming one of the top twenty MMA fighters in the country. And he can proudly say:

'I'm an ex-football hooligan.'

Debbie not only went on to become a twice-winning silver medallist in two Olympics, but has also been my staunchest supporter, dearest friend, and for thirteen years a co-director of Creativity in Sport. Her drive and enthusiasm for helping to improve quality of life for the most disadvantaged and challenging young people with complex problems has never waned. Today, she champions the work of Christians in Sport and Christians Against Poverty, and in her spare time, continues rowing and looking after the welfare of the competitors. Debbie enabled me to fulfil my ambitions, to spur me on through the difficult times, to innovate so many educational ideas and projects. I'm indebted to her.

There are too many people to thank who have made such an enormous impact on my life, including Andy and Dougie, who have given me such tremendous support, as well as the many individuals, organisations, teachers and friends who have offered me countless opportunities. And for Ben, my son, who has been at my side throughout much of my time teaching. I have so much to thank him for, whether it's for the filming, editing, our Creativity in Sport website, artwork, brochure and website for the London 2012 Bid, Joggy Bear videos and books, for the competitions, and for his many other numerous creative contributions that haven't even been mentioned in this book. He would patiently and prophetically say 'Not another project!' I couldn't have done it without him.

It's time now for me to change, but it's not going to happen; my passion just won't go away. The Covid virus has abated and I'm back teaching where I belong.

ACKNOWLEDGEMENTS

My heartfelt thanks and gratitude to my lovely family, friends and colleagues, who have encouraged and supported me throughout the writing of this book; writers Kathryn Knight and Sophie Ratcliffe for their initial, invaluable professional advice, to David James Smith and Alan Johnson whose expertise, enthusiasm and continued guidance spurred me on to complete it and to whitefox for helping me to publish it.

To Greg Dyke and Jane Tatnall, thank you for giving me the opportunity to 'Wake up Britain' on breakfast television for ten years, and Ian White for helping to refresh my memory with his extensive TV-am archive and website. To all the viewers, thank you for watching and especially those who joined in!

My grateful thanks also to Dougie Squires, Andrew MacTavish, Reverend Chris Russell, Eija Hughes, Julie Kapsalis, Andrew Middleton, Martin Clark, Karen Brown and the Thames Valley Police Force; to John Cosgrove, Katy Peters, Karen Salter, Gill Denham and the many headteachers and inspirational teachers who afforded me the luxury of implementing and developing my physical activity learning programmes in their primary and secondary schools, pupil referral units and prisons. Without the support and generosity of the Rotary Club, the Berkshire Community Foundation, corporate companies, and wonderful individuals including Catherine Stevenson and Charles Brims, none of it would have been possible.

And finally, a big Joggy Bear hug and thank you to my huge extended family of past pupils who have played such a major part in my life.